STREET GANGS THROUGHOUT THE WORLD

STREET GANGS THROUGHOUT THE WORLD

By

HERBERT C. COVEY, Ph.D.

College of Continuing Education
University of Colorado, Boulder

CHARLES C THOMAS • PUBLISHER, LTD.
Springfield • Illinois • U.S.A.

Published and Distributed Throughout the World by

CHARLES C THOMAS • PUBLISHER, LTD.
2600 South First Street
Springfield, Illinois 62704

©2003 by CHARLES C THOMAS • PUBLISHER, LTD.

ISBN 0-398-07428-3 (hard)
ISBN 0-398-07429-1 (paper)

Library of Congress Catalog Card Number: 2003050397

Printed in the United States of America
CR-R-3

Library of Congress Cataloging-in-Publication Data

Covey, Herbert C.
 Street gangs throughout the world / Herbert C. Covey.
  p. cm.
 Includes bibliographical references and index.
 ISBN 0-398-07428-3 -- ISBN 0-398-07429-1 (pbk.)
 1. Gangs--Cross-cultural studies. I. Title.

HV6437.C68 2003
364.1'06'6--dc21
                                        2003050397

To my family, friends, teachers, and colleagues—Bob Hunter, Scott Menard,
Lori Gorshow, Cindy Mason, Kenneth Berry, Malcolm Klein, Blaine Mercer,
Paul Lockman, Robert Franzese, Mark Rousseau, Wayne Wheeler,
and
Chris, Kelly, and Marty Covey

INTRODUCTION

This book is about street gangs throughout the world. Although a substantial amount of research on street gangs has been conducted over recent decades, research on street gangs in countries outside of the United States remains scarce. While research is scarce, no single volume can encompass and report on all that is known about street gangs throughout the world. However, it is important to gather what we know about street gangs together. My intent has been to discover what we know about street gangs throughout the world. This book summarizes some of the major works on street gang phenomena outside of the United States.

Over the years we have witnessed the development of street gangs in countries that historically did not have gangs. Officials in these countries are increasingly asking questions about street gangs and how to respond. Previous scholars have addressed the topic of the world's street gangs. For example, Hazlehurst and Hazlehurst (Eds.) prepared an excellent book titled *Gangs and Youth Subcultures: International Explorations* that focused on organized crime that occasionally references gangs. Malcolm Klein has written extensively about street gangs in Europe. His *The Eurogang Paradox: Street Gangs and Youth Groups in the U.S. and Europe* (2001) studies street gangs in countries outside of the United States, but the focus is on Europe and not the remainder of the world. Most of the literature on street gangs is in the form of chapters to edited collections, such as Malcolm Klein's, "Street Gangs: A Cross-national Perspective," in C.R. Huff's *Gangs in America III* (2002). Finally, Chapter 6 "Comparative Perspectives on Juvenile Gangs," of our book on *Juvenile Gangs* (Covey et al., 1997) continues to draw attention from scholars. While much has been written about organized crime in several countries, street gangs remain an unexplored topic begging attention. The topic of street gangs, with the exception of the United States and Europe, has not been adequately covered and summarized in a single work. While research on street gangs is being conducted in many countries, no one has taken stock about what is currently known.

This text is an effort to summarize some of the research on street gangs. The first chapter provides an introduction for the reader on the topic of street gangs throughout the world. The chapter addresses why the study of street gangs is important and the world demographic changes that will promote the development of street gangs. The chapter addresses important topics on the various definitions of gangs and youth subcultures. It addresses methodological issues, such as measuring the extent of street gang activity in different countries. The chapter also compares and contrasts street gangs with skinheads, mobs, causals, taggers, hooligans, and organized crime. The chapter makes basic observations about gang structures and Klein's dimensions and five structural patterns of street gangs. Finally, the chapter closes with a brief description of the roles of the community and mass media relative to street gangs.

Chapter 2 reviews some of the basic research on street gangs in the United States. This chapter provides only an overview of street gangs in the United States and does not provide much detail. While it would be impossible to provide adequate coverage of all of the literature on street gangs in a single volume, it is possible to highlight some of the main studies and recent findings regarding American street gangs.

Chapter 3 covers what is known about street gangs in Europe. Because street gangs have been present in some European countries for centuries, a special section is devoted to historical references to European gangs. Street gangs in Great Britain, Northern Ireland, Scotland, France, Scandinavia, the Netherlands, Belgium, Germany, and Eastern European countries are covered. Most of the materials in the chapter focus on street gangs in Great Britain.

Chapter 4 covers street gangs in the Western Hemisphere excluding the United States. The assumption is made that the United States warranted a separate chapter from its neighboring countries, although it has major influence on street gangs in the region. Street gangs in Canada, Jamaica, Brazil, Venezuela, Nicaragua, Trinidad, Ecuador, Tobago, and other countries are covered.

Chapter 5 addresses street gangs in Russia, India, China, Hong Kong (post-reunification), Japan, and other Asian countries. Russia was included in this chapter on Asian gangs to add balance to the chapter length. In addition, there is considerable information on street gangs in Russia that warrants special attention that would be lost if included in the chapter on street gangs in Europe.

Chapter 6 covers the immense continents of Africa and Australia and island countries in the Pacific Ocean. These countries and continents share little in common but for most a Southern Hemisphere orientation. The chapter includes sections on street gangs in South Africa and Papua New Guinea, and shorter sections on Kenya, Australia, New Zealand, and other Pacific Islands.

Chapter 7 is devoted to summarizing the main findings presented in the previous chapters. It compares information on what we know about street gangs throughout the world. The chapter covers trends and universals for all street gangs. When enough information is available, it uses Malcolm Klein's street gang dimensions to compare and contrast street gangs in different countries.

CONTENTS

STREET GANGS THROUGHOUT THE WORLD

Chapter 1

COMPARATIVE PERSPECTIVES ON STREET GANGS

When scholars think about street gangs, there is a tendency to view them as principally an American phenomenon. After all, researchers have conducted most of the world's research on street gangs and these gangs are known throughout the world. In addition, mass media images of street gangs are for the most part American based. Gang authorities Campbell and Muncer (1989) once characterized American gang research as taking a parochial view of gangs. Yet, we live in a world where some suggested decades ago that street gangs are an adolescent phenomenon in all cultures (Hardman, 1967). Irving Spergel (1990) concluded over a decade ago that street gangs were a trans-cultural phenomenon present with different manifestations in a diverse range of countries.

Although present in some countries, currently there is a void of research on street gangs in areas other than the United States (Hazlehurst & Hazlehurst, 1998). We face considerable gaps in information for South America, Africa, India, China, Japan, and other regions of the world. In addition, the research that has been translated into English about street gangs in other countries is often limited and outdated. Because street gangs have not garnered much attention, it is easy to conclude that street gangs are nonexistent or are effectively controlled in other countries. It also follows that the United States must be different from other countries because of its relative abundance of street gangs and corresponding research.

REASONS WHY STREET GANGS SHOULD BE OF WORLDWIDE INTEREST

One might question whether street gangs should be of any concern because so many of them do not persist for any great length of time. In addition, there are many other more important worldwide issues demanding our attention, such as civil wars, terrorism, and economic crises. However, although street gangs currently do not appear to be a worldwide pressing issue, there are many indications that they may become so in several countries.

Writing about the social ecology of gangs, Schneider (1999: 33) concluded, "The tipping point is an epidemiological term that explains how diseases must reach a certain threshold level, or a critical mass to spread epidemically. Before reaching that point they can be managed, but once the threshold is achieved, they become difficult to contain." Societies and communities may have "tipping points" at which street gangs are so numerous that they become a permanent fixture in the society. We may be witnessing a world where street gangs are becoming a permanent feature of the social landscape.

Some evidence for this may be found in changes in the world's demographic trends. Most street gangs are predominantly comprised of youth and young adults. Therefore, it is important to understand what is occurring to the world's population of youth. The increasing number of impoverished street children in the world is a major social problem that has definite ramifications for the spread and development of street gangs. Two decades ago, the United Nations Children's Fund (UNICEF) estimated that there were 40 million street children in the world, of which 25 million lived in Latin America (Tacon, 1982). The numbers of street children throughout the world are growing at an alarming rate. More recent reports estimate the number to be as many as 100 million youth living on the streets (United Nations, 1999). These homeless street children are the least likely to be employed or able to support themselves through legitimate means. Street gangs and law-violating youth groups provide options for many of these destitute youth. It is from this growing population of impoverished youth that street gangs across the world potentially find willing and eager recruits who have few socioeconomic options in life.

The United Nations (1999) reported that while the urban population of developed countries has doubled from 448 million in 1950 to 875 million in 1990, the urban population of developing countries quintupled over the same period from 285 million to 1.6 billion. A large portion of this urban population explosion is youth, who were the least equipped to cope with the stresses of urban areas. Many of these urban areas lack the infrastructures to meet the needs of youth, especially for those needing services. The result is that many youth fall prey to criminal exploitation and turn to crime for protection and survival. An avenue open to some urban youth is the street gang, which can provide some level of personal and financial security. Scholars have for decades observed that street gangs are more predominant in urban settings. Street gangs are and will become attractive options for youth lacking opportunity and facing impoverished futures. Street gangs will not only provide some, albeit modest, level of support, but also the social associations and security that many impoverished urban youth need.

In a similar vein, the world is developing an informal or underground economy. Several scholars have acknowledged and described informal economies in the United States and other countries that serve as alternatives to the formal economic structures that lack entry-level jobs for disadvantaged people. The world's growing youth population is expanding without corresponding increases in the demand for their labor. Improved health care and decreasing death rates are resulting in an increasing pool of unemployed and marginalized youth. Concentrations of these youth will diminish capital formation and economic modernization because they are economically dependent and less productive than their adult counterparts. Opportunities in some areas of the world for legitimate gainful employment have all but disappeared, leaving people, including youth, to rely on informal economies for survival. Informal economies are usually a combination of legitimate, such as cottage industries and open markets, and illegitimate activities, such as drug sales, prostitution, and crime. Street gangs participate in some of these illegitimate economic endeavors. For example, street gangs have increasingly become involved with illegal drug sales as part of the informal economy in the United States (Hagedorn, 2002) and other less developed countries (Portes et al., 1989; Rogerson, 2000).

Besides a growing worldwide population of youth at risk of joining street gangs, there are several other reasons why we should be interested in other countries. First, making cross-cultural comparisons has theoretical value. To assess whether theoretical explanations based on studies of American gangs apply to gangs in other countries, we must first determine whether the patterns of gang activity in other countries parallel patterns in the United States. In addition, a value of comparative gang research is that through the study of gangs in different countries, we gain an understanding of the role played by cultural factors in shaping gangs. Some have suggested that culture is second only to gender in understanding crime and delinquency (Beirne & Nelken, 1997). This might also be true of street gangs. If culture matters, then we would expect to see important differences among street gangs across the world. We need to consider how our observations and conclusions about American gangs should be modified by information from other countries (Campbell & Muncer, 1989; DeFleur, 1967a).

Evidence exists that some street gangs are internationally mobile. For example, we know that some Jamaican street gang members migrate to and from the United States. In the United States, there is rising concern that Asian gangs may become a major problem, as Southeast Asian and Hong Kong youths immigrate to the United States. It is also true, however, as Klein (1995a) and Van Gemert (2001) have noted, that the United States may be exporting gangs to other countries. However, this pattern is not true in all regions. For example, Malcolm Klein (2002) found no evidence of American gangs moving to Europe, although some European gangs modeled themselves after "American" style street gangs. Even when the street gangs do not move across international boundaries, youth who immigrate may be more likely to join or form new gangs upon arrival to new countries.

Increasing attention is being paid to the immigration of foreign gangs to the United States (Leo et al., 1998) and from the United States to other countries (DeCesare, 1999). Immigrant groups from Asia and Latin America, such as the Marielito gangs from Cuba, raise concerns that parallel issues raised in the 19th century concerning southern European immigration to America. Law enforcement is increasingly paying more attention to the immigration of youth and gangs to the United States. The media has been quick to pick up on the increased activities of the immigrant gangs to the United States (Leo et al., 1998). A central question will be whether the new immigrant gangs will become less prevalent as groups acculturate, as has been the previous pattern in the United States (Leo et al., 1998).

Another reason why we need to pay attention to street gangs is linked to their important role throughout the world in promoting racism and racial violence. In their collection of studies of racism and violence in Europe, Tore Bjögo and Rob Witte (1993) summarized a major finding of their volume by concluding that most of the racist violence in the world was perpetuated by youth gangs or individuals who were not affiliated to political organizations. Racism is most evident and real to victims at the street level compared to the larger political action group level. Members of minority populations may need to pay more attention to street level groups and gangs because they are more likely to pose an immediate threat than organized political movements. Racism and prejudice are typically carried out at the street gang or group level.

There are other important questions to be answered regarding street gangs. For example, how important is the host culture to gangs and gang activities? Are there some cultures or societies more conducive to street gangs than others (Hardman, 1967)? Do the processes of acculturation and integration eventually result in the disappearance of immigrant ethnic gangs? What aspects of street gang behavior, organization, and membership patterns transcend national boundaries? To what extent can an understanding of gangs in other countries help us to understand gangs in our own country? What roles do industrialization and urbanization play in the emergence of street gangs in developing societies? Answers to these and similar questions may help us obtain a broader understanding of street gang phenomena.

PROBLEMS OF COMPARATIVE STUDIES ON STREET GANGS

The study of street gangs in different countries poses a complex set of methodological considerations for the scholar. Problems exist in the equivalence of measurement, definitions, sampling variation, and the validity of data, as well as problems in the conceptualization and operationalization of gangs and the measurement of gang prevalence and activity. For example, does the term *dacoit* in India mean the same as "gang" in the United States? For English speaking only audiences, an added problem is the language barrier. Relatively little of the international research on gangs has been translated into English.

Undoubtedly, there are linguistic and conceptual issues when crossing national and cultural boundaries. Crime and delinquency may have different meanings based on culture and law (Janeksela, 1992; Janeksela et al., 1992). For example, different countries define adult and juvenile status differently, so that a juvenile in one country is an adult in another. Gangs also may be defined differently in different countries, as Clinard (1960) observed when he attempted to study gangs in Sweden. Authorities, researchers, and journalists frequently use inconsistent definitions of gangs, which add to the confusion. In some countries, law-violating youth groups can be mislabeled street gangs. In the United States and other countries, it is common to identify these groups as street gangs when in fact they are not. Malcolm Klein (1995a) uses the term "gang-like" to describe some of these groups.

Vaz (1962) conducted a study of Parisian gangs in the 1960s and concluded that relying on official delinquency and gang statistics is risky across national boundaries. Some countries may suppress information about street gangs. For example, before the 1980s, the Soviet Union officially failed to formally recognize the existence of youth gangs and subcultures. Therefore, statistics on street gangs in the Soviet Union have been rare to nonexistent. Europeans and Americans tend to not view some street gangs as true gangs because they do not conform to the distorted media portrayals of gangs as being tightly knit, highly organized, violent, and leader-directed groups (Klein, 2001). Thus, street gangs in Europe, as well as other countries, may not always be viewed as such by the general public. In some countries, the quality and quantity of law enforcement data on gangs vary over time. The definition of what constitutes a gang, or gang behavior, often varies (Cavan & Cavan, 1968; Kinnear, 1996). According to Klein (1995a), commingling of terms such as gangs, self-defense groups, peer groups, delinquent youth groups, street gangs, youth gangs, and so forth, presents another problem for researchers. Also, just as scholarly and public interest in street gangs in the United States has fluctuated over the decades, it has fluctuated in other countries as well. Consequently, the amount of research and literature varies over time, making it difficult to know what is occurring.

Although obstacles exist, it is still valuable to periodically take stock of what we think we know about gangs. Over time, as street gangs spread and there is no indication that they won't, our knowledge base will need to expand and conclusions become stronger. The value of studying gangs in different countries and in different periods should not be underestimated, as it poses a significant challenge.

APPROACH OF THIS REVIEW

This review of what we know about street gangs throughout the world is based on previous systematic research and information provided by media sources. It relies in part on recent work by Malcolm Klein et al. (2001) and many of his professional associates working on the topic of street gangs in Europe. When enough information was provided by the original sources, street gangs also were classified according to Klein's dimensions of street gang structures (Klein, 1996; 2001). In addition, other important information was collected for this review.

Each source was reviewed for the following gang characteristics: (1) County or specific region of gang within a country; (2) Whether the gang was urban or rural; (3) Whether the source was a systematic research study or mass media report. More credence was given to true research efforts than media accounts of gangs, but in some cases, the media accounts are the only information we have until gang research is conducted in these areas; (4) Whether there was enough information to classify the groups as true street gangs, youth subcultures, or law-violating youth groups. Insofar as the sources permit, when definitional issues arise as to whether a group resembles a gang or alternative organization, some judgment was necessary. Consistent with Klein et al. (2001) and Klein (2001), hooligans, biker gangs, organized crime, and political movements were not considered to be representative of street gangs. The review does provide some coverage of these groups, when appropriate. Some skinhead groups were considered street gangs, if they met other criteria for being a gang; (5) The main focus of the gang was reviewed, be it drug sales, violence, territory, social, drug use, community honor or status, power, racial prejudice, profit, hatred, or combination of these. Consistent with most research on street gangs in the United States, most of the gangs that are described have strong social aspects to their operations and focus. With few exceptions, street gangs throughout the world tend to be predominantly social organizations; (6) The impact of the host culture on the street gang. In some countries, cultural influences play an important role in the gang's operation. These cultural factors and influences, when identified, are noted; (7) Characteristics of gang members, such as age, gang-related tattoos, income level, gender, ethnicity, and migrant status, were reviewed; (8) Characteristics of the gang's structure, such as size, duration, subgroups, leadership, hierarchical or horizontal structure, processes, and age-grades; (9) Known organized crime relationships, if present, were described. While many do not, some street gangs have established business or social relationships with organized crime organizations in their respective countries. It should be noted that some scholars do not make clear distinctions between street gangs and organized crime. Thus, they refer to gangs when they are really referring to criminal organizations and vice versa; (10) Characteristics of the victims of gang offenses. When information on who the gangs targeted for crime was provided, it was noted. Typically a rule of thumb is that street gang members usually victimize others that are similar to themselves in income, ethnicity, gender, etc. This is not always true for street gangs that have racism or political causes on their agendas; and (11) Community or official responses to the gangs, such as denial, passive acceptance, repression, prevention, and active support. We know from years of research in the United States that the larger community's response to street gangs plays a major role in shaping their character. Typically, the more repressive the community, the more cohesive the gang. Likewise, community denial of a gang problem can later haunt the community, as gangs become more omnipresent and criminally active. The community response represents an important dimension for understanding gangs. In addition, it is of interest to know what gang intervention and prevention strategies have been tried and work in different countries.

Very few studies have addressed all of the previous items, hence more often than not, the materials reviewed provide a limited view of the street gangs. In addition, researchers and journalists do not cover the same aspects in the same manner. Street gang research is not uniformly conducted across national boundaries let alone within countries, thus observations and interpretations may differ. For example, research on street gangs in South Africa is characterized by differing opinions about the role of apartheid in shaping gangs.

CULTURES, SUBCULTURES, AND STREET GANGS
IN OTHER COUNTRIES

Certain themes recur in the work of researchers on street gangs in other countries. One key theme is the role of the host culture in determining the nature of street gangs and group delinquency. An operating assumption of many researchers is that culture influences the structure and nature of youth subcultures, group delinquency, and street gangs. Consequently, we would expect street gangs to differ across national and cultural boundaries. Similarly, scholars often regard youth subcultures as important influences on youth. It should be noted that in some of the cross-national research on gangs, what are described are more likely to be youth subcultures rather than street gang phenomena.

An assumption underlying the work of some international gang researchers is that rapid social change, resulting from urbanization, industrialization, and the modernization of nations, undercuts the existing social order and leads to increased social problems such as poverty and crime. This orientation may be traced to Durkheim (1933) and other scholars and social critics who viewed rapid social change as a source of social problems and deviant behavior (Merton, 1957; Parsons, 1977). From this perspective, we would expect to find higher levels of street gang activity in the more industrialized and urbanized countries. An alternative explanation for the increase, however, is that the more urbanized and industrialized countries have more extensive and better record-keeping systems that capture gang data and consequently feed the illusion that there is more street gang activity.

The roles of urbanization and modernization in generating a cultural milieu for crime and delinquency have received attention from comparative criminologists. Known in some circles as developmental theory or the Durkheimian-Modernization perspective, it views modernization and urbanization as disruptive to the populations of developing countries and promotes the development of street gangs of marginalized youth. An underlying theme is that the breakdown of the prior stable normative order leads to increased criminal activity, such as criminal gangs. Concepts of social disorganization, anomie, division of labor, industrialization, and urbanization help explain cross-cultural variations in crime (Clinard & Abbott, 1973; Durkheim, 1933). A focus is on rapid development in ill-prepared areas as being an over-riding factor in the rise of street crime and gangs. As development occurs, the migration of populations to the cities for work puts stress on the urban infrastructure. Urban areas appear to be generally more conducive environments for the rise and persistence of street gangs, regardless of country.

Another perspective is from the Marxian point of view. It views the spread of the capitalist mode of production as promoting the formation of criminal activities, including criminal street gangs. The inherent inequalities and social classes present in capitalistic economies create socioeconomic conditions ripe for the formation of street gangs. This view sees third-world populations as exploited by the industrialized world and kept in perpetual poverty. Crime becomes a drastic but natural adaptation to this exploitation as little wealth finds its way to the impoverished sectors of the population. Street gangs represent one adaptation to the exploitation. For example, industrialized countries produce consumer goods that are desired by low-income youth. Without the means of making enough money to purchase these consumer goods, such as stereo equipment, sports clothing, electrical gadgets, automobiles, etc., youth turn to crime. Thus, street gangs are a creation of macro-level socioeconomic relations between those that have and those that have not. Street gangs typically draw most of their membership from those that have not.

A third perspective is labeled the Ecological-Opportunity view (Neuman & Berger, 1988; 1997). It ties macro-level changes in socioeconomic structures to micro-level explanations of crime through the concept of opportunity. At the societal level, different societies present different opportunities and conditions for crime (and street gangs) to occur. Crime increases when evolutionary processes create a societal surplus of material goods that can be stolen. At the micro-level, when opportunities for individuals or groups are blocked, crime becomes an option. Street gangs are simply a mechanism used to take advantage of the absence of legitimate economic opportunity in a climate of surplus wealth.

Another theme in much of the comparative literature is the role of immigration in the formation of street gangs. Immigrating youth commonly find it difficult to integrate into the host society because of differences between their cultural backgrounds and the culture of the host society. Consequently, immigrant youth may join or form gangs as an alternative to their immediate assimilation into the host culture. Immigrant language and cultural differences may fuel the need for youth to join gangs of similar youth, particularly if they are confronted by problems of socioeconomic discrimination and rejection. The formation of new ethnic street gangs with each corresponding new wave of immigrants to the United States illustrates well this pattern. The immigration of foreigners also promotes reactions from threatened groups, including the formation of racist and ethnocentric groups and street gangs. This pattern of response to immigration is typical of skinhead groups and gangs that target recent immigrants in several European countries.

Regardless of what perspective one takes, all would agree that the mass media, multi-nationalism, global trade, the open exchange of information all contribute to a shrinking planet and promote the exchange of ideas and social groups, such as street gangs. For example, youth in South Africa and other countries have access to images of street gangs in the United States. Some youth find these images attractive and choose to imitate what they learn about regarding gangs. They have embraced the American street gang style, a pattern that occurs throughout the world.

Another theme that recurs in the cross-national literature on gangs is that key historical events, such as wars, have major impacts on juvenile delinquency, subcultures, and street gangs. For example, World War II appears to have had major effects on group delinquency in Europe. Some European youth lost one or both parents to prison or death during the war, and found it necessary to band together to survive (Cavan & Cavan, 1968). World War II not only affected delinquency rates, but also increased the extent of group and gang delinquency in Europe (Fyvel, 1961). The current civil wars in Africa and Asia undoubtedly mirror this pattern.

DETERMINING THE EXTENT OF STREET GANG ACTIVITY IN THE WORLD

We know that street gangs have been identified in countries outside the United States, especially in Europe. In most countries, however, street gang activity is not as extensive as it is in the United States

(Hood & Sparks, 1970; Mayo, 1969). Over 30 years later, few would argue that the United States continues to dominate the worldwide street gang scene. National studies on street gangs are virtually nonexistent outside of the United States. Therefore, students of street gangs in other countries often must rely on mass media accounts and antidotal evidence of street gangs in their respective countries. It is well known that there are clear risks of relying solely on the mass media or hearsay evidence regarding the extent and nature of street gangs.

More fundamentally, there is no consensus about what constitutes a gang, and how it differs from a subculture or a group of individuals. Several definitions have been used to refer to gangs, and the term gang has been broadly applied to a variety of different collections or aggregates of individuals (Bynum & Thompson, 1988; Covey et al., 1997; Horowitz, 1990; Johnstone, 1981; Kinnear, 1996; Klein, 1971; Loeb, 1973; Spergel, 1984, 1990; Stafford, 1984).

One of the most difficult questions to answer about gangs is how prevalent and extensive is current street gang activity in the world, let alone the country we know the most about, the United States. In the United States, very few studies have addressed the question of street gang prevalence on a national scale. Most current American research focuses on individual gangs or ethnic groups (Horowitz, 1990), rather than on national data with a few notable exceptions, such as Klein's work (1995a; 1995b.). Some suggest that it may be impossible to answer the question, given the diversity in definitions of what represents a gang (Bookin-Weiner & Horowitz, 1983; Spergel, 1990). Siegel (1989:177) typifies the common perception that "Today, the number of gang youths appears at least in these major cities (Philadelphia, Los Angeles, and Chicago) to be at an all-time high." Earlier research reported declines in gang activities in some cities and stability of gangs in other American cities (Spergel, 1990). Davis (1978) and Miller (1980) suggested that American gang membership and activity had increased, and that the extent of the gang problem was underestimated in the 1970s. A more recent estimate is there are about 800 cities with about 10,000 gangs and perhaps as many as a half-million members in the United States (Klein, 1995b).

Varying methods used to define gangs and to count gang members make estimates of their extent terribly unreliable. In addition, research indicates that gang membership fluctuates considerably over time. Thus, who is in or out of a gang changes on a regular basis. To complicate matters even more, media attention to gangs appears to be cyclic. The media since the mid-1980s have shown considerable interest in gangs. Does this mean gangs have become more prevalent or have we just noticed them more because they are more newsworthy? This has created a context in which it is difficult to determine whether gangs are as active, as prevalent, and growing as fast as the mass media would suggest.

While determining the extent of street gang membership in the United States is difficult, it is even more challenging in other countries. Most American researchers must depend on police records or court records, or in some cases, self-report data. Klein (1971) suggested that these sources of data are often inaccurate. In the United States, official data is not systematically collected on gangs at the national level, and at most local levels, it is based on incidents and definitions of what constitutes gang activity or gang-related activity that vary across jurisdictions. In addition, when they are picked up by the police, gang members may deny membership and nonmembers may incorrectly be identified as gang members. Citizens have been reluctant to report on gang activities, serve as witnesses, or cooperate with authorities. Johnson, Webster, and Connors (1995) attribute this to three basic factors: fear of retaliation from the gang, not wanting to be labeled a "snitch," and personal involvement of the victim or witness in gang activities. Klein and Maxson (1989) noted that defining "gang-related offenses" by law enforcement agencies and other officials is likely to vary across U.S. jurisdictions. As an alternative to official statistics, researchers sometimes rely on small-scale or local studies (Bookin-Weiner & Horowitz, 1983). Most of the gang research from other countries parallels that of the United States, as it tends to be ethnographical and local.

The study of contemporary gangs in the United States is beset with methodological problems that are also likely confront gang researchers in other countries. Generalizations about cross-national crime always involve methodological and measurement issues (Clinard & Abbott, 1973; Neuman & Berger, 1988; 1997) let alone measuring the extent of gangs and gang-related crime.

To complicate matters even further, Klein (1995b) suggests that street gangs operate in a variety of cycles. Sanders (1994) also observed a cyclical pattern to gang activities in San Diego. Block and Block (1993) found that gang violence in Chicago was cyclical over a

26-year period, with periodic increases, perhaps as gangs sought to expand territory. Gangs and gang activity fluctuate in cycles. For example, in the late 1960s, gang activity decreased but increased in the 1980s. Klein pointed out that the extent of gang activity increases and decreases according to a number of factors including but not limited to seasonally, research attention, political climate, media attention, and gang members' self-regulation. Similar cyclical patterns may operate in other countries; we simply do not know.

GANGS, GROUPS, AND YOUTH SUBCULTURES

The difficulty of distinguishing between group and gang delinquency has been a major problem for American gang research (Kornhauser, 1978). Ever since social scientists began to study gangs, the definition of what constitutes a gang has been imprecise (Covey et al., 1997; Stafford, 1984). Early uses of the term were very general, and the term *gang* has sometimes been used to signify a group of close associates or friends with no criminal intentions (Bynum & Thompson, 1988). Over 35 years ago, Empey (1967:33) observed that, "The term 'gang' is so overworked and is so imprecise that its use in scientific discourse may very well be questioned." More recently, Miller (1982) asserted that there has never been anything close to a consensus on the definition of a gang by scholars, criminal justice workers, or the general public. Just as it is true for the United States, it is true for other countries.

Underlying the imprecision in the use of the term "gang" is the finding that most juvenile delinquency is typically committed in the company of friends, and solitary acts are the exception, not the rule (Erickson & Jensen, 1977; M. Harris, 1988; Short, 1968). The size of the group involved with group delinquency, however, is usually small. Miller (1982) estimated that of all crimes committed by groups, pairs of individuals committed two-thirds, and only one-third involved three or more perpetrators.

Gang authority Walter Miller defined gangs as:

A youth gang is a self-formed association of peers, bound together by mutual interests, with identifiable leadership, well-developed lines of authority, and other organizational features, who act in concert to achieve a specific purpose which generally includes the conduct of illegal activity and control over a particular territory, facility, or type of enterprise. (Miller 1982:315-316)

Illegal activity is an element of the definition of gangs proposed by Miller (1975). According to Miller, a gang is a group of recurrently associating individuals with identifiable leadership and internal organization, identifying with or claiming control over territory in the community and engaging either individually or collectively in violent or other forms of illegal behavior. Miller's definition distinguishes gangs from friendship groups, athletic teams, and the like, and is based on criteria used by criminal justice personnel with working contact with gangs (Campbell & Muncer, 1989). It is the street gang's orientation to illegal activity that is the driving force behind our interest in gangs.

In his earlier work, Malcolm Klein (1971:13) defined an adolescent gang as, ". . . any denotable adolescent group of youngsters who (a) are generally perceived as a distinct aggregation by others in their neighborhood; (b) recognize themselves as a denotable group (almost invariably with a group name); and (c) have been involved in a sufficient number of delinquent incidents to call forth a consistent negative response from neighborhood residents and/or enforcement agencies."

More recently, Klein defines a street gangs as:

> A street gang is used to indicate a group-accepted and acknowledged orientation toward anti-social or criminal activities. It includes some specialty-focused groups such as street-level drug sales groups but not organized, upper level distribution systems and cartels. It includes some hate groups such as a number of skinheads, but not terrorist groups. It excludes prison gangs, motorcycle gangs, football hooligans, and the many youthful groups at school and elsewhere that may occasionally dabble in delinquent activities but not orient themselves around these. (Malcolm Klein 2001:61)

Malcolm Klein's definition would not clearly distinguish gangs from law-violating youth groups, as defined by Miller. Klein (1995a) believes that setting and style are more defining characteristics of street gangs than age. According to Klein (1995a, 2001), street gangs are qualitatively different from other youth groups. Klein observes that for some youth, street gang membership becomes their master identity. Further, Klein has found that most street gangs tend toward moderate levels of organization. However, street gangs are not noted for their rigid and hierarchical organizational structures. Leaders change and gang codes of conduct are weakly enforced. Street gangs commit a wide variety of crimes instead of specializing and most are minor offenses. Klein's work, consistent with other gang research findings, notes that gang membership results in higher levels of offending.

GANG DELINQUENCY AND GROUP DELINQUENCY

Most research on street gangs in the United States suggests that gangs are loose affiliations with little cohesion and unstable memberships (Jansyn, 1966; Klein and Crawford, 1967). The implication is that because they are loose and fluctuating, it is difficult to get one's arms around their nature and they are often confused with non-gang delinquent groups. The gang vs. group issue is seldom addressed in modern American literature (Klein et al., 2001). This is true in other countries as well and the implication is that many nongang groups are wrongly labeled as gangs.

Walter Miller contrasts gangs with law violating youth groups, which he defines as "an association of three or more youths whose members engage recurrently in illegal activities with the cooperation and moral support of their companions" (Miller, 1982:313). This definition of law-violating youth groups does not include structure or territory, two important elements of Miller's definition of youth gangs. Spergel (1984:200) similarly defined delinquent groups as "an association of two or more youths, usually between the ages of ten and seventeen years, who are engaged in acts defined as illegal." Spergel's definition of delinquent groups is less restrictive than Miller's, insofar as "recurrent" activity and "cooperation and support" of others in the group are not included in Spergel's definition, but are in Miller's.

Research has consistently found delinquency to be a group phenomenon in the United States and other countries, such as Russia (Pridemore, 2002). Most American delinquent youth have delinquent friends and most delinquent acts are committed by groups of delinquents rather than individuals acting alone (Elliot et al., 1985; Kornhauser, 1978; Short & Strodbeck, 1974). Delinquent acts often occur within a group context (Erickson & Jensen, 1977; Giordano et al., 1986; M. Harris, 1988; Short, 1968; Zimring, 1981). Consequently, distinguishing gang from non-gang crime or delinquency can be difficult.

In the United States, the distinction between group and gang delinquency is an area of disagreement among scholars and public authorities (Fagan, 1989). Using the distinction proposed by Miller between gangs and law-violating youth groups, we know that groups conduct most delinquency, not gangs (Klein & Crawford, 1967; Morash, 1983;

Yablonsky, 1959). Campbell (1991:12) suggested that many of the gangs described by Thrasher (1927) were "little more than social clubs that from time to time engaged in some suspect activities." Lerman's (1967) research on juvenile delinquents in New York found that until the age of 14 or 15, most boys committed delinquent acts with small groups of close associates. This pattern continued in later years with increasing numbers of youths committing delinquent acts alone. Miller (1977) noted that street crime is often committed by small, informal groups of teenagers and not true gangs.

The fact that much delinquency and crime is committed by groups, which may or may not represent true street gangs, clouds our understanding of street gangs in different countries. What would be defined as a street gang in the United States may be viewed as a law-violating youth group in many other countries. It is also important to note that most law-violating youth groups do not evolve into gangs.

GANGS AND YOUTH SUBCULTURES

In addition to a concern with street gangs, some scholars have linked collective youth law violation to youth subcultures. At times, the terms "gang" and "subculture" have been used interchangeably and imprecisely. Subcultures characterize groups within a society, but not the whole society, and they have patterns of values, norms, and behaviors that have become traditional within the group, but which may deviate from the values, norms, and behaviors of the larger society. Campbell and Muncer (1989:272) offer the following definition, "Youth subculture has come to denote a geographically diffuse social movement of teenagers and young people who share a common set of values, interests, and a tacit ideology, but who are not necessarily dependent on face-to-face interaction with other members and do not have any rigid criteria of entry, membership, or obligation." Specific to youth, Campbell and Muncer (1989) defined youth subculture in terms of values, ideology, interaction, and membership criteria. Based on their definition, gangs can be distinguished from subcultures because the latter are less dependent on face-to-face interaction among members, less geographically centralized, and have less rigid criteria of entry, membership, or obligation.

Subcultures may be important frames of reference that youths and other groups use to interpret their social worlds. Although gangs often reflect subcultures in values, norms, and behaviors, and although subcultures may have gangs as adherents, the two are nevertheless different. Subcultures are not organized to the same extent as gangs, and they lack the face-to-face interaction that characterizes gangs, according to most definitions of gangs (Pfautz, 1961). Gangs form within larger subcultures that may be organized racially, ethnically, politically, religiously, or economically. For example, Skinhead gangs may be regarded as part of a white supremacist (political and racial) subculture, but they are only one manifestation of that subculture. Not all white supremacists are members of skinhead gangs—indeed, not all skinheads are necessarily members of skinhead gangs.

HOOLIGANS, CAUSALS, MOBS, AND STREET GANGS

A term often used throughout the world that encompasses a wide variety of meanings including delinquents, soccer fans, social deviants, criminals, and street gang members is hooligan. The term hooligan originated in the nineteenth century from an Irish immigrant family named Hooligan. The family preyed on residents in the East End of London. Hooligan became used as a descriptor of any criminal or rowdy behavior. Sports-related violence and hooligan-like groups are well established in European history, dating back to the ancient Greeks and Romans. In England, the recent rise of hooliganism has been tied to the Teddy Boys, football (soccer), and skinhead subcultures.

The term hooligan also is common in Europe, Russia, Australia, and English-speaking countries with the exception of North America. Hooligans, sometimes referred to as "hools," are predominantly a European phenomenon. Most of the time hooligans are violent soccer fans who often dress similar to skinheads. They are known to shout racist chants and taunt in soccer stadiums. Hooligans have been known to join forces with skinheads and punks and engage in violent events. The hooligan phenomenon is described in detail by Bill Buford (1990) in his ethnographic account *Among the Thugs*. Buford views hooliganism as a form of quest that gives males an excuse to go berserk for a cause, which is often soccer.

British and European hooliganism on the surface and street level can seem similar to street gangs. For example, the Chelsea Headhunters are a notorious hooligan group in London. Similar to some types of street gangs, the Chelsea Headhunters have a hierarchical leadership structure. They clearly identify themselves as members of a group similar to street gangs. They have a sense of territory. The group makes plans for "aggro" (aggression or violence) on opposing teams' fans and rival hooligans. This soccer hooliganism may evoke riots, playing field (pitch) invasions, assaults, vandalism, alcohol-related offenses, use of weapons, muggings, arson, and even homicides. Victims are generally opposing soccer fans or hooligans representing other teams.

A question might be raised as to whether hooligans should be considered street gangs? The answer depends on a number of criteria. Hooligans, similar to street gangs, clearly identify themselves as members of a group, can be criminal, have a sense of territory, have more than two members, are multi-functional, distinctive dress indicating membership, have leaders, face-to-face interaction, are on-going (lasting), and otherwise share characteristics common to street gangs. Hooligans, however, may or may not be viewed as street gangs by the larger community. The numbers of hooligans involved in soccer brawls and assaults suggest that they operate more as organized mobs than true street gangs. Occasionally, they operate in small groups that on the surface resemble street gangs. According to Kersten (2001), soccer hooliganism is territorial and is similar to a war where participants take risks and engage in combat. The territory is the soccer field and immediate surrounding area. Hooligans from other areas with other soccer teams are seen as the invaders of this territory and hence as opponents.

Some of the characteristics of hooliganism suggest they are not gangs. Kersten (2001) noted that in many respects hooligans were different from street gangs because they act more like mobs. According to Kersten, hooligans lacked fixed hierarchies, had no rules or orders, were comprised of a wide variety of subcultural groups such as neo-Nazis, skinheads, and punks, and members being in a mob act violently as individuals. Similar to mobs, hooligans had a high degree of spontaneity in their action. Hooligans are certainly viewed as criminal groups by the communities and groups they victimize. Perhaps the answer as to whether they are street gangs or not lies more with the communities where they reside and victimize. Using community perception as a criterion, Hooligans do not seem to be street gangs. While hooligans do commit crimes, they otherwise do not function as street gangs and are generally not labeled street gangs by the general public. Malcolm Klein (2001) recently excluded hooligans as being representative of street gangs and British law enforcement agencies would concur (Hazlehurst & Hazlehurst, 1998).

In France, "casuals" are similar to hooligans. They are violent youths who occasionally engage in assaults at soccer matches or in surrounding areas. According to the Anti-Defamation League (1995), casuals are usually white youth that exhibit racist and anti-Semitic attitudes and actions. They, unlike skinheads, usually do not associate themselves with Nazism. The casuals seem to be more opportunistic and less enduring than the hooligans. They conform better to Walter Miller's notion of law violating youth groups than true street gangs. The characteristics we find of street gangs, such as on-going face-to-face interactions and a sense of group membership are essentially absent from casual groups.

DIFFERENCES BETWEEN STREET GANGS AND ORGANIZED CRIME

The various relationships between street gangs and organized crime and their corresponding definitions are important to the student of street gangs throughout the world. Just as definitions of gangs differ, so do definitions of organized crime organizations. There are no consistent definitions of organized crime, syndicate crime, or professional crime, and consequently, distinctions between common street gangs and organized crime organizations are sometime blurred when the two transact. The definitional problems associated with the term gang are paralleled by those of organized crime. Definitional issues are further clouded by the media, scholars, and law enforcement, by the practice of calling organized crime organizations gangs. In addition, the picture is further clouded because some street gangs work for organized crime and others claim organized crime affiliations, whether real or not.

As is the case with gangs, numerous definitions of organized crime exist. Maltz (1985:24) suggests the following characterize organize crime: (1) corruption; (2) violence; (3) sophistication; (4) continuity; (5) structure; (6) discipline; (7) multiple enterprises; and (8) involvement in legitimate enterprises. Abadinsky (1990: 4-5) states that organized crime refers to groups of criminals having all or most of eight attributes: (1) is nonideological; (2) is hierarchical; (3) has a limited or exclusive membership; (4) is perpetuitous; (5) uses illegal violence and bribery; (6) demonstrates specialization/division of labor; (7) is monopolistic; and (8) is governed by explicit rules and regulations. In Abadinsky's view, the goals of organized crime are not political but power and wealth.

Good examples of how the distinction between organized crime and street gangs becomes blurred are the relationships between triads and street gangs. Law enforcement typically views triad groups as meeting all of Abadinsky's criteria for organized crime. Triads are generally viewed as highly organized criminal enterprises that are distinctively different from common street gangs. According to Main (1991) triad societies are varied in their makeup and can range from street gangs to highly organized groups. It is common for triad leaders to not be too involved in the operations of street gangs. Triad leaders typically do not dictate the types of crime subgroups, such as street gangs, are involved in. Triad leaders may or may not share in the profits of subgroups and street gangs.

Few would debate this characterization of triads; however, it is also known that street gangs model themselves after triads but in no way represent true organized crime. Does a street gang, by adopting a few notions of what it is to be a triad, represent an organized crime organization? The answer is without hesitation no. Is a street gang that puts in "work" for an organized crime a street gang or simply an extension of the organized crime structure? The answer is, if the street gang functions more characteristically as other street gangs, then it should be labeled as such. However, if the degree of control exercised by the organization is extensive, then the group could justifiably be labeled organized crime. In general, organized crime organizations, such as triads, do not typically consider street gangs full participants in the organization as much as contractors hired to carry out crimes.

Shelden, Tracy, and Brown (1997) provide other distinctions between street gangs and organized crime groups. They note that street gangs tend to have younger members, are largely social most of the time, are involved in legal as well as illegal activities, and have subsets involved in crime. Organized crime groups operate differently and are constituted solely for economic gain through illegal activities. Organized crime groups also commit illegal acts as a whole group rather than as subsets.

STREET GANGS AND TAGGER CREWS

A form of group that some would consider to be street gangs are labeled tagger crews. In the United States, tagger crews, also known as "toys," or "piecers," "housers," "graffiti bands," or "posses," are one of the newest and fastest rising delinquent groups. In Los Angeles in 1993, law enforcement estimated that there could be as many as 30,000 taggers and slightly over 400 tagger crews operating (Glionna, 1993). Tagging and gang graffiti are not limited to the United States and are found in other countries.

Taggers are typically armed with cans of spray paint, felt pens, and increasingly, weapons. They mark property with their tags which are stylized initials of group members. Groups of taggers, most commonly referred to as crews, go out on "bombing runs" and mark property with their tags. They also mark over the tags of others which forms a type of competition that can led to conflict among tagger crews. Taggers are caught up in a competition with others to locate their tags in high-risk and visible areas.

The painting is usually done in groups called crews but is also done by individual members of crews acting independently of the group. Usually nonviolent, taggers may operate in the same areas as more violent, territorially oriented street gangs without serious conflict with those gangs (Klein, 1995a), but some have become more violent in nature, carrying weapons for defense, and some more violent gangs have added tagging to their repertoire of illegal activities. Tagger crews do not claim any specific "turf," and do not usually attempt to keep other taggers out of areas in which they have been active. Crossing out the tags of other taggers appears to be more the exception than the rule.

According to Wooden (1995), some of the characteristics of tagger crew are that they: (1) do not have detailed organizational structures; (2) change names; (3) lack initiation rituals; (4) are not territorial; (5)

come from all socioeconomic backgrounds and races; and (6) have changing membership as taggers move from crew to crew. All of these and other features, Woodson proposes, make tagger crews something other than a street gang. But it is also true that taggers are involved in law violating behavior, have face-to-face interaction with each other that continues over time, associate for other reasons other than tagging, although tagging is the central reason, have a sense of group membership, may have a sense of identity, share common goals, and have a sense of status within the group (the reputations of successful taggers). Are taggers true gangs? The evidence is mixed and will require more research and a consistent use of the definition of what represents a gang. What is clear is that in many countries throughout the world and especially Europe, tagging and gang graffiti are present.

CONCLUSION: DEFINITIONS OF STREET GANGS

The absence of consensus on the definition of the term gang has an impact on what we conclude about gang behavior. Decker and Kempf-Leonard (1991) suggest that public perception of the seriousness and scope of the gang problem is influenced by the definition being used. If a broad definition of the term is used, then a wide variety of groups, such as college fraternities, play groups, street corner groups, and other collections of individuals can be defined as gangs, and we are likely to conclude that gang activity is widespread. Miller (1982) argues that the use of very narrow definitions of gangs have resulted in gross underestimation of the extent of gang behavior.

This book will generally use Miller's definition of law-violating youth groups, Campbell and Muncer's (1989) definition of subcultures, and Klein's definition of street gang. Klein's definition of gang is reasonable, useful in distinguishing gangs from groups, and contains elements common to many other definitions. It also provides a reasonable balance between excessively restrictive and overly broad definitions. Although the book will try to adhere to these definitions, many of the works cited in this book may not. When researchers are describing gangs but are probably really covering law-violating groups, it will be noted.

KLEIN'S DIMENSIONS AND FIVE STRUCTURAL PATTERNS OF STREET GANGS

Malcolm Klein (1996, 2001) suggests that there are reliable dimensions that can be used to describe street gangs. These dimensions are size, age range, duration, territoriality, and criminal versatility. These dimensions are represented in various combinations of five street gang structural patterns. The following table summarizes Klein's street gang dimensions and street gang structures. Klein's work is a useful tool in understanding street gang structures, as they exist throughout the world.

Table 1
KLEIN'S CHARACTERISTICS OF FIVE GANG STRUCTURES

Dimension	Traditional	Neo-traditional	Compressed	Collective	Specialty
Duration	Long-lasting	10 Years or Less	Short History	10 to 15 Years	Under 10 Years
Size	Large	Medium to Large	Small	Medium to Large	Small
Subgroup	Distinct Subgroups	Distinct Subgroups	No Subgroups	No Subgroups	No Subgroups
Age Range	Wide		Narrow	Medium to Wide	Usually Narrow
Territory	Strongly Territorial	Strongly Territorial			Territorial
Other					Narrow Criminal Focus

[Klein 2001:65]

Although some patterns of gang structure, including loose organization, fluidity of leadership, and ambiguity of membership, appear to prevail in contemporary American and other gangs, there is considerable variation in the patterns. In particular, certain types of street gangs, based on patterns of illegal behavior or on ethnicity, appear to have more formal, rigid, hierarchical organization than others.

Leadership functions vary with the situation, and may be assumed by different individuals in the same gang and by individuals with different strengths or weaknesses in different types of gangs. Membership in some types of gangs is ambiguous; in others, there are clear distinctions between members and nonmembers. Altogether, the variability in gang structure is consistent with a more general pattern of variability in the street gang phenomenon.

DEMOGRAPHIC CHARACTERISTICS OF GANG MEMBERS

Even with all of the cultural and national variation in street gangs, gangs can be characterized as predominantly male, young, urban, lower income, marginalized, and often ethnic minority. Braithwaite (1989) notes the facts are essentially the same in most societies. He observed that crime is disproportionately a male phenomenon, committed by young and urban individuals. The weaker the individual's attachment to school, lower educational attainment, downward social mobility, weaker family relationships, and stronger associations with offending groups, the greater the likelihood of offending. The same factors are also common to most street gangs throughout the world.

Although females participate in street gangs, they have historically taken secondary roles to males (Campbell, 1984a). This pattern may, at least for the United States, be changing as females are taking more active leadership roles and becoming more involved with gangs than in the past. Street gangs in the United States may be getting both older and younger in terms of the typical age range of members, as gang members remain in the gang longer, and as younger members are recruited to insulate older members from more serious criminal penalties. Although American street gangs have increasingly moved to suburban areas and to smaller cities, they remain predominantly an urban, central city phenomenon. This pattern is generally true for gangs in countries outside of the United States. Lower-class minority group members are more likely to be identified as gang members, a fact which may at least in part reflect a bias in the way official statistics are produced, but which, even according to self-report data, accurately reflects a disproportionately high probability that lower-class, minority group youths will become involved in gangs. Finally, ethnicity and nationality continue to matter. For example, in Europe, ethnic minorities comprise the majority of street gang members. Klein (2001:135) writes:

> In most cases however, it is the refugee and immigrant populations, first as well as second generation, which are found in these gang structures. The list is very long: Afro-Caribbean, Algerian, Antillean, Croatian, Filipino, Iranian, Italian, Moroccan, Pakistani, Russian, Somali, Surinamese, Turkish, and Vietnamese.

COMMUNITY CONTEXT AND PUBLIC REACTIONS TO STREET GANGS

Central to the issue of street gangs in modern society is the image of gangs in the broader community. The word gang or its equivalent is a convenient catch phrase used by the mass media. In a content analysis of the media's treatment of gangs over a four month timespan in the United States, Fasilo and Leckie (1993) found the media depicted gangs and their activities as widespread, a threat to society, and a new phenomenon. They discovered stories were along ethnic lines, were not historical, and resulted in an unjustified fear of gangs. These patterns likely occur in other countries as well.

Public reaction to gangs does much to shape the nature of gangs and gang behavior. Community perceptions may be critical to the definition and perception of groups as gangs. According to Miller (1974:263), "Put in general terms, if youth groups in a particular community appear clearly to present a problem, they are perceived as gangs; if they do not, that community has 'groups' but no 'gangs'." Its external environment and community (Short, 1976a, 1976b) shape every group, including a gang.

Public or community responses to street gangs can be antagonistic and hostile, when gangs are viewed as negative forces to be addressed. Communities oppose street gangs through force and antigang suppression efforts. Communities may also ignore or be apathetic toward street gangs, at least to the point that gangs are not viewed as significant threats to the social order. Communities have also been known to view street gangs as partners. For example, this pattern occurs in Papua New Guinea and Northern Pakistan, where communities are supportive of local street gangs. Communities and gangs may operate in a spirit of mutual cooperation working toward common goals and objectives. Communities have supported street gangs by not cooperating with law enforcement officials, hiding firearms or drugs, providing social support, protecting gang members from authorities, and informing gang members of law enforcement activities. In return, street gangs have been known to offer protection from outside threats and corrupt businesses, and have provided financial support to their respective communities.

The perception of the nature and extent of gangs in society is largely a function of the mass media (Miller, 1981). The media can and often does help shape public perceptions of street gangs. Media portrayals and false depictions of gangs have been criticized by a number of researchers (Decker & Kempf-Leonard, 1991; Hagedorn, 1988; Horowitz, 1990; Zatz, 1987). Parks (1995) and Prothrow-Stith (1991) have suggested that the nature of violence associated with gang behavior may have resulted in its being distorted and exaggerated by the media.

The mass media play a dominant role in creating moral panics. Zatz's (1987) study of gangs in Phoenix found that law enforcement agencies, with the help of the press, were able to create an overreaction or "moral panic" over Hispanic street gangs. Moore (1991) noted that American Hispanic gangs originated and have existed in contexts of periodic moral panics that shape public perceptions of gangs. Cohen (1973; 1980) traced the development of mod and rocker youth cultures in England and offered similar findings. Takagi and Platt (1978) studied Chinese street gangs in San Francisco's Chinatown and contended that youth groups are incorrectly labeled as gangs by the press and the criminal justice system.

Another relationship between gangs and the community is that the community may contribute to the gang's group cohesion (Klein & Crawford, 1967; Yablonsky, 1970). The more the community reacts to the gang and takes actions to undercut it, the more the gang solidifies into a cohesive group, becoming stronger in the face of adversity. Klein and Crawford (1967) proposed that eliminating external forces which contribute to gang cohesion may help reduce the gang problem and may even lead, at least temporarily, to the elimination of gangs (Klein, 1995a). Gangs, they believe, are internally unstable and tend to break apart when external threats decline.

The role of the American mass media is important in understanding gangs and their relationships with the community. Hollywood and other sources of mass media have done much to shape our perceptions of gangs. In the decades since the 1950s, images of gangs have emerged from movies such as *The Outsiders, Colors, The Lords of Flatbush, West Side Story, Romper Stomper, Boyz'n the Hood, New Jack City, American Presidents, Rumblefish,* and *The Wild Ones.* Another gang movie, *American Me*, portrayed an account of one gang member's experiences in a youth and prison gang in California. Some, such as Marlon Brando's leather-jacketed character from *The Wild Ones*, have created perceptions and stereotypes at the international level. French and German youth modeled their behavior and gang style after these Hollywood images of gangs. In the Netherlands, Van Gemert (2001) found many street gang members had copies of the American journalist Leon Bing's *Do or Die* (1992), which sensationalizes the street gang lifestyle.

Music also plays a mass media role in the shaping of gangs throughout the world. American gangsta rap and hip hop music, which more often than not, promotes and romanticizes street gang values and culture have helped spread American street gang culture to other countries. The distorted view of street gangs portrayed by this music adds fuel to the formation and imitation of street gangs in other countries. One only needs to walk through any major city to hear the pervasive influence of "gangsta rap" and hip hop music that promotes the street gang lifestyle.

CONCLUSION: THE CHALLENGES OF STUDYING THE WORLD'S STREET GANGS

An essential point of this chapter has been to underscore the importance of studying street gangs throughout the world. The United States is not alone in having street gangs and they exist or are developing in many countries. In spite of their presence or emergence, research on street gangs in other countries continues to be rare. Only recently have scholars from different nations come together to help bridge the gap of current knowledge about street gangs in different countries (Klein et al., 2001).

Current research on street gangs presents us with a blurred picture because of the paucity of good information on street gangs at the national and international levels. Many studies of gangs give us depth in the workings of individual gangs but provide little information about the extent and nature of gang activity. Official sources give us a biased and inconsistent picture of gang activity may vary from one jurisdiction to another. Coming up to speed on street gangs throughout the world will be no small task. Numerous definitional and methodological issues will need to be addressed. Cross-comparisons of street gangs are beset with problems. Basic questions, such as the extent to which street gangs are present and their involvement in crime in some countries, may never be answered for some countries.

Nevertheless, we should be very concerned with street gangs throughout the world, as all indications are they will expand or already have done so in a number of countries. This expansion should be expected as the world's burgeoning population of impoverished youth with dismal prospects for wealth and success will likely turn to street crime and gangs for support. If expansion occurs and all indications are it will, our current knowledge about street gangs throughout the world leaves us ill equipped to respond and address gangs and their corresponding crime. It is thus paramount to begin the process of collecting information about street gangs throughout the world.

Chapter 2

STREET GANGS IN THE UNITED STATES

The question has often been asked whether American street gangs are unique or share characteristics with other street gangs throughout the world. Clearly, street gangs have been more common in the United States than any country in the world. It is also true that American street gangs, at least as far as the media has influence, have had a profound role in shaping street gangs throughout the world. American street gangs, for better or worse, have served as models for other street gangs, indirectly through the media or directly through the movement of populations.

ETHNICITY AND AMERICAN STREET GANGS

In America, ethnic youth have formed street gangs to adapt to the demands of American life. Members of ethnic minority groups seem to be overrepresented in American street gangs (Miller, 1975; Stafford, 1984). In a Klein et al. (1995) survey of research on contemporary street gangs, they concluded that about 85 percent of street gang membership was comprised of youth of color. One police department study of New York gangs found that 55 percent were Hispanic and 36 percent were African American, with the remainder being white non-Hispanic or Oriental (Collins, 1979). However, recent evidence reported to law enforcement agencies indicates that Anglos now represent a greater share of gang membership than they have in the past (Egley, 2000).

Furthermore, street gangs tend to be racially exclusive (Miller, 1975), although some racial mixing does occur (Yablonsky, 1970). All

African American (Miller, 1962; Short & Strodtbeck, 1965), all Hispanic (Erlanger, 1979; Moore, 1978; Moore et al., 1983), Vietnamese (Morgenthau, 1982), and Chinese (Joe, 1994; Joe & Robinson, 1980; Takagi & Platt, 1978) gangs have been well documented. Although street gangs comprised of ethnically mixed members exist (Fleisher, 1998; 2002), ethnically homogeneous gangs remain the most common pattern in the United States (Klein, 1995a; Knox, 1993). Summarizing previous gang research, Jackson (1989) concluded researchers should continue to look at the variations in gangs and gang behavior across ethnic lines because important differences exist among ethnic groups. Some researchers continue to find ethnicity and race useful in understanding American gangs (Johnson et al., 1995), especially within the context of multiple marginality (Vigil & Yun, 2002). Others, however, suggest that race and ethnicity may not be useful in understanding all gang phenomena. For example, Maxson and Klein (1994) found that ethnicity was not particularly useful in predicting the structure of American street gangs. This does not mean that ethnicity is not useful in understanding who joins gangs, how ethnicity is interpreted by members and outsiders, and the values articulated by gang members.

SOCIOECONOMIC BACKGROUND AND AMERICAN STREET GANGS

It is generally agreed that the racial and ethnic composition of the street gangs reflects the composition of the inner city neighborhoods from which street gang members are drawn. Some of the ethnic divisions are also linked to socioeconomic status. The relationship between socioeconomic status and delinquency, including gang delinquency, is controversial. Short and Strodtbeck's (1974) research on Chicago gangs found that lower class boys were the most delinquent. Johnstone (1983) found that low-income communities were more likely to serve as recruitment areas for street gangs. In part, whether there are substantial differences by socioeconomic class may depend on whether official or self-report statistics are used (Elliott & Ageton, 1980; Elliott & Huizinga, 1983). Although street gangs appear to be primarily a lower class phenomenon, there is evidence of the existence of middle class gangs (Coleman, 1970; Chambliss, 1973; Vaz, 1967). Stover (1986) noted that Los Angeles and Detroit police reported problems among middle class suburban youths, as well as lower class youths from the central city.

FEMALE PARTICIPATION IN AMERICAN STREET GANGS

Gang research has consistently found that although American females join youth gangs, they do not do so to the degree that males do (Miller, 1975, 1977; Short, 1968). Although historical evidence documents female participation in gangs since their inception, female participation in gangs has been relatively rare and minor compared to male involvement. Recently, female participation in street gangs has been documented in a number of locations in the United States. Researchers have documented female gang membership in Boston (Giordano, 1978; Morash, 1983), Philadelphia (Brown, 1977), New York (Campbell, 1984a, 1984b; Goldstein et al., 1994; Hanson, 1964; Rice, 1963), Southern California (M. Harris, 1988; Moore, 1978), Los Angeles (Bowker & Klein, 1983; M. Harris, 1988; Murphy, 1978), and other cities (Miller, 1973; Rice, 1963).

Although historical evidence indicates female involvement in gangs, their participation rates have been comparatively low in the United States. Miller (1975) reported that no more than 10 percent of gang membership in major American cities was female. Conklin's (1989) summary of research on gangs estimated that males outnumbered females as gang members by a ratio of 20 to 1. Gang researcher Anne Campbell is cited by Mydans (1990) as estimating about 10 percent of gang membership is usually female (A. Campbell, 1991). These low estimates of female participation have been supported by other research (Campbell, 1984a; Short & Strodtbeck, 1974). Goldstein et al. (1994) concluded that males continue to outnumber females at a ratio of 20 to 1.

Some more recent research on street gangs indicates higher rates of female participation. For example, Esbensen, Huizinga, and Weiher (1993) found females represent about 20 to 46 percent of gang members in a Denver sample. Bjerregaard and Smith (1993) found female gang members constituted 22 percent of gang members in Rochester,

New York, and Fagan (1990) found that 33 percent of gang members were female. Females represented about 38 percent of the G.R.E.A.T. sites (Esbensen & Winfree, 1998). Criminal justice data on offenses committed by gang members supports the lower levels of participation of females in gangs and gang delinquency. Esbensen and Huizinga (1993) reported that female gang members were likely to report lower levels of delinquent activity than males. Arrest statistics consistently indicate lower arrest rates for females than males in gangs (Spergel 1986). Summarizing much of the contemporary research on street gangs, Klein et al. (1995) noted the ratio of females to males can range from one female for every male to one for every 10 males.

Other gang studies in the United States report that female membership in gangs is much more common than in the past (Curry, 1998; Esbensen et al., 1999; Howell et al., 2002; Maxson & Whitlock, 2002; Moore & Hagedorn, 2001). A confounding factor in all of these estimates is that there is evidence that females may claim to be in gangs and dress like gang members, even when they are not really members. The Los Angeles Sheriff's Department found that in some of the most hard core gang areas, females will wear gang colors and claim they are gang members when in fact evidence shows that they are not (Operation Safe Streets, 1995).

THE STRUCTURE OF AMERICAN STREET GANGS

Street gangs, like other groups in society, must perform certain functions to survive. They must recruit members, provide for the well-being of their members, make decisions about immediate (and perhaps long-term) goals and lines of action, and settle internal disputes. There is considerable variability in how different gangs approach these tasks. According to Stafford (1984), most researchers have found that American gangs are loosely structured, not very cohesive, and without clearly defined leadership roles. Some gangs, however, are more highly structured, especially Hispanic and Asian American gangs in the United States (Chin, 1990a, 1990b; M. Harris, 1988, 1994; Moore, 1978; Vigil, 1988). It also appears that gangs that focus on profitable property crime, as opposed to drug use, violence, or other activities, tend to be more formally organized.

Spergel (1990) and Klein (1971) have described patterns of *vertical* and *horizontal* structure or alliances in gangs. Vertical structure refers to hierarchy, and includes differentiation between leaders and followers, and differentiation between age groups, who may move from one level to another, or from one gang to another, as they get older. Horizontal structure refers to distinctions that are not vertical in nature, including linkages with the neighborhoods from which gang members are drawn and the combination of different, separate gangs into "nations," "supergangs," alliances, or confederation. According to Spergel, horizontal structure is the more common pattern in contemporary American gangs. Within these broader structural patterns, Spergel (1984a) found that gangs tend to be imitative of structures in the larger society: families, businesses, and the military.

Typically, American gangs consist of a small core of five to 25 members who are most active in gang activities and from which the leadership of the gang is drawn, and a set of peripheral or marginal members, more or less strongly affiliated with the gang, more or less frequently involved in gang activities, and more or less committed to the gang (Hagedorn, 1988; Hardman, 1969; M. Harris, 1988; Klein, 1968; Spergel, 1990; Vigil, 1988). Counting only core members, most gangs are fairly small, typically 20 or fewer members (Davis, 1978).

AMERICAN STREET GANGS, DRUG SALES, USE, AND VIOLENCE

A considerable body of research on American street gangs has focused on the relationships between gangs and drug sales, drug use, and violence. American street gangs have been involved in the distribution and sale of illegal drugs for years, although the earlier research was not able to confirm this without serious reservations. Some authors found limited involvement in drug trafficking by street gangs, but they were unable to substantiate claims that these gangs were more heavily involved in the drug distribution (Chein et al., 1964; Spergel, 1964). In addition to these earlier findings there were reports that gangs looked down on drug abusers, and consequently prohibited use among their own gang members. Of particular concern to these gangs were individuals who used and sold heroin, since they were viewed as threats to their own neighborhoods (Short & Strodtbeck, 1974; Spergel, 1964).

By the late 1970s and 80s, the information on the role of American street gangs in drug trafficking began to change. Moore (1978) found that drug trafficking was more common among gang than nongang members, a finding also supported by other scholars (Dolan & Finney, 1984; Spergel, 1984). The 1980s were marked by a number of violent crimes that were reported to be associated with street gangs and drug sales. The rise in media interest in the "Crips" and the "Bloods" and their alleged involvement in the illegal sale of hard drugs fueled the concerns and fears that gangs were becoming more dangerous as a result of their role in the illegal drug market. A number of studies during the 1980s reported the increasing involvement of street gangs in illegal drug trafficking. Hagedorn's (1988) study of Milwaukee-based gangs reported that most gang founders and gang members had engaged in the selling of illegal substances. Klein et al. (1991) reported that street gangs in Los Angeles were more heavily involved in selling rock cocaine than were groups other than gangs. Cooper (1987) also found a connection between street gangs and trafficking in rock cocaine. Some have suggested that gangs have grown in membership due to the significant amounts of money members could make in drug trafficking (Fagan, 1989; Padilla, 1992). Esbensen et al. (2002:39) observed, "Drug trafficking has been widely attributed to gangs, and there is considerable agreement that gang youths are significantly more active in this arena than are nongang youths."

A number of other studies have described the relationship between American street gangs and drug sales. Terry Williams (1989) conducted an extensive ethnographic study of a Latino gang's involvement in the cocaine trade in New York City. In another study, Skolnick et al. (1990) interviewed incarcerated gang members in Northern California and found that street gang members did not necessarily organize for the purpose of selling drugs. Decker and Van Winkle (1994) report that gang members in St. Louis, Missouri, are heavily involved in drug sales, but that drug sales are seldom well organized. For example, Mieczkowski (1986) and Cooper (1987) found evidence of street gang drug trafficking (heroin and crack cocaine) and violence in Detroit, Michigan.

Some gang research leads us to a different conclusion. In a review of 26 years worth of gang-related homicides in Chicago, Block and

Block (1993) found that few gang-motivated homicides were related to drugs. In one period, out of 288 gang-related homicides occurring from 1987 to 1990, they found that only eight were tied to drugs. Most gang-motivated homicides were linked to conflicts over territory. This observation parallels that of Klein et al. (1991) in Los Angeles, who found a weak relationship between street gangs, drugs, and homicide. In addition, Moore (1991) suggests that the high number of homicides involving the sale of drugs should not be considered gang violence because the motive is competition for money and not traditional gang objectives. Finally, Sanders (1994) observed that gangs like the Crips were violent long before they became involved in cocaine distribution. Drug sales only added to the violence that was already occurring.

American Street Gangs and Drug Use

The relationship between American street gangs and drug use is heavily documented in the literature (Dolan & Finney, 1984; M. Harris, 1988; Klein & Maxson, 1985). In a systematic study of drugs and gangs, Fagan (1989) found a positive association between drug use and serious violence by gangs. Drug use was widespread and violent behavior occurred, but violence was independent of drug use and sales. Feldman et al. (1985) reported that the nature of drug use among Latino gangs in San Francisco varied according to their relationship to violence. The authors developed a typology of these gangs, classifying them as "fighting gangs," "entrepreneurial gangs," and "social gangs." The "fighting gangs" were reported to be occasional drug users, and drug use was said to have a minor relationship to violence. "Entrepreneurial gangs" were more concerned with drug trafficking as a method of attaining money for the purpose of social status, and only occasionally used drugs heavily. Violent behaviors were also only occasionally related to the presence of drugs. Finally, "social gangs" used drugs for recreational purposes, and rarely if ever were involved in fighting or violence.

There is research that challenges the assumptions that gang members are frequent users of illegal substances. Fagan (1989), in his review of the literature on drugs and gangs, noted that although some street gangs are actively involved in drug sales, they have strict codes against the use of addictive drugs like heroin by gang members.

Mieczkowski's (1986) Detroit-based research found that heroin use by teenage drug runners was prohibited by gang norms, and that violence, along with sanctions that eliminated monetary rewards were used to discourage gang use of heroin. Although gang members did use other illegal substances, such as cocaine and marijuana for recreational purposes, the abuse of heroin was definitely looked down upon and viewed as a threat to gang stability and security. Chin's (1986) research on heroin trafficking Chinese street gangs in New York City reported that gang members rejected the use of heroin, and that the gangs had rigid rules that included punishment by violence for using heroin. Cooper's (1987) research on street gangs that were involved in selling crack cocaine in Detroit reported that gang members were prohibited from using drugs, since this was believed to pose a threat to gang economic efficiency, as well as exposing them to the police. More recently, Waldorf (1993) studied gang drug use and sales by interviewing a sample of 300 gang members in San Francisco. He found that African American gang members reported almost universal participation in drugs sales, predominantly sales of crack and marijuana. He also found that African American gang members believed that crack use was bad business and was dangerous because it is addictive. Waldorf (1993:5) wrote, "Black gang members tend to avoid injectable drugs (heroin, cocaine, and methamphetamines) and psychedelics; they concentrate on alcohol and marijuana and only a small percentage use cocaine and crack." He (1993:5) also found, "Latino gang members use a broader range of drug-alcohol, marijuana, heroin, cocaine and PCP and seldom use crack as they consider it a black drug." Latinos or Hispanics reported selling marijuana, cocaine, and heroin; only a small number reported selling crack.

AFRICAN AMERICAN STREET GANGS

African American street gangs have been a feature of major cities throughout the United States for many years (Covey et al., 1997; Drowns & Hess, 1990). Recent research on African American gangs includes Hagedorn's (1988) study of African American gangs in Milwaukee, Labov's (1982) study of African American gang terminology and structure, Campbell's (1984b) study of New York gangs,

Dawley's (1992) ethnographic description of the Vice Lords in Chicago, Huff's (1989) work with African American gangs in Cleveland and Columbus, and Cureton's (2002) ethnographic work with the Crips in South Central Los Angeles. Perkins (1987) conducted a historical study of the evolution of African American gangs in Chicago. Reinhold (1988) studied the "Bloods" and the "Crips" across metropolitan areas. Brown (1977, 1978) studied African American female gangs in Philadelphia, and also studied gangs as extensions of the family. Keiser (1958) studied African American gangs in Chicago, seeking to discover why youths joined gangs. Short and Strodtbeck (1974) examined the relationship between African American and European American gang members and their respective communities. Johnstone (1981, 1983) studied factors that influenced recruitment to predominantly African youth gangs in suburban Chicago. In spite of all of this research, some scholars suggest that we continue to know relatively little about African American street gangs (Klein et al., 1995).

The Bloods and the Crips, two predominantly African American gangs, were the most widely known youth gangs operating in the United States in the late 1980s and early 1990s. According to Sanders (1994), the Crips were the first African American gang to emerge as a major force. The two gangs are identified by their respective colors with the Bloods wearing red and the Crips wearing blue in their clothing. Colors other than red and blue, such as green (in it for the money) or purple or have been adopted in some specific metropolitan areas. Each gang has its unique sign language, called flashing, which serves to reinforce gang identity. For example, Crips form the letter C and Bloods the letter B with their hands to indicate their affiliation. Bloods and Crips also use language (or argot) to reinforce their gang identities. For example, Crips greet each other with "cuzz" (cousin) and use the initials "BK" to mean Blood Killer. Crips will intentionally avoid using the letter B in writing and spoken language. Bloods use the term "Blood" (once a sort of generic greeting between African Americans, possibly derived from the term "blood brother" or suggesting "blood" kinship, that is, a common heritage or racial background) as a greeting and the initials "CK" to mean Crip Killer. They will avoid the letter C in writing or talking.

The Crips are also known for their intragang rivalries and violence. Fights between Crips factions were said to be responsible for up to one-half of all intergang fights in the Los Angeles area (Baker, 1988).

The Bloods were formed largely in response to the Crips. Violent encounters between the two groups are well-documented and led to much of the public concern over the two gangs. The Los Angeles County Sheriff's Department (LASD) observed that the Bloods fight the Crips and the Crips fight other Crips, but the Bloods do not typically fight other Blood gangs. The LASD (1995) estimated that there were over 12,000 members of the Crips and the Bloods in California Youth Association facilities or on parole.

Crip and Blood gangs typically have loose and informal structures. "Old Gangsters" (OGs) or "shot callers" sometimes assume leadership roles. Characteristically, the gang member with the most money, women, drugs, and other desired objects receives the most respect from other gang members. Gang members with the most respect and power are said to have "juice." The size of the Crip and Blood gangs varies from as low as five to as high as 1,000 members (Operation Safe Streets, 1995).

Crips and Bloods refer to their gangs as "sets" and the neighborhoods they operate in as *hoods*. Both gangs are territorial, but territory is linked more to drug distribution than to identification with particular neighborhoods. The Crips and Bloods in Los Angeles are reported to have direct contacts with major drug importers and use southern California as a major cocaine and crack shipping center (Porché-Burke & Fulton, 1992). Both groups mark territory with graffiti, which often has coded and violent messages.

Crips and Bloods draw their membership from African American "wannabes." The gangs sometimes attract members from grade school-aged youth and some authorities have found that some gang members may continue their affiliation well into their forties (Operation Safe Streets, 1995). Many youth have adopted Crip and Blood subcultures in terms of dress and identity, thus making the extent of true Crip and Blood activity in the United States impossible to accurately estimate. Many street gangs spread out throughout the country attach Crip or Blood to their gang names and identities without any connection between their gangs and the Crips and Bloods. This practice was found by Sanders (1994) in San Diego where Filipino gangs used African American gang culture with no real connection. In the United States, there is a fair amount of imitation going on, with gangs using the "Crip" or "Blood" label to try to enhance their status. Similar appropriation of gang names to enhance gang status occurs in prison gangs (Fong et al., 1996).

Similar to the Bloods and the Crips has been the creation of two alliances of gangs in the Midwest, known as People and Folks. During the mid-1980s, a Chicago gang known as the Latin Disciples, a racially mixed gang allied with the Black Gangsters Disciple Nation (BGDN), a gang consisting mostly of African American males, formed the Folk Alliance. Shortly thereafter, the Latin Kings, who were mostly Latino men, and the Vice Lords, who are almost all African American men, formed the People Alliance (Block & Block, 1993). Other gangs belonging to the Folk Alliance include the Black Disciples, Blank Gangster Nation, Young Latins, Simon City Royals, and Gangster Disciples. Gangs belonging to the People Alliance include Black P Stone Nation, and Loco Boys, among others.

Hagedorn's (1988) study of African American gangs in Milwaukee stirred a surprising amount of controversy. Hagedorn proposed that gangs in Milwaukee were a new phenomenon evolving from the growing African American underclass. Hagedorn explored the role the underclass plays in creating and perpetuating street gangs. He found that there was continued adult involvement in Milwaukee gangs, in contrast to the more usual pattern of "maturing out" of gang involvement with age. Hagedorn (1988:111) suggested that adult participation in gangs in Milwaukee was a product of the evolution of the underclass, "It is the contention of our study that increased gang involvement by adults is largely due to the drastically changed economic conditions in poor minority neighborhoods." Gang members participate in gangs longer, and fail to "mature out" in their early twenties, because there are so few good jobs and opportunities to provide alternatives to gang involvement. Gang leadership varied with the gang, and each age group had its own leaders, according to Hagedorn. Some gangs collected membership dues and had initiation rites. Only a small portion of time was devoted to criminal activities.

Hagedorn addressed the question of how gangs formed in Milwaukee and suggested that street corner and break dancing groups crystallized into gangs as a result of intergroup conflict, followed by media accounts often highlighting racial tension as a source of conflict. Authorities such as the police provide an additional source of negative reaction, and help to promote the crystallization of the group into a gang. Hagedorn described at length the changing relationship of gangs to their neighborhoods. According to Hagedorn, gangs have a lower sense of community than gangs in the past did. He proposed that ". . .

a number of factors have more recently acted to weaken this tie between gang and neighborhood" (Hagedorn, 1988:134). Hagedorn reported that gang members neither valued nor necessarily lived in their gang neighborhoods. They were alienated from their neighborhoods and from other members of their own ethnic groups. The lack of community awareness and allegiance, according to Hagedorn, is partially a result of school integration policies that moved youths out of their home neighborhoods into schools across town. This lack of neighborhood loyalties was further reinforced by the increased mobility afforded gang members by automobiles and mass transit systems.

Other Studies of African American Gangs

Johnstone's (1981) secondary analysis of youth gangs in the African American suburbs of Chicago provides another view of gangs. He found that the type of community influenced the prevalence of gangs. Gangs were more prevalent in areas with large concentrations of poor families, large numbers of youths, female-headed households, and lower incomes. Johnstone focused on racial tension among gangs and found that the prevalence of conflict did not increase with racial tension, as some might expect. Poverty appeared to have more explanatory power in understanding gang involvement and conflict among African American and European American youths in the suburbs.

Huff (1989) viewed African American gangs as a product of the underclass in Cleveland and Columbus, Ohio. Gang members were economically and socially disadvantaged youths. Huff's research on predominantly African American gangs found that members were usually 14 to 24 years old, with some gang members as young as 10 or as old as 30 years old. Gangs were age-graded, and started through some of the same patterns (break dancing clubs or informal social groups) or were started by the movement of ex-members of gangs into communities. Huff reported that there were three different types of gangs: hedonistic, instrumental, and predatory. Drug use was common to all types of gangs, but the emphasis placed on drug use was different in different types. Predatory and instrumental gangs were involved in property crimes. Gang structure was typically loose.

Campbell (1984a) researched a New York City group labeled by police as a gang. The "Five Percent Nation" adopted Islam as a way of life, was predominantly African American, and had both political and religious goals. A second gang described by Campbell was the "Sex Boys," which included both African and Hispanic Americans. This gang engaged in turf wars with neighboring gangs and committed crimes such as robbery. The gang had a core group of about 10 members and was estimated to have a total membership of about 100.

In a study of violent gangs in Chicago, Spergel (1984) reported that African American youth gangs were more homogeneous than gangs of other ethnic backgrounds. In Chicago, Curry and Spergel (1988) found that the number of homicides attributed to African American gangs rose from 61 in 1978-81 to 160 in 1982-85. It is possible, for instance, that more homicides are being attributed to gangs, even though the rate of gang homicides has not changed. Curry and Spergel also found that African Americans contributed proportionally less to the gang homicide rate than did Hispanics. They attributed this finding to greater social disorganization among Hispanics, who were relatively recent immigrants to Chicago, in contrast to the African Americans who had resided in Chicago for a longer period. In the Los Angeles area, however, Spergel (1990) suggested that gang homicides were disproportionately committed by African Americans rather than Hispanics.

HISPANIC AMERICAN STREET GANGS

We probably know more about Hispanic than any other American street gangs. Hispanic gangs have received considerable attention from scholars in recent decades (Erlanger, 1979; M. Harris, 1988, 1994; Moore, 1978; Moore, 1991; Moore et al., 1983; Rodríquez, 1993; Vigil, 1988, 1990; Zatz, 1985, 1987). Much of the focus on Hispanic gangs has been on the important role their cultural heritage plays in their lives, in and outside of gangs. It has been suggested (Operation Safe Streets, 1995) that to some Hispanic adolescents and adults, the street gangs are a way of life. Hispanic gangs have existed in the United States since the turn of the century, and may have become a way of life for some Hispanics (Heller, 1966; Paz, 1961). Mary Harris (1988) found evidence of Hispanic gangs, whose members were called pachucos, in the "barrios" (neighborhoods) of Los Angeles going back more than 60 years (Vigil, 1988, 1990). An important feature of Hispanic gangs in southern California is that they have become institutionalized in the social fabric of the Hispanic barrio subculture (Vigil 1988).

Moore et al. (1983) identified reasons why Hispanic gangs in Los Angeles are different from the gangs studied by Thrasher in the late 1920s. Specifically, these gangs are longer lasting and sometimes span several generations (M. Harris, 1988; Moore, 1991; Vigil, 1988). Some of the gangs and gang members have not assimilated into the larger American culture, and maintain cultural characteristics that are distinctively Hispanic, usually Mexican American. In addition, some gang members stay in the gang until middle age, which until recently has not been typical of most gang participation.

An important focal point of gang researchers has been the question of the ability of American Hispanic youth to obtain status from the larger society. Many of the studies on Hispanic gangs have concluded that Hispanic youths are marginal to the mainstream society and must find status through gang membership. However, this is not always true. Horowitz and Schwartz (1974) and Horowitz (1982) found Chicago Hispanic gang members to be adept at assuming socially desirable roles. These gang members could attain status and success in the larger society and had socially acceptable alternatives to gang membership, but they still participated in gangs. This suggests that marginal Hispanic youths could adapt quite well to the mainstream. Other studies by Mary Harris (1988) and James Diego Vigil (1988), however, seem to underscore the importance of marginality in gang formation. Vigil (1990) notes that there is a historical linkage between the term "Cholo" and the concept of marginalization. The essence of this is that Hispanics are not fully integrated into the mainstream socioeconomic and cultural system. They are marginal because of discrimination, prejudice, and cultural differences.

Hispanic Gang Characteristics

The longevity of some Hispanic street gangs is exceptional, such as with the White Fence gang of southern California that has existed for several generations. Some authors have suggested that Hispanic gangs may be a way of life in some barrios (Heller, 1966; Paz, 1961).

Hispanic gang members and marginal Hispanic youths are sometimes referred to as cholos (for males) or cholas (for females) (M. Harris, 1988, 1994; Vigil, 1988). Contemporary cholos and cholas carry on the tradition of barrio gangs in southern California, but not all cholos or cholas are gang members.

Gang members have a preferred style of dress that conveys gang membership. Popular among gang members are khaki pants and Pendleton® shirts. Pants are usually worn baggy and either "sagged" or high on the waist. Shirt collars are often buttoned down. These styles change over time and are likely to be modified. The general adoption of this and other styles of gang attire by nongang youth results in some individuals' being incorrectly identified as being in gangs. Klein (1995a) argues that this adoption of gang styles is problematic, beyond any confusion it may engender in identifying gang members, insofar as it positively reinforces gang culture in the larger society.

Controlling or protecting turf, specifically in the barrio, is a major concern of Hispanic street gangs. Hispanic gangs claim to view themselves as protectors of the neighborhood from threats or aggressors, including government agencies, law enforcement officials, and rival gangs (Operation Safe Streets, 1995). Moore (1978) found that Hispanic gangs emphasized protecting their neighborhood from outside gangs. Hispanic gangs are territorially based, so that the name of the gang and neighborhood are often the same (Moore, 1978). Residence, although important, is not a necessary or sufficient condition for barrio and gang membership. Some gang members may live outside the barrio because they or their parents have moved, but they may still continue to be members of the gang in the old barrio (Moore et al., 1983).

The identification with territory finds expression in a number of ways. Graffiti and specifically *"placas"* or stylized gang signatures are common in Los Angeles and other areas. *Placas* mark the boundaries of gang territories and warn other gangs to stay away. The importance of *placas* to gangs has been acknowledged for years, and some intervention programs are based on this fact.

Hispanic gangs, like other street gangs, are involved in the use and sale of drugs. Mary Harris (1988) found drug use to be very extensive in Hispanic gangs, with PCP, alcohol, and marijuana being the most prevalent drugs. PCP or "Angel Dust" preceded the present crack epidemic in the barrios (Rodríquez, 1993). Drug use by Hispanic gangs has been attributed to alienation (Bullington, 1977; Moore, 1978). According to Moore (1978), drug and alcohol use enhance the youth's sense of belonging in the group. Heroin use has had a long history (since the 1950s) among southwestern Hispanic gangs (Moore, 1991). Heroin use is more typical of older gang members (*veteranos*), while PCP is more often used by younger gang members (Operation Safe Streets, 1995). Drug use among Hispanic gang members is very much a social activity. Vigil (1988) likened drug use to a social lubricant.

American Hispanic gangs have been characterized as being very violent and vengeful. Joan Moore (1978; 1991) has argued that all Hispanic gangs are fighting gangs. While much of the violence is between rival gangs, fights among gang members, whether they are male or female, sometimes occur within the gang. Gang rituals such as "walking the line," where a violator of a gang rule must run between two lines of gang members while they beat him or her with sticks, have also been reported (Horowitz, 1982). Some of the reasons for gang violence include invasion of territory, rivalry over dating, sports, and gangs backing up individuals over personal matters (Moore, 1991). Revenge has been identified as an important motive for Hispanic youth gangs. Gang wars between rival barrios have been known to persist for decades. When barrio gang members are attacked or killed, their gang usually tries to avenge the attack.

As noted earlier, Curry and Spergel (1988) found that in Chicago, Hispanic gangs accounted for a disproportionate share of gang homicides. Spergel (1984) found that of 55 identified violent gangs, 33 (60 percent) were Hispanic, 15 African American, and seven white ethnic. From 1978 to 1981, approximately 60 percent of gang homicide victims and perpetrators were Hispanic, and 30 percent were African American. Hispanic gang members were more likely to be involved in homicides with multiple victims; African Americans were more likely to be involved in homicides with a single victim. Similarly, Bobrowski (1988) reported that in Chicago the number of Hispanic gang members suspected in 82 gang-related homicides outnumbered African American gang members, even though African Americans comprised 41 percent of the city's population and Hispanics only 16 percent. As noted earlier, there is some regional variation in this pattern, and Spergel (1990) reported that in Los Angeles, homicides committed by African American teenage gangs far outnumbered homicides committed by Hispanic youth gangs.

One characteristic of Hispanic gangs which has received considerable attention is the role and importance machismo plays in the gang and the larger community. Definitions of machismo differ, as does the importance researchers have attached to it (M. Harris, 1988). One of the basic assumptions of machismo is that its emphasis on masculinity and violence helps explain why Hispanic gangs are violent, male, and involved in displays of masculine prowess. Erlanger (1979:235) reported that while there is a Hispanic subculture which differs from the dominant American culture, it does not ". . . require or condone violence." Rather, Erlanger concludes, it is not so much Hispanic values, but social structural factors and estrangement from larger society that contribute to violence. In this context, research suggests that Latin American gangs have historically been less violent than their North American counterparts but may be in the process of becoming more violent and more similar to Hispanic gangs in the United States.

Some authors suggest that Hispanic gangs differ from other gangs in many respects, including their emphasis on machismo and the importance of identity with the barrio. In addition, Hispanic gangs tend to be modeled after the extended family. They have a sense of *carnalismo*, or brotherhood, among members (Moore, 1978; Vigil, 1990). Hispanic gangs have been characterized as highly cohesive with members having strong loyalties to the gang. Mirandé and López (1992:25), noting that Hispanic gangs are very cohesive, commented, "What made them different is not that they were "foreign," more violent, or innately criminal but that they were more cohesive and such cohesion was intensified by the fact that Mexican youth existed in a hostile environment."

Hispanic gangs are predominantly male, although there are female gangs and mixed gender gangs. Most research suggests that gender segregation among gangs is the most common pattern. Male gangs will often have female auxiliaries, who frequently take their titles from the male gangs. The age at which youths join Hispanic gangs has been placed as low as eight or 10 years old (Horowitz, 1982), or 11 and 12 years old (Chavira, 1980). Some Hispanic gangs begin recruiting members from grade schools. Most Hispanic gangs consist of teenagers, but gang membership is known to last well beyond age 20 for some members. Gang membership is divided about every two years into age-grades, cohorts, cliques, or *"klikas."* As children get older, they pass with their age cohort from younger to older *klikas* of the gang (M. Harris, 1988; Horowitz, 1982; Moore et al., 1983; Vigil, 1988). Moore (1991:45) noted that "each clique forms while its predecessor is active and visible on the streets." She then added, "It forms, generally, with the sense that it can match or outdo its predecessor." Leadership within the *klikas* is informal, loosely organized, and lacks a clear, solid chain of command. Moore (1978) places much importance on the role of age in defining Hispanic gang structure.

Hispanic gangs have a variety of rituals associated with entry and exit from the gang. Initiation rites often include attacks on the individual. These rites are called "courting in" or "jumping in." The degree of violence of the initiation may differ according to the residence of the initiate, with nonbarrio individuals being subjected to more violent initiations (Moore et al., 1983). Gang tattoos are also viewed as part of the initiation into some Hispanic gangs, as are the wearing of gang colors (Horowitz, 1982). The tattoos usually identify the individual's barrio and gang membership. Tattoos also represent a sign of the individual's toughness and commitment to the gang. Another measure of commitment to the gang is the individual's willingness to back up or fight for other gang members. Members not willing to support other gang members during fights or respond to outside threats to the gang are viewed as disloyal.

As the gang member participates in gang activities, there is an internalization of values, which evolves into a shared sense of common destiny. This latter appears to be more characteristic of Hispanic gangs than other gangs. Hispanic gang membership is more often linked to the larger Hispanic subculture than other types of contemporary gangs are linked to their ethnic subcultures. The gang provides a sense of belonging and a sense of identity. This identity is sometimes expressed in the notion of *La Vida Loca* (The Crazy Life). The crazy life is what we call the barrio gang experience. It is a lifestyle born out of the pachuco gangs of the 1930s and 1940s and the cholos. Although meanings differ, it is often meant to convey a sense of a life out of control and fatalistic. It is frequently symbolized in a triangular tattoo of three small dots usually located on the gang members hand. Each dot represents one of the words in the La Vida Loca phrase.

The social nature and functions of Hispanic gangs are well documented in the literature on Hispanic gangs (M. Harris, 1988; Horowitz, 1982; Horowitz & Schwartz, 1974; Moore, 1991). Extensive exchanges and mutual obligations reflect gang cohesion and longevity of relationships (Horowitz, 1982). These ties of trust and mutual support may help explain why Hispanic gangs tend to endure longer than other gangs. It should be noted that even though Hispanic gangs do tend to endure longer than other ethnic gangs, gang relationships change over time, as gang members marry, raise children, and find work (Horowitz, 1982). The adult gang member may maintain a dual commitment to the gang and to the conventional world.

Vigil used the concept of "multiple marginality" to explain the existence and persistence of Mexican American gangs. He proposed, "The multiple marginality framework better allows for descriptions and interpretations of particular (and perhaps peculiar) facts of people, time, and place" (Vigil, 1988:10). The multiple marginality approach stresses historical-structural and cultural-ecological criteria influencing the formation and nature of gangs. The recognition of the marginality of the population from which gangs are drawn is critical to understanding gangs. Vigil concluded by noting that the multiple marginality approach to gangs is capable of incorporating many other theoretical explanations for gangs. Vigil viewed previous gang theories as failing to consider the historical development of gangs.

Vigil recognized and stressed the community context of the barrio in the emergence and persistence of gangs. The barrio, in Vigil's view, separates Mexican American youths from mainstream society. There is also a strong sense of identity in the barrio. Vigil (1988:91) noted that the barrio and "*familia*" (family) are sometimes used interchangeably by youths. This sense of barrio or territory is highly refined in the minds of youths and at times promotes violence between rival barrio gangs. The continued importance of the barrio in Vigil's gangs stands in marked contrast to the de-emphasis of the importance of the neighborhood by Hagedorn's gangs.

Discrimination in schools, family difficulties, a poor labor market, poverty, gang subculture, and Cholo subculture are factors viewed by Vigil as contributing to the formation of youth gangs. Vigil observed that gang youths, more frequently than other youths in the barrio, find themselves in problematic situations in the home (e.g., disruptive families) and school (e.g., school failure). The gang fills the voids created by disruptive families, poor schools, and a hostile mainstream society (Vigil, 1988). Also, Vigil found that male family gang members had more influence than peers on the decision of youths to join gangs. Instead of being a reinforcer of conventional morality and norms, the family could thus be a source of pressure for gang membership.

Padilla (1992, 1995) conducted a study of a Puerto Rican gang, the Diamonds, that was involved in drug sales in Chicago. Padilla found that members were involved in street level dealing as part of the gang and also as individuals acting independently of the gang. The gang started out as a violent gang but over the years became more involved in the sale of drugs. Youths turned to the gang searching for employment that paid better than the legitimate jobs available to them. They believed that they could not make enough money working in conventional jobs to pay for the material things they wanted. They also did not believe that education would help them. Members in this gang, and others as well, perceived the gang as a business, and in that context, attached importance to ethnic and group solidarity. Padilla concluded that street dealing did not really pay the members much better than conventional jobs because few members actually made much money from their dealing.

Martin Sánchez Jankowski (1991) conducted a study of Hispanic gangs in Los Angeles, New York, and Boston that focused on how street gangs emerged as the result of a particular type of social order linked with low-income neighborhoods. These neighborhoods were organized around intense competition for scarce resources. The underground economy of drug sales played an important role in the gangs operations in the community. Jankowski concluded gang members had a defiant individualistic character.

It is important to acknowledge the presence of the very large 18th Street gang. This street gang or, perhaps more appropriately, this large affiliation of street gangs formed under the same name, has a major and growing presence in the United States as well as the western hemisphere. The gang may be larger than the Crips and Bloods combined. It formed in the 1960s in the Pico-Union section of Los Angeles, an impoverished area known to harbor recent and poor immigrants. One of the reasons for the gang's formation was a protective response to attacks from local Hispanic street gangs on immigrants to the area. Comprised mostly of Latino members, the gang is open to others from different ethnic backgrounds. Professor Jose Lopez is quoted as stating the gang breaks with tradition and has opened up to blacks, Samoans, Middle Eastern immigrants, and Anglos (Connell & Lopez, 1996).

Since its formation, the gang has spread to other cities in California and other states, such as Utah and Oregon. Some South and Central American countries report gang members claiming affiliation with the

18th Street gang. Assistant U.S. Attorney Gregory Jessner described
the gang's organizational structure as comprised of older members
(*veteranos*) who oversee a loosely organized network of cliques whose
members are intensively loyal to the gang's values and goals (Connell
& Lopez, 1996). It falls short because its loose structure of being organized crime but does have known links to the Mexican Mafia.

AMERICAN WHITE ETHNIC STREET GANGS

We know relatively little about white ethnic gangs other than what
the mass media have provided or from outdated studies. Historically,
this is ironic given that many of the first gangs in the United States
were mostly white ethnic youths from European countries. The Irish,
Polish, Italian, and other European countries all found representation
in nineteenth century American gangs (Asbury, 1927; Thrasher, 1927).
As these immigrant groups assimilated into the American culture, the
number of people involved in street gangs declined. One frequently
cited study of gangs in New York City estimated that European
Americans represented only about 9.3 percent of gang members
(Collins, 1979). Klein's (1995a) study of cities reporting the existence
of gangs found only 10 percent of the cities reported the presence of
predominantly white ethnic gangs. The relative absence of white ethnic gangs in official studies may be a product of a number of factors
including the difficulty in identifying them (Friedman et al., 1976) and
biases in reporting and public perception (Chambliss, 1973). The
absence in some urban areas, such as San Diego, of an identifiable ideology or cultural history may help explain why white ethnic gangs are
absent or rare (Sanders, 1994).

Recently the media and researchers have reported the existence of
a variety of suburban white ethnic gangs, including "Stoners,"
"Satanics," "Punks," and white supremacist gangs (Dolan & Finney,
1984; Wooden, 1995). The variety of white ethnic gangs may be partially attributed to their broad range of organizing foci such as racism,
drugs, satanism, neo-fascist ideology, fighting, and motorcycles
(Goldstein et al., 1994). In addition, since the mid-1980s, there have
been reported increases in white ethnic, middle-class gang activities in
suburban Los Angeles (Conklin, 1989), some of which are white

supremacists and others of which are satanist gangs. A common thread running through the descriptions of these different gangs is a general rebellion against adults and conventional society. Alienation from and rejection of mainstream society are common themes in much of the research on white ethnic gangs. This pattern is not new; Short and Strodtbeck (1974) noted that white ethnic youth gangs were more rebellious, sexually delinquent, and involved in drug use than African American gangs in Chicago.

American Skinhead Street Gangs

One type of predominantly white street gang that has received attention recently in the press is the "Skinhead" gang. Relatively little is known about the nature and prevalence of skinhead gangs. Some researchers have raised the issue of whether skinhead gangs are really gangs or are simply members of a neo-fascist youth subculture (Hamm, 1993). What is most likely is that some skinheads are members of law violating youth groups, others street gangs, and yet others only the skinhead subculture. What all experts agree on is that race and ethnic issues seem to be at the core of many skinhead groups. Either skinheads are racist or they make a special point of declaring they are nonracist. We know that they have been reported in several cities with names such as the "Confederate Hammer" in Dallas, "DASH" (Detroit Area Skinheads) in Detroit, and "CASH" (Chicago Area Skinheads) and "Romantic Violence" in Chicago. Other American cities have reported skinhead group activity.

A comparison of supremacist and traditional street gangs, according to Grennan et al. (2000) shows that they share much in common. For example, they noted that both are concentrated in economically deprived urban areas. Members are poorly educated and believe they are persecuted and discriminated against by social institutions. Members tend to come from abusive and dysfunctional families. However, according to Grennan et al. (2000), typical street gangs differ from skinhead and white supremacist gangs in some important ways. Street gangs often engage in illegal activities to circumvent formalized structures of oppression while white supremacist gangs target them. Skinheads attack those groups and organizations that they believe are unfairly benefiting from their (skinhead) oppression.

Typical street gangs lack ideological consistency present in some skin-head gangs. Most victims of street gangs are socioeconomically simi-lar to gang members, whereas supremacist and skinhead gangs attack victims that in some way are different.

Different estimates of the number of skinhead gangs and gang mem-bers vary widely (Moore, 1993; Mydans, 1990; Reed, 1989) because there are no reliable data from which to estimate skinhead gang mem-bership. Most authorities agree that the numbers of youths joining skinhead gangs is growing, but the absolute number remains small in the United States. The numbers of skinheads are low enough in most cities and areas that they do not have sufficient numbers to stake claim to territories. Rather, as Moore (1993) noted, they tend to float from city to city, as is the case in Florida where skinhead gang members have migrated between Tampa and Orlando. Skinhead gangs usually consist of European American youths who are non-Hispanic, non-Jewish, Protestant, working class, low income, clean shaven, and mili-tantly racist and white supremacist. Skinheads are often motivated by changes in racial diversity occurring in their communities and the attention they receive by the media (Wooden, 1995).

Most authors trace the evolution of the skinheads as a subculture to the 1970s and the working class in Great Britain. The roots of the skin-head movement in England can be traced to the 1950s and the Teddy Boys who wore Edwardian coats and tight pants. An interesting twist is that the original skinhead look can be traced back to Jamaican immi-grants to England who wore their hair very short and played their own type of music. Known as Rude Boys, their hairstyle and music would eventually be adopted by white working class youth (Wooden, 1995). The basic values of the original skinheads were those of the British working class (Taylor & Wall, 1976). The British working classes were very concerned about the invasion of foreign immigrants to England. Immigrants were seen as destroying British society and taking needed jobs from citizens. The skinhead subculture expanded to the United States during the late 1970s and early 1980s (Moore, 1993).

Skinheads typically attack immigrants, gay men and women, and other groups judged to be weaker or threatening. Such attacks were viewed by some skinhead, white supremacist, and neo-Nazi groups as a form of initiation of members into the gang. In the United States, increased skinhead violence in recent years, much of it anti-Semitic, has been reported in Portland, Tampa, San Diego, Hartford, and other cities (Sears, 1989). The violence ranges from beatings and abduction to murder. Skinhead violence has been a common theme in reports about skinheads (Came et al., 1989a, 1989b; Coplon, 1988).

American skinheads may be identified by their physical appearance, which typically includes shaved heads, Nazi insignia, heavy jeans that are rolled up over the boots, heavy steel tipped boots (Doc Martens), suspenders, and leather clothing which is often marked with racist and white supremacist slogans. Some youth will have tattoos of swastikas, a circled letter "A," and "666," the satanic mark of the beast. Skinheads use their suspenders to convey meaning. Suspenders worn down mean the wearer is ready to fight. The color of the suspender may also mean what group the wearer is against. For example, yellow suspenders may mean the wearer is against the police or the color green against people who are gay. Similar to other gangs, youth are often jumped in to the gang. White shoelaces may represent white pride, red laces white power, and yellow the wearer hates police. Membership in skinhead gangs ranges in age from 16 to the early 20's. Members frequently come from working class broken homes, but some skinheads are from middle-class backgrounds. Moore (1993) suggests that skinheads from working and middle-class backgrounds want and need a firm identity and a sense of belonging to something similar to an extended family. Some skinheads overtly reject the upper class and material wealth, and appear to believe that opportunities for them to attain wealth and status are closed. Some research has identified being labeled a "bully" as one of the most common predictors of youth belonging to racist skinhead groups (Wooden, 1995).

CONCLUSION: AMERICAN STREET GANGS

Much has been written about street gangs in the United States compared to other countries. Most of the world's knowledge about street gangs reflects what they are and are not in the American context. Few would question the assertion that American street gangs serve as role models for street gangs throughout the world. Even though street gangs throughout the world reflect their host cultures and countries, at the core, they draw much of their style from American street gangs. Therefore, a good starting point for reviewing the world's street gangs is how they are represented in the United States.

There is no American street gang reflective of all street gangs in the United States or the world. Even within the United States, the combinations and variations in the American street gang seem at times to be endless. Although there is no one gang representative of all gangs, there are features about gangs in America that at least on the surface seem to shape the nature of gangs in other countries. For example, most American street gangs are not typically highly organized, formal, one-dimensional, or solely organized for the purpose of committing crimes. These same features, or characteristics if you will, are present in many street gangs in other countries.

In a racially and ethnically divided American society, street gangs organized along racial and ethnic lines seem inevitable. American street gangs appear to evolve out of primary friendship groups, and to the extent that segregation in our neighborhoods and schools leads to racially and ethnically homogeneous friendship groups, we may also expect it to lead to racially and ethnically homogeneous gangs. This is especially true when, in addition to skin color or country of origin, we add the language barrier experienced most acutely by Hispanic and Asian American communities with continuously high rates of immigration (and thus high prevalence of individuals who do not speak English as a first language). Eliminating racial, ethnic, and linguistic segregation would not, in all likelihood, eliminate gangs, but it would probably eliminate race, ethnicity, and language as criteria for gang membership, and result in more racially and ethnically heterogeneous youth gangs. All of the street gang structures identified by Malcolm Klein (1995a, 2002) can be found in North America. The variety of forms of American street gangs, at times, seems endless.

Chapter 3

STREET GANGS IN EUROPE

Street gangs, though not as common as they are in the United States, have existed throughout much of Europe over the centuries. Several European nations, such as Great Britain, France, Germany, the Netherlands, Sweden, Hungary, Czech Republic, and others, have reported the presence of street gangs. Skinhead and neo-Nazi groups, some of which operate as street gangs, can be found in several European countries, including Denmark, Belgium, Czech Republic, Finland, Austria, France, Germany, Ireland, Italy, Slovenia, Spain, Norway, Slovakia, Portugal, Poland, Luxembourg, Bulgaria, and the balance of European countries (Anti-Defamation League, 1995).

Although references are made to street gangs in Europe, determining the true extent of their presence is difficult. As Malcolm Klein (2001) noted, Europeans frequently deny the existence of gangs because the gangs they see do not fit stereotypical depictions of leader-dominated, well organized, violent, and cohesive groups found in American film and mass media. American street gangs typically do not fit these stereotypical images either. Yet, a closer look reveals that there are clear examples of street gangs in many European countries. Hence, Klein et al. (2001) referred to the situation in Europe as being the "Eurogang Paradox," because, although street gangs existed, authorities did not always recognize them.

The presence of street gangs in many European countries is important but also is the noted absence of such gangs in other European countries. Writing in 1996, Klein noted the absence of street gangs in much of Europe such as Spain, Finland, Holland, and Slovenia. However, Hoyst (1982) wrote a decade and half earlier, that a large share of the criminal offenses could be attributed to gangs in Spain.

What should we make of a 1997 news report on teenage girls belonging to a violent street gang in Barcelona (Deutsche Presse-Agentur, 1997)? The gang reportedly had members as young as 12 and old as 16 and was involved in assaulting youth at school and dance clubs. Was this 1997 gang an exception or indicative of other female street gangs in Spain? Do Spanish street gangs appear and disappear over time, were they ever present, are they rare, or simply overlooked? Since Klein's early work on European street gangs, there is mounting evidence that street gangs are beginning to form to a greater degree in many of these countries. The relative absence of street gangs in some countries, such as Spain and Portugal, might be attributed to a number of factors that require further study.

HISTORICAL REFERENCES TO EUROPEAN GANGS

Street gangs or prototypes of gangs have probably been around much longer than most people would believe. For example, more than 1,600 years ago, Saint Augustine (AD 354-430) made reference to perhaps a type of adolescent gang in his *Confessions* (St. Augustine, 1949). Saint Augustine described his own involvement in criminal activities as a member of a group of youth. Morales (1992) noted that Saint Augustine believed that crimes committed as a group seemed more rewarding. During the Middle Ages, youth groups sometimes formed and engaged in delinquent acts. Some of these youth groups only hint at being gangs (Capp, 1977), while others clearly were gangs (Bellamy, 1973; Cockburn, 1977; Hanawalt, 1979; McCall, 1979). Chaucer used the term gang in his writing as early as 1390 (Klein, 1995a). Historians generally agree that gangs were common during the 14th and 15th centuries, at least in Great Britain. For example, Shelden et al. (1997) concluded the first known youth gangs in recorded history appeared in London during this period, as England shifted from an agrarian to industrial society.

Gang crime is relatively obscure during the Middle Ages because of the different practices of classifying offenders. In 14th century England, Hanawalt (1979) found that criminals and criminal gangs were often sadistic and violent. These gangs stole livestock, committed robbery, extortion, rape, and numerous other offenses. Material gain was a clear motive for gangs in the Middle Ages (Bellamy, 1973; Hanawalt, 1979; McCall, 1979). In the 14th century, some of the gangs studied by Bellamy (1973) averaged about six members, came from all walks of society including the gentry, had internal organization, defined leadership, a hierarchical structure, and specialization of roles. Members were often related. Bellamy cited the example of the Coterel gang, whose core was comprised of James Coterel and his brothers. Membership in these gangs was interlocking. Gang members moved from gang to gang, and gangs sometimes cooperated on larger criminal endeavors. It is evident from the historical record that gangs of the Middle Ages were every bit as violent as contemporary gangs. The principal difference is that gang homicides in the Middle Ages were more physically direct and personal than today's drive-by shootings.

Not all medieval youth groups operated entirely outside the law. Youth groups known as "Abbeys of Misrule" because they drew their membership from abbey or trade schools existed in medieval France. These groups participated in violent football games, fights, and socially condoned activities. There is evidence of similar youth groups in England but with less organization than those in France (Capp, 1977). Germany and Switzerland also had similar groups (Gillis, 1974). Often these youth groups viewed their role as being the guardians of social morality; they performed social control functions and had the support of the community.

One practice of these groups was the *charivari*. Charivaris were mob-like demonstrations usually directed toward deaths, scolds, cuckolds, and upcoming marriages between mismatched couples (Davis, 1971). They enforced the existing social order but could also be part of religious, political, and economic protests (Shorter, 1977; Thompson, 1984). The principal motive of *charivaris* was to disrupt the community and harass the victims until they paid a bribe to quiet the commotion. The *charivaris* were similar to gangs in the respect that youths were identified with a specific group, performed delinquent acts, and acted in unity as a gang would. English church and court records indicate that while many of the activities of these youth groups were condoned by adults, some acts were clearly criminal (Capp, 1977). The records show that gangs of youths rioted and battled with rival gangs from other schools and abbeys until as late as the 17th century.

During the 1600s, English gangs with names such as the Hectors, Bugles, and Dead Boys fought each other and damaged property

(Pearson, 1983; Spergel, 1995). These gangs wore colored ribbons to identify themselves. In Germany during the 17th and 18th centuries, bandits did not operate exclusively on their own but were typically members of gangs, or at least of delinquent or criminal groups. Gang activity usually involved four to six members, with no criminal court records indicating more than 12 members involved in a single gang incident (Danker, 1988). These groups were organized for crime and had specialists in certain areas, but lacked well-defined leadership and had no gang induction ceremonies.

The Industrial Revolution had an effect on street gangs in England and other countries. The slums spawned by the Industrial Revolution were known to harbor street gangs such as the "Redskins," the "Black Hand," and the "Beehives" in England (Fyvel, 1961). Other 19th century English gangs included the "Gonophs," "Fagins," and the "Swell Mob" (Whitfield, 1982). According to John Gillis (1974), from 1770 to 1870 urban working class youth gangs with strong neighborhood affiliations vied for supremacy and control of territory. Gillis suggested that these gangs established themselves as basic units of British youth culture during this period. Gangs of youth, with members aging between 14-20 years, had a sense of territory and fought rival gangs for turf. These street gangs took on names of their neighborhoods. In Manchester England gang life was known as "scuttling," which was fuelled by the wish of gang members to assert their supremacy of one neighborhood over another. Gillis likened street gangs to a type of school for the poor, as gangs brought youth together into a learning situation.

Andrew Davies (1998) studied the street gang the Beehive Boys that operated in Glasgow, Scotland during the 1930s. In the 1930s, high unemployment and a struggling economy characterized Glasgow. Davies cautions us that although the Scottish economy was in poor shape, Glasgow's violent street gangs cannot be solely attributed to the poor economic climate. He noted that street gangs had a long history in Glasgow predating the poor conditions of the 1930s. He also discovered that in the case of the Beehive Boys, some members continued to be active members of the gang well into their 20s and 30s, as work was scarce in Glasgow. Lacking work, some Beehive Boys became involved in organized crime as a means of support.

In the period after World War II, youth gangs or youth subcultures were present in England and other European countries (Campbell et al., 1982; Cavan & Cavan, 1968; Fyvel, 1961). In countries devastated by war, such as France, Germany, and Belgium, youth gangs flourished. Statistics are unreliable for this period, but it appears that World War II had major effects on rates of delinquency and street gang activity in European countries (Cavan & Cavan, 1968; Louwage, 1951). In Great Britain, the British Empire following WWII had basically dissolved and waves of immigrants moved to the British Isles from the colonies. These and other post-war changes created ripe conditions for street gangs to develop (Etter, 1999). Groups of British youths pillaged, worked in the black market, and became involved in prostitution, theft, and vagrancy. Economically motivated delinquent and criminal acts were a method of surviving for groups of youths who had lost their homes, lost one or both patents, and lost their means of support (Cavan & Cavan, 1968; Fyvel, 1961). Similarly, Jungk (1959) found orphaned and abandoned children joining street gangs for survival in the chaotic post-atomic environment of Hiroshima following the war.

STREET GANGS IN GREAT BRITAIN

Little is currently known about street gangs in Britain and some have suggested the reason for this is a social denial of their presence (Mares, 2001). Some scholars deny street gangs are present even though gangs have been a feature of the British landscape for centuries. In England, true street gangs probably started in the 19th century. Burt (1925) reported that during the first quarter of the 19th century, dangerous delinquent gangs were present in England. The 19th century was the Victorian age, and the period of Charles Dickens, an astute observer of British society and street life. Dickens provides a plausible account of what street gangs of the Victorian period may have been like in his book *Oliver Twist.* The street gang portrayed by Dickens consisted of a loosely organized group of youths who were led by adult leaders who provided shelter and food in return for a share of the earnings. The members specialized in different street crimes, such as picking pockets and other forms of theft, to support the gang. Roaming the streets during the day and staying in dirty lodges with prostitutes, drunkards, and adult criminals may have been common. In England, according to some historical evidence (Sanders, 1970;

Tobias, 1967), groups of boys lived independently of their parents, sometimes in settings not unlike those portrayed by Dickens. The street gang's main purpose was to provide a collective way to cope and survive in Victorian society.

Other youths formed casual partnerships with other boys in non-hierarchical and temporary groups (Tobias, 1967). Picking pockets, theft, burglary, and begging were often used to support these law violating youth groups. Members usually specialized in specific types of delinquent and criminal behavior, such as cut pursing (cutting money pouches loose from people's belts) or picking pockets. These groups were relatively small, typically ranging from two to five members (Sanders, 1970).

Some street gangs were highly territorial, well organized, with regular meeting places, age-graded, hostile to outsiders, and took on neighborhood names and occasionally had female satellites (Gillis, 1974), much like contemporary street gangs. According to Gillis (1974), from 1770 to 1870, urban working-class youth gangs based on neighborhood affiliation and competing for supremacy and control of turf developed into a basic component of youth culture in Great Britain. Similar to contemporary gangs, immigrant groups and other minorities were sometimes the targets of 18th and 19th century English street gangs (Humphries, 1981). These characteristics, plus involvement of street gangs in illegal activity, particularly violence and theft, persisted into the 20th century.

Andrew Davies (1999) offers a description of 19th century English "scutter or hooligan" street gangs. The 19th century hooligan subculture was working class, out-of-control, and defiant of authority. Hooligans were known for their drunkenness, disorderly conduct, brawling, and assaults (Pearson, 1983). Hooligan gangs became associated with street battles among themselves and law enforcement. Pearson noted the early hooligans wore a distinctive style of clothing, including bell-bottom trousers, colorful neck scarves, caps, heavy boots (with steel toecaps), studded leather belts, and "donkey fringe" haircuts. They focused on maintaining positive social relationships within their peer group.

They fought over territory with rival hooligans in "scuttles." A "scuttle" refers to a gang fight. These 19th century English gangs were mainly concerned with control over territories and neighborhoods. Scuttle gangs attacked members of rival gangs over territorial disputes.

Long-running feuds among these street gangs led to prolonged violence in some areas. Characteristics of scuttle gang members were that they were usually aged between 14 to 19 years, were working class, and had strong identification with specific neighborhoods. These Victorian street gangs were mostly male but included some female members. British society viewed these female gang members as stark contradictions to the mainstream Victorian expectations of appropriate female behavior. Some historians have perceived female gang members as "molls" or simply girlfriends of male gang members with little involvement in the gangs. According to Davies (1999), this perception is inaccurate because females were much more involved in the conflict and operation of the gangs than once thought.

Over the decades, numerous studies have been conducted on street gangs in Great Britain (Downes, 1966; Gillis, 1974; Patrick, 1973; Scott, 1956). For example, in the mid-1950s, Scott (1956) interviewed criminal youth who were known by authorities to have at least committed group offenses. He classified them into adolescent street groups, structured gangs, and loosely structured groups. He found some youth belonged to groups of five to 30 members aging from 14 to 18 years. Mostly male, some allowed females to participate in the groups and gangs. The groups all opposed conventional values and rigid organizational structures. The groups and gangs generally lacked well-defined leaders.

Downes' (1966) research on subcultures and gangs in Britain found no evidence of organized delinquent gang subcultures, an idea touted in much of the American gang literature of the 1960s. Instead, he found British youth were alienated from middle-class institutions such as school and the workplace. Because of their relative level of deprivation and lack of opportunity, these youth rebelled but did not establish formal gangs. In 1966, Downes characterized the situation at the time as the "gang myth" and objected to the application of the term gang to British youth. He concluded gangs were nonexistent and Britain was relatively gang-less. Downes' conclusions mirror some those referenced four decades later by Klein et al. (2001) that denied the existence of street gangs in Europe. Others besides Downes, such as Parker (1974), found little evidence of highly structured and offense-oriented street gangs.

Almost 50 years ago, gang membership appears to have little effect on delinquency in London (Downes, 1966). Cavan and Cavan (1968) reported that only about 11 percent of the offenses in London's courts were gang related. Like street gangs in other countries, British gangs' primary activities are not delinquent in nature, but consisted of hanging out and socializing (Patrick, 1973; Willmott, 1966). When gang members committed crimes, they were usually attributed to small cliques within the gang (Downes, 1966; 1996). Although British gangs had "punch-ups" or gang fights, the violence did not generally reach the severity found in contemporary American gangs. More recently, there is some evidence that this pattern continues. Sanders (1994) recently noted the lack of gang violence in London.

Labels attached to British youth gangs and subcultural groups have included "Teddy Boys" (Short & Strodtbeck, 1974), "Skinheads" (Knight, 1982; West & Farrington, 1977), "Mods," "Punks," "Rude Boys," and "Rockers" (Whitfield, 1982). Some researchers have suggested that these groups represent subcultures rather than true gangs (Campbell et al., 1982; Campbell & Muncer, 1989; Short, 1968). Others believe that youth street gangs are very much a part of the British scene (Whitfield, 1982). The debate will likely continue in the foreseeable future.

As early as the late 1950s, British "Teddy Boy" or "Teds" gangs were active in racially motivated attacks on West Indian immigrants (Fyvel, 1961). Symbolically, they saw their role as defender of the streets and responded to any threats to their space and socioeconomic status. The Teds attacked Cypriot and black people during the 1950s. Café owning Cypriots were seen as a threat because they had become economically successful. The Teds also perceived blacks as being relatively economically successful. The Teds were comprised of working class youth with a musical preference for American rock and roll music. The Teds were known for their intense loyalty to each other, which can be viewed as a reaffirmation of traditional slum working-class values and a strong sense of territory (Downes, 1966). Their style of dress was decisively English.

By the early 1960s, the Teddy Boys were replaced by the Mods, who had yet another distinctive style of dress. The "Mods" and their counterparts, the "Rockers," continued to be active in the 1960s and 1970s. The Mod subculture was primarily interested in music, appearance, alcohol, and drugs. According to Hebdige (1976), the Mods focused on the pursuit of leisure. Their drug of choice was methamphetamine (speed). In contrast were the Rockers who were more interested in motorcycles, leather clothing, and had more in common with the American motorcycle gangs of the 1950s. Rockers wore black leather jackets, liked the "greasy look," and held macho values. The Rockers typically came from families with unskilled and manual labor jobs (Burke & Sunley, 1998). They viewed Mods with contempt as spoiled rich kids. It has been suggested that the Mods and the Rockers crystallized into well-defined subcultures with corresponding gangs partly in reaction to accounts published in the British press (Cohen, 1973). Representative gangs from the two subcultures occasionally fought each other in well-publicized fights along the southeastern coast of England (Cohen, 1973; Knight, 1982; Moore, 1993).

The Mods eventually broke down into "Hard Mods" and "Smooth Mods." The former adopted wearing heavy boots and short hair and evolved as a precursor to the skinheads (Moore, 1993). In the mid-1960s and 1970s, Rastafarian youth groups linked to West Indies culture were called "Rudies," or "Rude Boys." They emerged and were influential in shaping the developing skinhead subculture (Hebdige, 1976; Knight, 1982). Their short hair and style of dress, which includes heavy black boots, leather and denim clothing, and an overall air of toughness identified these Rudie gangs.

British Skinheads

The skinhead gangs observed throughout the West are thought to have originated in Great Britain in the 1970s (Brake, 1974; Burke & Sunley, 1998; Clarke, 1976; Moore, 1993) and specifically East London (Brake, 1974). Moore (1993) contends that English skinheads set the early style for similar groups in the United States. The history of the skinheads in Great Britain has been covered well by a number of scholars (Hebdige, 1976, 1979; Knight, 1982; Moore, 1993).

In England and other European countries, there is a strong association between skinheads and football (soccer) teams. Skinheads are primarily a working class movement that sometimes expresses itself in street gangs. Moore noted (1993) that in England, skinhead youth grew up with the worst schools, cockney subculture, working class values, and low incomes. Within the cockney lifestyle, skinheads are thought to have adopted certain dominant values such as toughness, football, ethnocentrism, and bravado (Brake, 1974).

The British skinheads emerged in a climate of increasing prices, unemployment, and an increasing minority and immigrant population. Their shaven heads (cropped hair) from which they derive their name and their distinctive style of dress characterize many skinheads, both male and female. The short hair was thought to offer an advantage in fighting because opponents could not grab their hair. The characteristic skinhead uniform includes black leather clothing, hobnailed boots (Doc Martens), army greens, Ben Sherman shirts, chains, swastikas, braces (suspenders), and tattoos (Knight, 1982). The working class background is symbolized in skinhead clothing a number of ways, such as the use of two crossed hammers on some clothing.

Much of the skinhead subculture is designed to instill fear, via dress, gait, vocabulary, and ideology (Young & Craig, 1997). Brake wrote of British skinheads:

> Aggressive working-class puritans in big industrial boots, jeans rolled up high to reveal them, hair cut to the skull, braces, and a violence and racism [that]earned them the title 'bovver boys,' 'boot boys' on the look out for 'aggro' (aggravation). Stylistically they have roots in the hard mods, forming local gangs called after a local leader or area. Ardent football fans, they were involved in violence on the terraces against rival supporters. They espoused traditional conservative values, hard work, patriotism, defense of local territory, which led to attacks on hippies, gays and minorities. They became a metaphor for racism. (Brake 1985:75-76)

Unlike most American skinhead youth who have grown up under relatively comfortable economic conditions, the British skinhead youth have lived in a steadily declining economy. Because so many British working class youth have been affected by the lack of opportunity and declining economy, significant numbers of skinhead youth are present in Great Britain. Because of their relative concentration, British skinhead youth are able to form a critical mass much easier than their counterparts in the United States, where skinhead youth are more dispersed across the country (Moore, 1993).

The British skinheads are a violent subculture that, like their American skinhead counterparts, express racist attitudes and hostility toward the upper-class and established political authority. Skinheads generally believe minority groups and immigrants are taking over Great Britain. These targeted groups are seen as taking jobs away from the British working class and, correspondingly, from skinhead youths.

British skinheads engage in "paki-bashing" (attacks on Pakistani and other nonwhite immigrants) and are also known to be aggressive toward youths from other British subcultures, for example, the punks and hippies (Brake, 1974; Campbell et al., 1982; Knight, 1982). References to skinhead and other white British youth prejudice towards Asians, such immigrants from Pakistan are abundant (Carey, 1985). Immigrants of Pakistan are convenient targets because of their "exotic" clothing, food, religion, and language. They also represent an easy population for scapegoating. British skinheads have targeted other groups besides immigrants. They often view people who are homosexual as corrupt and vicious and hippies as lazy and unclean (Burke & Sunley, 1998).

The main skinhead political organization in Great Britain is named Blood and Honor, which was founded in 1987. Other hard line racist groups are named the Combat 18 group and the British National Party (BNP). In addition, links between the National Front, a British neo-fascist organization, and skinhead youth have been suggested by research (Buford, 1990). However, skinhead violence may have very limited formal links to political organizations or movements. Bjorgo and Witte (1993:11) conclude that, "A major finding of this volume is that most racist violence is perpetuated by youth gangs or individuals not affiliated to political organizations." Bjorgo and Witte discovered that street-level gangs and individuals were more influential in shaping skinhead activities and violence than well-organized political movements.

It is important to note that much of the skinhead violence is directed toward Asians in general. In Great Britain, "Asian" includes a broader range of peoples than in the United States, where Asian typically refers only to far-eastern peoples. In Great Britain, Asian also refers to Pakistani, Indian, Southeast Asian, and far-eastern peoples. The ethnicity of those groups and gangs attacking Asians in Great Britain is not restricted to whites or white skinheads. Journalist Gwynne Dyer (1999) found that black youth joined whites in attacking Asian peoples. Black West Indies origin people share a common language and religious background with white British white society; thus they have more in common compared to their Asian victims who often come from non-English-speaking and Christian backgrounds.

Case Examples of Other Types of British Street Gangs

Media reports on British gangs and hate crimes are not restricted to skinhead violence on Asian and African ancestry immigrants. Reports of Asian or Afro-Caribbean street gangs attacking whites in some cities have been written (Burkeman, 2000; Vasagar et al., 2001). These attacks are characterized as being racially motivated and retaliatory for past violence by white street gangs or groups on Asian or Afro-Caribbean immigrants. The media have reported that some immigrant street gangs have established "no go" zones for white British youth. Allegedly, any white entering these zones runs the risk of victimization. These allegations of "no go" zones controlled by street gangs of youth are likely overstated according to some media sources (Vasagar et al., 2001). What is evident is that for some, racism fuels conflict or at least tension between different racial groups and gangs in some British cities. Control over drug trafficking territories may also be motivating some of the violence between street gangs (Hopkins, 2000; Vasagar et al., 2001). The media have noted wars between Asian and Afro-Caribbean street gangs with motives being debated as to whether the issues are racial or drug sales related (Burkeman, 2000).

Studies of British street gangs include Stephen Humphries' (1981) work, where he used oral reports to study British street gangs. His analysis revealed that street gang members were working-class youth who had a shared sense of oppression and inequality. The gangs represented an avenue for comradeship, opportunity for status, and a way to pass time. Gang members had a sense of membership and belonging. Outbreaks of violence among rival gangs occurred in the poorest areas. When the economy declined, street gang violence increased. The lack of opportunity to obtain material goods helped drive gang members to committing property crimes such as theft.

Debbie Archer (1995) studied criminal female street gangs in South London. These female street gangs were involved in criminal offenses, such as shoplifting, assault, mugging, and robbery. Gang members wanted to gain respect from peers. The gangs claimed territories, which they viewed as providing them with power and control. They marked their territories with gang graffiti or tags and defended these areas from competitors. Gang members spent most of their time hanging-out with other members in their territories, consistent with street gangs throughout the world.

Characteristics of the gang members included being from female single-parent households, beginning ages of around 13 to 14 years, Afro-Caribbean, inner city, poor and not involved in school. Many members were pregnant by their mid-teens. The gang members wore different clothing from nongang members. For example, the Peckham Girls wore gold sun-visors, pink fluorescent leggings, red blouson jackets, baseball caps, nose-studs, streaked hair, and multiple earrings. These trappings were viewed by the members to flaunt their individuality at the same time as identifying them as gang members. Their clothing distinguished them from the general public.

Archer (1995) reported membership varied, but for the "Peckham Girls," it was about eight to nine members. Gangs had "ring leaders," who were typically arrested more often than the other members. She did not find any links of these street gangs to organized crime. One of the gangs described by Archer, the "Gunners," gave members a sense of empowerment and support because it focused on attacking males in the community who had victimized females. They targeted males who had sexually assaulted neighborhood females. Archer found that the community basically tolerated these female gangs. Archer found the primary response from law enforcement was to crack down on the gangs but failed to keep data on gang activities.

Malcolm Klein (2001) found true street gangs in Manchester and London. According to Klein, these gangs were mostly comprised of foreign-born members of Chinese, Pakistani, Indian, or Jamaican ancestry. Unlike street gangs in other European cities, these gangs were not from the suburban outskirts, but from the inner areas of the cities. They, unlike their continental counterparts, were very territorial. Klein reported the street gangs focused on the sales of drugs. They used violence to gain marketing advantages in their territories. They preferred to sell hashish and heroin.

Dennis Mares (2001), using Klein's gang typology, found examples of compressed and neotraditional gangs in the greater Manchester metropolitan area. Mares collected ethnographic data on street gangs in Manchester from 1997 to 1998. His research covered three distinct areas of the city. In Moss Side, an impoverished neighborhood close to the city center, his research found street gangs that were violent and had conflicts with rival gangs. The gangs were heavily involved in the sale of drugs. Mares noted that as these gangs became increasingly involved in the drug trade, they became more violent. Even thought they were involved in drug sales, the gangs were not totally organized around drug sales but were very socially oriented. The members used street gangs to establish and maintain social relationships. The gangs were not hierarchical and had no formal leaders, although older members were respected more and wielded more influence. The gangs had about 80 members, but only 40 were generally active much of the time. Ethnically, about 80 percent of the members were of Afro-Caribbean ancestry. This high representation of Afro-Caribbean gang members was reflective of the neighborhood's ethnic composition. The ages of gang members ranged from 10 years to the early 30s. Besides drug sales, members were involved in other crimes such as auto theft, protection rackets, and robberies. Mares (2001), using Klein's typology, considered these gangs as being neotraditional in type.

Mares (2001) also studied another type of gang in a different section of Manchester. In the poor section called Wythenshawe, Mares found an example of a compressed gang. This gang had about 25 members, including some females. Members were about 90 percent white and aged between 14 years to early 20s with most maturing out during the early 20s. This gang had no formal organization, no formal leaders, and was territorial. The gang was involved in drug sales, but its involvement was minimal. The gang's other crimes included auto theft (for joyrides), extortion, shoplifting, and other forms of minor crime.

The final area of Manchester that Mares (2001) studied was the Salford district. Salford is a working-class district of Manchester. In Salford, Mares concluded the gangs were similar to those found in Moss Side. Mares (2001) again used Klein's typology and concluded these gangs were neotraditional. These gangs were violent and territorial. The gangs named themselves after streets or neighborhoods. The gangs protected their territories from other rival gang members. Gang members worked hard at developing reputations through their aggression and criminal accomplishments. They had members ranging from 10 to 25 years of age. The gangs were involved in auto thefts, robbery, theft ("crash and carry"), and drug sales.

Summarizing his research, Mares (2001) concluded that the street gangs he observed reflect historical class relations within Britain. Being a member of the working class in Britain implied being "hard." Being "hard" meant the individual needed to be strong, tough, and powerful. To the poor and working-class youth of Manchester, street gangs provided a great social mechanism for youth to establish and maintain an image of being "hard." Street gangs enhanced this tough powerful image though the use of violence and criminal activities.

Journalists have identified other types of street gangs in England. For example, Neil Berry (1988) reported on the presence of young radical Sikh gangs in London. Members of the Sikh religion base their beliefs on ideas formulated in the Punjab region of India. Many adherents of Sikh religion reside in London. The Sikh followers dress and live in styles that set them apart from mainstream British society. For example, Sikh's wear long white garments, white turbans, and carry long daggers. In Southall, violent Sikh gangs, such as the Tuti Nang, operated in the late 1980s. According to Berry, these street gangs were not politicized but conveyed traditional Sikh images and styles. Members were male and young. Other than violence, Berry (1988) does not elaborate on the criminal activities of these gangs.

Ross (1972) wrote journalistic account of street gangs in London. Ross indicated that "mugging gangs" were mostly comprised of two to three adolescent boys. These mugging gangs had regular "patches" of territory where they victimized individuals. These boys were school dropouts who were basically unskilled inner-city youth. Their focus was on obtaining money to support their interests. They committed crimes such as theft and simple robbery.

Another journalistic account of London's street gangs provides some information about one street gang involved in a murder of a law student (Morris, 2002). According to Morris, the gang members came from broken homes and were well known to the police. All lived in the poor section named Peckham. They were of Mediterranean origin and had been bullied by other youth until becoming bullies themselves. They joined together to defend themselves from bully attacks. The gang's image was important to members and they wore clothing reflective of "American" gangster culture. Their weapons of choice were baseball bats, axes, and knives. Gang members were known to "jook" victims, which means stab them in the leg to hurt and terrorize them. They sold or ran drugs for an adult drug gang from the same area. They had assaulted females, whom they judged to be more vulnerable, and demanded money to support their habits.

Another form of English gang is known as the yardies. Yardies, who control much of the cocaine trade in England, first appeared in the late 1980s (Vasagar & Hopkins, 2000). Speculation is that a yardie gang fled Jamaica to live in Great Britain as Jamaican police increased pressure (Roth, 1997). Yardie gangs, as they are called, operate in certain sections of London and rural areas of England and Scotland (Roth, 1997). Yardie gangs are mostly comprised of Caribbean-African males and are heavily involved in the crack cocaine and heroin trade. They are known to have violent battles with competitors over the control of drug distribution (Wright, 1999). Yardie gangs have loose organizational structures and are generally disorganized (Vasagar & Hopkins, 2000). However, the issue of just how well organized Yardie gangs are is unresolved (Roth, 1997). The problem of Yardie gang violence was significant enough in London that Scotland Yard set up a special program called Operation Trident to investigate several homicides and control mounting violence between Yardie gangs.

Some scholarly attention has focused on the British youth subculture associated with European football (soccer). This subculture has been typically characterized by ethnographic-based research as being violent, racist at times, ethnocentric, nationalistic, substance abusing, and more mob-like in nature than being similar to true gangs (Buford, 1990). Buford's (1990) personal account of his membership in a Scottish gang underscores the importance of alliance to soccer teams to some gangs. Recent evidence indicates that "football" hooligans may be branching out into drug sales and distribution. Burke and Sunley (1998) noted potential hooligan involvement in ecstasy and LSD distribution in Europe.

Malcolm Klein (1995a) reported on the existence of Chinese drug gangs with ties to the Chinese triads, Jamaican drug gangs involved in hashish and heroin sales, plus some Indian and Pakistani conflict gangs in rivalry with one another, in London. Jamaican posses reportedly migrated to England during the mid-1970s (Gay & Marquart, 1993). These posses, besides involvement with the drug trade, were also involved in the production and sales of false documents, such as passports and visas. The posses also provided fellow posse fugitives from the United States with shelter. Manchester has a similar pattern, with considerable violence associated with drug sales.

British Community Responses to Street Gangs

The British have responded to street gangs in a variety of ways. The British have emphasized gang law enforcement rather than prevention strategies. British authorities, similar to their counterparts in other countries, often chose crackdowns on street gangs as the primary response. This enforcement has been directed to reducing the drug trade and corresponding gang violence. Law enforcement agencies have also attempted to curb violence between rival soccer teams, hooligans, and street gangs that have allegiances to specific neighborhoods or soccer teams.

Besides law enforcement crackdowns, British reactions to street gangs include alternatives to strict law enforcement. For example, one program used unemployed school dropouts to reach gang members (Wainwright, 2000). The program used youth action groups to negotiate peaceful deals among rival gangs and the police. Official data suggest the program was reducing citizen fear and emergency calls. The youth action groups were small teams that worked the neighborhoods to prevent gang violence and crime. The program attributed much of its success to the teams' abilities to relate and listen to gang members' concerns.

The British media have had a dramatic response to gangs over the years. The early literature on moral panics was based on observations of the British media's response to youth subcultures and gangs of the 1950s and 1960s (Cohen, 1973, 1980; Jefferson, 1976). The British press has had a long history of sensationalizing the news related to youth. Currently, media reports of other forms of street gangs are present. For example, there have been press reports of female Bosnian gangs operating throughout Britain. These gangs of six to 12 members used children to distract victims and cause scenes. These distractions and scenes were useful in committing robbery and other property crimes.

The British contribution to the worldwide phenomena of street gangs has to be the evolution of skinhead gangs. British skinhead and corresponding gangs have served as a model for similar street gangs throughout much of the world, at least in those countries with sizable Caucasian populations. Equally important is the response to such gangs and movements by the victims. The victims of racist and skinhead violence have sometimes formed gangs. This pattern of the persecuted reacting to gang violence by forming defensive gangs is expanding in Europe. This pattern is similar to what happened with the Pachucos in southern California, the zoot suiters in the 1930s and 40s, the Irish, the Polish, and other minority immigrant groups to

America. It is also similar to what is occurring in Germany with the Turkish Power Boys gang.

In sum, street gangs in Great Britain have been found to be more loosely organized and unstructured than American street gangs (Campbell, 1991; Cohen, 1980; Morash, 1983; Scott, 1956; Spencer, 1964), with the possible exception of some Scottish gangs (Patrick, 1973; O'Hagan, 1976). Patrick (1973) did report that the gangs in Glasgow formed major alliances in the 1960s. Although some gangs have a sense of territory (Wilmott, 1966), formal leadership may be absent, and some gangs do not identify themselves as being gangs (Downes, 1966; Scott, 1956). Again, some of the Scottish gangs may be the exception (O'Hagan, 1976). The Scottish gang described by Campbell (1991) partially based membership, as did other gangs in Glasgow, on whether individuals were Catholic or Protestant. The gangs tend to be small; Cavan and Cavan (1968) estimated the typical size of British youth gangs to be three or four members. Age-grading appears to be present in some gangs, but not in others. Membership is typically drawn from lower or working class backgrounds (Campbell, 1991; Knight, 1982). There is disagreement on the extent to which subcultures are well developed, and to which gangs are able to flourish, in British as opposed to American society (West, 1967; Campbell & Muncer, 1989). The diversity of reported findings about British gangs suggests considerable variation in the size, degree of organization, cohesiveness, and structure of British gangs. Klein (2001:68) best summed the street gang situation in England by stating, "Most are minority and/or immigrant groups clearly located in inner-city, deteriorating areas." He added, "The days of the Mods, Rockers, and Teddy Boys are long gone."

STREET GANGS IN NORTHERN IRELAND AND IRELAND

The street gang picture in Northern Ireland is unclear. In a climate of on-going political and religious disputes, the civil strife in Northern Ireland masks the true extent and nature of Irish street gangs. In Northern Ireland, Michael Montgomery (1997) identified groups of delinquent youth as street gangs or groups. These youth gangs, referred to as "hoods," were comprised of impoverished Catholic youth who typically had been kicked out of school by age 14. They were also considered to be out of control of their families. The youth were involved in the theft of automobiles. The youth considered the stolen automobiles as being symbolic of power and their rejection of society. They typically stole automobiles to use for reckless joyrides. They did not carry weapons but drove stolen vehicles so carelessly that the vehicles represented a serious safety risk to communities.

The hoods challenged not only police authority but also the Irish Republican Army (IRA). The IRA was known to violently punish hoods involved in criminal activities. The gangs' cohesion, consistent with what Klein has reported for years regarding American street gangs, was found to increase as external efforts to repress their criminal activities increased. Harsh punishment seemed to reinforce their criminal identity and motivate them to retaliate even more against the community. Montgomery's (1997) research into the nature of hoods in Northern Ireland does not provide enough information to determine whether these groups of youth are true street gangs or simply law-violating youth groups.

Other references to street gangs or law violating youth groups can be found in the Irish press (*Belfast Telegraph*, 2001). In Ireland, the media describe "Los Angeles" style street gangs operating in Dublin. The street gangs victimize commuters on Dublin's mass transit system, called DART (Maguire, 1999). The gangs attack other youth and DART staff in the evenings. The gangs often have robbery as a motive for their attacks. Again, it is unclear whether these groups represent true street gangs.

STREET GANGS IN SCANDINAVIA

In the late 1950s, gangs called the *Skinnknutte* operated in Scandinavia (Fyvel, 1961). In Scandinavian countries, youth groups and perhaps street gangs similar to the *Skinnknutte* have developed since the 1950s. In Denmark, they were referred in their early days as Green Jackets. The Green Jackets were known for their assaults on immigrants. In Norway, skinhead gangs and violent motorcycle gangs are present and documented. Street gangs do not have a strong presence in Norway but may in the future with immigration, discrimination, and economic trends helping create divisions within Norwegian society. Klein's (1995a) review of the gang situation in Europe and elsewhere suggests that American-style gangs, skinhead gangs, and law-violating youth groups maintain a stable and, in some countries, an expanding presence in the European countries.

Examples of Street Gangs in Sweden

Jerzy Sarnecki (1986) conducted early research on Swedish law-violating youth groups that, due to the scarcity of information, were identified by others as street gangs. Although labeled gang research, Sarnecki was actually studying loosely affiliated and changing youth groups that were involved in criminal activities. Klein (1995a) reported on episodic skinhead activity, plus what we (following Miller, 1982) have called law-violating youth groups of second-generation Turks, Yugoslavs, Moroccans, and others (children of guest workers and asylum seekers) that may be evolving into street gangs in Sweden. Sweden has patterns similar to those described for Australia (loosely formed groups of wandering youths in public places) and American-style taggers.

Eventually, true street gangs developed in Stockholm (Klein, 1996, Sarnecki & Pettersson, 2001). After Sarnecki's (1982, 1986) ground breaking work in the 1980s, Klein (2001) found evidence of street gangs in Swedish housing projects. These street gangs were comprised of second-generation immigrant youth from Moroccan, Yugoslavian, Greek, Lebanese, or Turkish backgrounds. The gangs were not territorial and did not engage in gang rivalries. The street gangs did have a strong sense of group identity and adopted special ways of displaying their gang membership. Gang members were known to ride mass transit systems to the inner city where they committed crimes of theft, robbery, mugging, and other property crimes. Klein (2001) referenced one media account of a *Skarholmen* gang, which he observed fit the immigrant commuter gang model. The gang reportedly commuted to the inner city to commit crimes and then return home. In Stockholm, there appear to be two general types of gangs—skinhead and immigrant gangs. Most of these gangs had young members (teens to early 20s), were small (10-40 members), and were not violent.

Tore Björgo (1993) described Swedish white supremacist or racist gangs involved in violent crimes such as assault, vandalism, and arson against out-groups. The typical out-groups include foreigners, refugees, immigrants, ethnic minorities, and asylum seekers. White supremacist gangs viewed these groups as threatening to traditional Swedish culture and more importantly working class jobs. Sweden had experienced years of economic downturns and declines in employment opportunities that aggravated the situation. However, Tore Björgo (1993) noted that racist attacks started before the economic downturns. Members of these gangs used alcohol as their primary social drug, which was often the common denominator for their street violence.

Street gang members were mostly male and projected a tough and violent image. Many relied on Nazi symbols, slogans, and signs for effect. On this latter point, these street gangs had no formal ideology per se, only hostility toward those "invading" their country. Björgo concluded that these youth gangs were responsible for most of the racist violence in their areas. The youth gangs appear to be primary perpetrators of terror against targeted groups. These street gangs lacked formal structures and were very unorganized. Community responses to these street gangs ranged from support to rejection.

Examples of Street Gangs in Denmark

Little research has been conducted on street gangs in Denmark. One exception is a study by Arne Stevns (2001) who researched street gangs in Copenhagen. Stevns found there were about 15 to 20 street gangs known to authorities in Copenhagen. The gangs ranged in size from five to 20 members and lacked fixed organizational structures. The gangs had strong group solidarity. Stevns identified different types of gang members such as "key" members, whose role was to instigate criminal activities; "members," who carried out crimes; and "hang-arounds," who occasionally participated in street gang conflicts and activities. Stevns found that gang leadership was fluid, changing, and situational.

Copenhagen's gang members came from immigrant families that were poorly integrated into mainstream Danish society. They were in a word, marginalized. These youth and their families lacked formal educational backgrounds. They felt marginalized from and discriminated by mainstream Danish society. Gang members were between the ages of 15 and 20 years. The gangs' crimes of choice were street robberies, violence, property damage, assaults on police, theft, and extortion.

Stevns (2001) reviewed some of the Danish programs in place to address street gangs in Copenhagen. Stevns noted that prosecution and investigation of gang-related crimes was a high priority in Copenhagen. Copenhagen's police also emphasized community policing and crime prevention approaches towards the street gangs. The use of personal advisers (*Bonus Pater*) to prevent street gang activities was a gang intervention and prevention strategy. The *Bonus Paters* worked directly with youth to help them secure jobs and be involved in pro-social activities. Youth were encouraged to participate in youth clubs. The Danish approach to gang prevention emphasized integrating marginal youth into mainstream Danish society.

Examples of Street Gangs in Norway

Similar to the rest of Scandinavian countries, few studies have been conducted on street gangs in Norway. There are numerous media references to Norwegian adult motorcycle gangs that are not true street gangs. One exception is a study by Inger-Lise Lien (2001). Inger-Lise Lien studied immigrant street gangs that operated in and around Oslo. Immigrant gangs are a relatively new phenomenon that surfaced during the 1980s in Norway. According to Lien, these gangs were violent and engaged in criminal activities including robbery, assault, possession of weapons, and violence. The street gangs were territorial and had conflicts with rival gangs. Lien observed that the gangs were not locked into their neighborhoods and traveled all over the metropolitan Oslo area to engage in violence and gang fights. The street gangs used violence as a symbolic tool to convey their frustration with and reaction to mainstream Norwegian society. Some gangs specifically targeted white Norwegian youth, who they viewed as weak, to convey their anger and obtain respect. Lien (2001) found that street gang membership was correlated with higher levels of criminal offending. This pattern is consistent with most gang research (Covey et al., 1997).

Inger-Lise Lien found that gang members came from low-income neighborhoods of Oslo where unemployment was very high. Street gang members aged between 13 to 18 years. The gangs were often male youth with Somali, Vietnamese, Filipino, Pakistani, and Iranian ethnic backgrounds. The gangs organized along ethnic lines; however, some gangs were of mixed ethnicity. Organizational structure for all of these street gangs was minimal. Oslo's street gangs valued masculinity, respect, and most importantly, honor. In the case of honor, Lien suggests that the gang members were hyper-concerned about their honor. The absence of status in their new countries may have fueled their emphasis on respect and honor.

She also noted that white Norwegian youth also formed gangs and groups, such as the neo-Nazi groups called the Vikings, the Skinhead Boot Boys, and Aryan Brotherhood. In earlier research, Bjorgo (1997) found Norwegian boys became skinheads following periods when they were harassed by other youth and excluded from friendships. Consequently, they sought membership in groups of peers that would accept them. With their membership in such groups, they felt they gained respect, a sense of belonging, and social status. They dressed and acted in ways to promote fear, which was an important part of their public image. Antiracist street gangs were also present in Oslo.

In summary, many of the street gang issues in Norway hinged on ethnic and social differences. Immigrant ethnic gangs can be viewed as a response to the lack of full integration and social acceptance into mainstream Norwegian society. White ethnic racist gangs the perceived immigrants as threatening to the established Norwegian social order. Norwegian youth also join white ethnic gangs or immigrant gangs to feel socially accepted.

BELGIAN STREET GANGS

Criminal youth gangs were reported to exist in Belgium in the 1960s (Fyvel, 1961). More recently, Malcolm Klein (2001) discovered limited evidence of traditional street gangs in Brussels. According to Klein, these gangs formed age-graded strata that were linked together by territory. However, as he noted, his evidence was not based on personal verification.

Belgian authorities use a relatively broad definition of gang. A gang is defined as "a group of minors whose behavior disturbs the public order and security" (Vercaigne, 2001: 288). The implication of this broad definition is that some Belgian youth are labeled gang members even when they are not involved in criminal activities. Police in Brussels are required to report on gang activity by district. The police in Brussels developed a typology of four types of gangs: the gang with a leader, the spontaneous gang, the ghetto gang, and criminal organization. The fact that the police took time to develop a typology suggests that Brussels may be experiencing a variety of developing types of gangs or law-violating youth groups.

In Brussels and other urban areas such as Ghent and Antwerp, Vercaigne and Goris (1996) described the existence of hardcore youth gangs involved with drug and gun sales in the 1990s. They identified various "types" of street gangs including delinquent gangs, gangs with leaders, spontaneous gangs, ghetto gangs, youth gangs, and splinter gangs. Some of these "types" are similar to what Walter Miller would refer to as law-violating youth groups rather than street gangs. For example, in describing splinter gangs Vercaigne and Goris (1996), observed, ". . . small groups of youngsters from different neighborhoods who quickly gather in view of particular activities (for example, car jacking) and who disperse quickly when the police appear. This pattern is more typical of law-violating groups than street gangs.

Vercaigne and Goris (1996) reported that street gang members were youth who lived in deteriorated neighborhoods and came from immigrant minorities. They had considerable leisure time and thus had many opportunities to commit street crimes. Vercaigne and Goris found the degree of organization varied with each street gang. They observed that gang organizational structure, leadership, and sense of territory had diminished since the mid-nineties. Vercaigne and Goris found no links between street gangs and Belgian organized crime.

In 1997, Conny Vecaigne noted the development of "splinter" gangs in Belgium's main cities of Brussels, Ghent, Mechelen, and Antwerp. Her description of Belgian gangs reported of youth that came together to commit crimes and then broke apart. These youth gangs were known as "splinter" gangs because they dispersed following their committing street crimes. Also referred to as "clans," they were comprised of young males who were involved assaults and drug or weapon sales. The clans had defined leaders and carried weapons.

Belgian responses to these gangs have been enforcement oriented. In 1991, the Belgian Attorney General established a special task force to dismantle youth gangs. At the other end, some officials have denied their presence (Vercaigne & Goris, 1996). Some Belgian officials have been concerned over having a moral panic or overreaction to the gangs. They believe that street gangs were not a serious problem that demands a formal response. Nevertheless, the primarily Belgian response has been gang repression strategies.

Vercaigne (1997) commented that community response to the clans has ranged from total denial to overreaction. Belgian perceptions of gangs depend on how the term gang is used by officials and the media. Much of the media's attention has been devoted to distinguishing Belgian street gangs from their American counterparts. Vecaigne noted that this leads to both minimizing and exaggerating the gangs as a problem. She suggested that moral panics regarding the gangs have occurred in some locations. However, she also observed that the public's demand for repression is currently weak but may change with the increase of street gang activity.

Conny Vercaigne (2001) has raised important questions about whether a moral panic regarding street gangs might be evolving in Brussels and other Belgian cities. Perhaps the gang problem is not as extensive as media and police would suggest. Other media and police have concluded that street gangs are developing. Weitekamp (2001) noted that the existence of police gang units, gangs with names, and four types of gangs being identified by authorities all suggest that the gang situation in Belgium is real and not imagined or a creation of media hype.

STREET GANGS IN THE NETHERLANDS

The Netherlands had gangs called the Nozems in the late 1960s (Baur, 1964). Baur concluded that these youth groups were similar to the German *Halbstarke* and French *Blouson Noires* and further that highly integrated street gangs were not present in the Netherlands. He did observe that some peer groups wore distinctive clothing and had a preference for loud motorcycles. Much of these gangs' behavior and style was modeled after media images of American street gangs.

More recently, experts have reported on the presence of street gangs in the Netherlands (Came et al., 1989b; Gruter & Versteegh, 2001; Klein, 2001; Van Gemert, 2001). According to media depictions reviewed by Klein (2001), these gangs tended to be small, comprised of teens and young adults, were criminally versatile, adopted American street gang styles of dress (Crip/Blood), were territorial, called themselves posses or sets, and had O.G.s (seasoned leaders). All of these characteristics suggest modeling by Dutch youth after African American street gangs.

Gruter and Versteegh (2001), who surveyed police regarding their perceptions of different types of youth groups, including street gangs in The Hague, reported similar findings. The police classified four types of groups as troublesome, non-serious criminal, serious criminal, and gang-related criminals. Gruter and Versteegh found that some of these groups adapted and imitated American Crip-styles of music, clothing, names, argot, and gestures. Of the four groups they found, the less criminal groups were motivated by recreation and prestige while more serious groups and street gangs were motivated primarily by financial gain via crime. The Hague's street gangs were less violent and armed than their American counterparts. They did not fight over the control of territory. Gang members were predominantly male Moroccan youth ranging from 15 to 20 years of age. These street gangs had weak organizational ties but had recognizable leaders.

Another summary by Frank Van Gemert (2001) parallels the Dutch gang observations of Klein and Gruter and Versteegh. Van Gemert found that Dutch youth were enamored by American mass media images of street gangs available through television, film, and music. For example, copies of the books *Monster* (Shakur, 1993) and *Do or Die* (Bing, 1992) were owned and cherished by some of the gang members. These mass media books tend to glorify the gangster image of violence, being cool, bad, mean, and having bravado. They also served the youth as examples of how to model their lives as street gang members.

Van Gemert reviewed the court and police records relating to three "American" style street gangs arrested in The Hague and Rotterdam. Two of the street gangs from The Hague were predominantly adolescent males, who were black, and mostly from Surinam and the Dutch Antilles. All were born in Holland, but Van Gemert concluded that their families' immigrant backgrounds played a role in their gang associations. They were from low-income backgrounds and had difficulty adjusting to Dutch society. The youth were marginalized from mainstream Dutch society. The adolescents' average age was 15 years.

There were no identified fixed gang leaders, but members took on leadership roles when necessary.

Van Gemert (2001) found the street gangs from Rotterdam were similar to the two from The Hague. Gang members came from similar backgrounds and the same neighborhood. They were older (age 18), members of ethnic minorities, had gang-related tattoos, wore gang attire, and spoke a distinctive gang argot. They made references to "O.G.s" who served as leaders for the gang. Members of the gang marked the neighborhood with gang related graffiti. The gang required new gang members to commit a robbery to gain membership.

The crime of choice for these street gangs was "jackmoves" or street robberies. The gangs often became unnecessarily violent when committing these robberies. The gangs often targeted females for robbery because they could be easily overpowered by a small group of males. The gangs also committed thefts from businesses and sometimes used guns during robberies. Gang violence was not typically necessary for the gang to be successful, but it nevertheless occurred. Violence appeared to be an important component and requirement of gang membership.

Van Gemert (2001) concluded that some youth, especially those of Moroccan ancestry, were undoubtedly mislabeled as street gangs for simply hanging out on street corners. Traditional Moroccan cultural factors were not conducive to the formation of street gangs. If anything, they worked against the formation of gangs. Moroccan cultural practices encourage individualism and competitiveness and not group cohesion. Van Gemert noted that Moroccan youth hanging out together on street corners were simply youth socializing and not evidence of gang participation or membership. This hanging out by Moroccan youth did not represent street gang activity but nevertheless was labeled such by outsiders.

GERMAN STREET GANGS

We know that youth street gangs operated in Germany following World War II and were motivated by survival. Following the collapse of Germany at the end of World War II, groups of *Trümmerjuend* (youth in ruins) functioned as survival specialists that were involved in petty crimes and the sales of black market goods. They adopted American hairstyles, blue jeans, and music. These groups were likely true street gangs. In the 1950s, there were several youth riots by marginal youths called *Gammler*. These groups were loosely organized and were probably not street gangs, but were instead law-violating youth groups. The existence of youth street gangs called *Halbstarke* (half-strong) in Germany and Austria was noted by Short and Strodtbeck (1974), Fyvel (1961), and Cavan and Cavan (1968). The *Halbstarke* were white youth interested in rock and roll music and liked to promote a tough gang image.

During the early 1980s, scholars reported West Germany was experiencing increases in its rates of juvenile delinquency (Hotyst, 1982) and gang-related crime (Kaiser, 1983). The recent reunification of East and West Germany has given rise to a fear of increased crime and delinquency, including illegal activity by street gangs. Especially if observations linking industrialization and urbanization to gang delinquency are correct, the restructuring of the German economy, especially in former East Germany, is likely to generate pressures toward street gang formation and gang crime. However, Kersten (2001) warns that we need to exercise caution in viewing the rapid social change and cultural disorientation in Germany as giving rise to extreme violence and crime.

The picture of what is currently occurring in Germany with respect to street gangs is difficult to determine. Group delinquency always has been fairly common in Germany. Brunner (1974) found that group membership and processes played a central role in three types of youth crime in West Germany. In fact, it was estimated that 80 to 90 percent of all German juvenile crime involved groups of youths. Another reason is identifying the nature and extent of street gangs in Germany is confounded by the notion of the neighborhood clique. Neighborhood cliques of young Germans have been common throughout Germany and may or may not be classified as street gangs depending on one's definition. German neighborhood cliques do not consider themselves to be street gangs, nor do the neighborhoods in which they reside. The current literature separates cliques that occasionally commit delinquent acts from street gangs that are more heavily focused on crime and delinquency. Street gangs should be considered a unique form of clique.

David Huizinga and Karl Schumman (2001) described other differences between German street gangs, cliques, and their American street gang counterparts. Huizinga and Schumman asked the fundamental question of whether gangs or *bandes* exist in Germany. They concluded that German street gangs exist but not to the level as to generate widespread public fear. Using longitudinal self-report data from Bremen Germany and Denver, Colorado, Huizinga and Schumman found that 13 percent of school-aged youth surveyed in Bremen identified themselves as gang (*bande*) members. This compared with about 14 percent for Denver. In addition, Bremen youth reported longer duration of gang participation than the Denver sample, 2.3 to 1.5 years respectively. Street gang youth in Bremen were more likely to be delinquent and violent than nongang youth. Differences between street gang and nongang youth in the Denver sample were more pronounced. Street gangs in Bremen were less involved in drug sales and placed less emphasis on territory than their American counterparts. German street gangs fought more, spent more time together, and were more cohesive than neighborhood cliques (Huizinga & Schumman, 2001). In Bremen, street gang youth were more likely to be delinquent and violent than their clique counterparts.

Presently, skinhead street gangs exist in Germany (Came et al., 1989b). The Anti-Defamation League's (1995) report of skinhead activity throughout the world observed that loosely knit gangs of youth have been noted throughout many German communities. Although not a street gang event, in 1991, about 600 German racist and neo-fascist skinheads firebombed a home for foreign workers and assaulted Vietnamese and Mozambican workers (Levin & McDevitt, 1993). The German skinheads typically target Vietnamese, Gypsies, Turkish, Middle Eastern, and African immigrants for assault, firebombing, property crime, arson, and homicide. Neo-fascist groups, some of them appropriately labeled gangs, have also attacked Africans, Jews, and other "non-Aryans" in Germany. The German skinheads viewed immigrant groups as threats to the German culture and economy. Similar to skinheads throughout the world, they viewed immigrants as taking away jobs.

Concern for German skinhead violence is well documented in the German mass media. There is apprehension, according to the press, of skinhead gangs by East Germans. One *New York Times* story reported that East Germans were "startled" by the violence of West German skinheads (Binder, 1990). As in other countries, the skinhead gangs typically draw their membership from working class youth. The neo-fascist movement and corresponding values underpinning the skin-head gangs underscores the concern felt by some East Germans.

Joachim Kersten (1998) provided a detailed description of German neighborhood or turf, skinhead, and violent hooligan street gangs. Members viewed all of these groups or gangs as expressions of the "masculine" style. That is, members extorted their masculinity through their membership in these street gangs and groups. The first type of neighborhood or turf gang was conflict oriented and fought rivals to protect turf (neighborhoods). The second group, the skinhead gangs, viewed themselves as soldiers for a white (Aryan) Germany. These gangs saw their role to protect traditional German society and values by attacking immigrants and people with disabilities. Their heavy alcohol consumption fuelled some of their violence toward out-sider groups. The third group, the German hooligans, were also heavy involved in alcohol consumption. The hooligans developed rivalries with other hooligans and victimized locals and hooligans representing other sports teams. Their public image, according to Kersten (1998) was that of the Hollywood character Rambo, as they liked to present themselves as tough and invincible.

In response to the skinhead attacks, immigrant youths have formed street gangs or groups for self-defense. These include Turkish, Kurdish, Yugoslav, Polish, Lebanese, and Palestinian ethnic street gangs. Klein (2001) found second- and third-generation immigrant youth formed self-defense gangs to protect themselves against right-wing extremist groups, such as the skinheads. Klein's observations are mirrored in media reports (Fritz, 1992; Marks, 1992). Youth in these street gangs resided in the low-income and deteriorating areas of the inner cities. These gangs, Klein concluded, resembled traditional American street gangs in structure and organization.

Consistent with Fritz (1992) and Klein (2001), Hermann Tertilt (1997) provided a detailed case example of German immigrant street gangs. Tertilt reported on an ethnic street gang located in Frankfurt named the Turkish Power Boys. Applying Klein's typology to this gang, it is likely this street gang could be classified as a compressed gang. The Turkish Power Boys directed its violence toward German born youth. Tertilt speculated that the gang's violence was fueled by low self-esteem of gang members that resulted from negative German reactions to Turkish youth. The gang members were proud and defiant regarding their ethnic backgrounds and carried their cultural heritages on their shoulders. Given the pattern of attacks from neo-fascist and skinhead groups, it might be expected that these street gangs would have some bravado regarding their ethnic backgrounds. Tertilt (2001) later reported that street gangs in Frankfurt proclaimed their ethnic identities in their gang names, such as the Turkish Power Boys, Croatia Boys, Italy Boys, and Russ Boys. Other immigrant street gangs in Frankfurt named themselves after geographic areas of Frankfurt.

Tertilt (1997) found in the case of the Turkish Power Boys, members were second generation immigrants to Germany. Gang members ranged from 13 to 18 years of age. Some street gang members were delinquent while others were not. The street gang's criminal activities included shoplifting, truancy, drug abuse, auto theft, mugging, and other property crimes. The street gang was violent toward white Germans and was known to mug and steal leather jackets from German victims. White German victims were especially selected as victims as a reaction to the perceived mistreatment of people of Turkish ancestry by Germans. Tertilt noted that often the violence associated with the crime was unwarranted but was used by the street gang to humiliate German people. In short, the gang's violence was an act of hatred and revenge driven by a sense of injustice. The street gang's criminal behavior represented a minor gang activity and the gang was more social than criminal in orientation. The gang was not rigidly organized but relied on four individuals for leadership. Tertilt (2001:183) noted that the general population reacted to the Turkish Power Boys with "disdain," "incomprehension," and "shock."

Other ethnic street gangs may be present in Germany. Williamson (1996) reported that Vietnamese gangs have been involved in gangland type murders and the black market, especially the cigarette trade. Williamson did not determine whether these Vietnamese gangs are street gangs or evidence of more organized crime. Germany's neighbor, Austria, has similar patterns to Germany with violent skinhead groups and street gangs. During the 1980s, skinhead gangs aligned themselves with soccer hooligans to terrorize fans at soccer matches. These gangs also stormed dance discos and attacked random victims at street and subway stops (Anti-Defamation League, 1995). Foreigners were the most common victims of these assaults.

German responses to street gangs generally have been minimal and ambivalent. Reporting on these patterns, Klein (1995a) chillingly noted the low level of community control and the tendency of Germans not to intervene in what happens on the street, a pattern Klein finds reminiscent of the Kitty Genovese incident in the United States (in which a young woman was repeatedly attacked and eventually brutally murdered as onlookers did nothing, not even calling the police for help, for fear of "getting involved"). Even more darkly, this may remind some readers of an earlier period when good German citizens avoided getting involved and failed to intervene to prevent the persecution of Jews and other ethnic minorities in Germany before and during World War II. Recently, the German Government banned the international skinhead group Blood and Honor, which was known to promote racial hatred and violence. The group had an estimated 300 German followers and chapters in the USA, Australia, Great Britain, South Africa, and across Europe (Williams, 2000).

FRENCH STREET GANGS (BANDES)

Youth street gangs in France are relatively rare compared to the United States. Recently, one scholar even raised the question of whether youth gangs really exist in France (Esterle-Hedibel, 2001). Yet others identify street gangs as present, such as those found in the suburbs of Paris (Kroeker & Haut, 1995). Without too much debate, evidence suggests that street gangs have been present in France for decades in some form. Historically, the Nazi occupation terrorized Paris and left many older Parisians with vivid memories of street crime and violence. Following the war and similar to other European countries, groups of youth banded together to cope with the devastation of the war. While appearing to be street gangs, these groups of youth were probably criminal groups operating for financial gain and survival.

Like Great Britain, France has had street gangs that take on a wide variety of forms and characteristics (Lafont, 1982; Monsod, 1967; Vaz, 1962). According to Monsod, during the mid-sixties, gang membership was drawn from the ranks of the unemployed. Gang members tended to drop out of school and had lower levels of educational attainment than nonmembers. Vaz (1962) and Monsod (1967) observed that substantial differences existed between upper and lower class gangs in France.

French street gangs, like those elsewhere, developed their own argot and clothes to distinguish themselves from outsiders. However, like British gangs, French street gangs may be difficult to separate from French subcultures. The *Blousons Noirs* were characterized as a gang (Short & Strodtbeck, 1974) and as a subculture rather than a gang (Campbell & Muncer, 1989). These youth, named for their black leather jackets (blouson noirs), modeled their attire after images of the American motorcycle gangs of the late 1950s and early 1960s.

In the 1960s, Vaz reported the typical size of French street gangs to be five to eight members, but as large as 60 members. Monsod (1967) placed the size of French gangs at 15 to 20 members, with some gangs having as many as 40 members. Few females were involved in French street gangs, but some were members of male-dominated gangs. These French gangs placed less emphasis on age-grading than American gangs. Gang members ranged from their mid-teens to the early twenties (Monsod, 1967; Vaz, 1962). In Paris, Monsod reported a strong sense of social and territorial identity among French gangs in the 1960s. Gangs socialized and identified with specific areas of the city. Specific parks and neighborhoods were used as common grounds for Parisian gangs, and some gangs were even named after particular areas, similar to gangs in Los Angeles in the United States. By contrast, Vaz, in an earlier study, reported no sense of territory for French gangs.

Criminal activities of 1960s French street gangs included vandalism, theft, illicit sex, assault, and robbery (Monsod, 1967). Although fights did occur, violence was reported to be rare with most Parisian gangs (Vaz, 1962). Fyvel (1961), however, reported that violence was common with the *Blousons Noirs.* Monsod (1967) also reported drug and alcohol use was very high. Summarizing some of the research on French gangs up to the late 1960s, Cavan and Cavan (1968) reported that French street gangs were primarily adolescent, with few members under age 12 or over age 18. These gangs occasionally had adult leaders. They were impermanent, with little formal organization and only weak cohesion. Vandalism and theft were the most frequent crimes, and violence was rare. Females in gangs were rare, and usually took secondary roles to the male gang members. Delinquent acts were spontaneous and hedonistic. Membership was transitory and gangs formed or disbanded quickly.

Examples of French Street Gangs

According to Klein (1995a), the Blousons Noirs of earlier years have disappeared and have been replaced by American-style gang imitators called *casseurs* in Paris and Marseilles, Black African gangs (*zoulous*) in Paris, and Algerian gangs. These gangs define themselves by territory and ethnicity, wear unique clothing, listen to rap music, and are involved in crimes of violence on public transportation (buses and subways). In addition, during the 1990s groups of peers known as "posses" appeared in several metropolitan areas of France. These posses, comprised mostly of Antilleans and Africans, were involved in gang-like street fights (Esterle-Hedibel, 2001). The French media might have exaggerated the existence of these peer groups or possible violent street gangs. Esterle-Hedibel reported on two such street gangs residing in the suburbs of Paris. The gangs described by Esterle-Hedibel (2001) ranged from 30 to 40 members. These street gangs (*bandes*) would be classified as compressed gangs according to Klein's typology. The gangs were not highly spontaneous or organized. The gang members valued power, potency, and prestige in their community. The gangs used violence and property crimes to obtain what they valued.

The street gang members came from lower class areas of the city. Members were typically male and second-generation immigrants from Algeria (Maghrebine). The gangs named themselves with labels that reflected their ethnic backgrounds. The age of gang members ranged from 13 to 18 years, with most members aging out of the gangs when employed. A few females participated in the gangs but had low status and never assumed leadership roles. Gang members typically came from families with troubled backgrounds that often included domestic violence. These street gangs were opposed to the larger French society that rejected and discriminated against them. In a word, the gang members were marginalized from French society. Youth, whether in gangs or not, were negatively stereotyped by mainstream French society as "young-Arab-delinquents." In response to social rejection and attacks from outsiders, the street gangs formed for self-defense. Besides violence, the gangs were involved in crimes such as theft, assault, and motor vehicle theft.

Although street gangs have never been a major problem in France, the situation in France may be changing quickly. Mark Kroeker and

Francois Haut (1995) reported that Paris and other major cities, such as Lille and Marseilles, were developing street gangs similar to those found in Los Angeles. The French refer to these street gangs as *les jeunes*, which means young ones. According to Kroeker and Haut (1995), Parisian street gangs spend much of their time, similar to gangs throughout the world, simply hanging out. When involved in criminal activities, they typically sold crack cocaine and heroin. They were also involved in violent acts directed toward law enforcement agencies. Kroeker and Haut found that gang members migrated to the center of the city via the mass transit (Metro) to hang out and commit crimes. If they used weapons, the shotgun was the firearm of choice, as opposed to the American preference for handguns and semi-automatic weapons.

Kroeker and Haut concluded four factors have contributed to the rise of street gangs in Paris: low income high-rise public housing in the suburbs (banlieus), the embracing of American Hip-Hop culture and its corresponding negative attitudes, the development of mass rail transportation into the city, and expansion of narcotics trade. They also suggest that the immigration of people from Africa and the Middle East and their children were contributing factors, as the adjustment to French society for these groups was not always a smooth one.

It is the second generation of youth that represent the membership of Paris' street gangs. Besides African and Middle Eastern ethnicity, other characteristics of typical Parisian street gang members were that they were younger, often attended school, were poor, had parents on public assistance, and lived in suburban public housing. Kroeker and Haut indicated they did not have the traditional values related to work, such as strong work ethic.

The journalist Gwynne Dyer (1999) departs from Kroeker and Haut slightly by finding a wider range of ethnicity with the suburban gangs of Paris. Dyer found white French, Muslim, Yugoslavian, and Turkish youth participated in these suburban street gangs. Parisian street gangs did not use colors, signs, or symbols similar to their American counterparts. The gangs had adopted some of the American gang culture such as clothing and music. Parisian street gangs did mark their territories with graffiti similar to American street gangs. The gangs adopted names that were aggressive and had an in-your-face in tone. The street gangs displayed no strict organizational hierarchy but did have identifiable leaders. The leaders were typically the most violent or adept at selling drugs.

Victims of the gangs were primarily law enforcement agencies and businesses. The gangs were known to set up ambush fires to draw in police who would then be shot at by the gangs. Gangs would also overturn over police vehicles to incite law enforcement activity. Gangs would swarm police agencies when gang members were taken into law enforcement custody. Kroeker and Haut reported that setting police stations on fire was common. Gang members, while territorially based, committed crimes in other areas of the city. Gang members typically rode mass transit into inner city Paris to commit their crimes and then travel back to their home territories. An interesting aside is the apparent use of trained attack monkeys by some street gangs to intimidate rival gangs (Henley, 2000). As difficult as it is to imagine, one media source reported, some gangs have relied on trained monkeys to threaten and attack gang rivals. Trained monkeys have become weapons among some street gangs.

In a limited ethnographic study of Parisian youth, La grée and Fai (1987) focused on female participation in suburban gangs. They found that working-class suburban youth, including a small portion of females, turned to street gangs. These youth came from lower income or unemployed families that had experienced on-going financial stress. Gang members were frequently unemployed and had dropped out of school. Females joining these gangs became sex objects of the male gang members and held very low status. All of the youth felt marginalized and viewed the gang as a way to postpone the inevitable low paying jobs that awaited them in adulthood. The youth basically saw no way out of their low-income existence. Functionally, La grée and Fai (1987) concluded the gangs brought youth together on common social terms. They viewed the roles played by members of the gangs as being substitutes for conventional social roles and a means of suspending adulthood.

La grée and Fai (1987) found the street gangs valued the notion of "aggro" or aggression. The researchers, however, considered street gang violence a rare occurrence. Male gang members fought with rival gangs, but females were not allowed to participate physically or verbally in conflicts. Females in the gangs therefore played secondary roles to the males.

Other references to street gangs are present in the French media. One report by Henley (2001) describes a two-hour gang battle in the Paris suburb of La Defense. La Defense is an upper-end business and shopping suburb of Paris. Rival gangs used knives, hammers, and other weapons during this battle. It took over 200 riot police two hours to end the fighting. The street gangs involved in the conflict came from low income housing in other parts of the city. The two rival gangs selected La Defense as a neutral territory to stage their battle. Most of the gang members were between 15 and 18 years old. They had used mass transit to arrive at the location.

According to some media sources, street gangs are not limited to metropolitan Paris or the large French cities. A report in *The Guardian* (Jefferies, 2000) noted a number of teenage gang-related homicides in small communities, such as Drancy, Gaston-Rouleau, Courconnes, and other smaller French cities and towns. The article observed that street gang feuds developed among the highrise buildings, where unemployment was high and ethnic minorities rejected authority. Fuelled by a public gunfight between rival street gangs at the upscale business section, La Defense of Paris, citizens have protested against the sale of guns to youth and gang members (Jefferies, 2000, 2001).

Finally, any overview of French street gangs would be incomplete without mention of the Parisian pickpocket gangs. These street gangs focus on theft, robbery, and street fraud. The existence of pickpockets in Paris and other European cities is well documented. Gangs of small children have victimized pedestrians in certain parts of Paris for years, often gypsy in ethnic background, they pick the pockets of their victims. Most of these youth come from impoverished families, however, the media reports their involvement in crime has substantial financial rewards for some (Janssen, 1986). These gangs' main focus is to commit property crimes against distracted and unsuspecting victims, who are often tourists. A number of techniques are used by the youth to distract the victim, such as tossing blanketed bundles that appear to be infants at the victims and then grabbing their wallets or purses when the victim tries to catch the bundle.

Leadership of these street gangs is typically behind the scene adults, who organize and direct their activities. The adult leaders control the resources of the gangs and their takings. Police apprehension of these youth is difficult. When police arrest them, the youth often claim to be age 12. French law prohibits the prosecution of children under age 13, so many of these youth claim to be younger to avoid sanction. Without official documents to prove their true age, law enforcement officials can do little to sanction these youth. Another tactic to avoid apprehension and prosecution is for the youth to change names to confuse authorities. Law enforcement agencies may see the same youth over and over without knowing it and assume they are dealing with different youth when the opposite is the case. The problem of these pickpocket street gangs is not limited to Paris or other French cities, as they also operate in across Europe.

French Community Responses to Street Gangs

The official Parisian response to the street gangs has been primarily denial. This official denial may be a contributing factor to why we know so very little about French street gangs. In addition, in the neighborhoods outside of the city proper where the public housing projects reside, there is a high degree of tolerance of and ambivalence toward the gangs. Two possible reasons for these views might be offered. First, the gangs are inclined to victimize people and businesses outside of their neighborhoods in other sections of Paris. Second, the gangs contribute to the underground economy of these low-income areas by offering stolen goods at reduced prices to locals. To some low-income residents, the lower price of stolen goods is the only affordable means of ownership available.

In addition to denial, Parisian officials have not developed an organized strategy for dealing with street gangs. French law enforcement does not typically collect gang-related data and there are no specific gang-related court sanctions, or gang units in place. If anything, authorities have placed the blame on the rise of gangs not on the gang members but on larger economic and social conditions giving rise to gangs, such as racial and ethnic discrimination. Consequently, heavy law enforcement crackdowns on street gangs have not been the first official response.

This is not to suggest that attempts to curb the activities of street gangs are not present. Some French laws have been changed to permit authorities to prosecute adults for crimes committed by children under their direction. For example to inhibit pickpocket street gangs, French authorities now can prosecute adults for crimes committed by their children. Specifically, adults receiving public assistance can lose it if their children are caught committing crimes.

ITALIAN AND SICILIAN STREET GANGS

In the 1950s, teenage street gangs were present in major Italian cities (Cavan & Cavan, 1968). Short and Strodtbeck (1974) reported the existence of the *Vitelloni* in Italy. More recently, Sean Grennan et al. (2000) reviewed the relationship between street gangs and organized crime in Italy and Sicily. They found "crews" or criminal youth street gangs were involved in crimes such as credit card scams, burglary, and high-jacking of goods. These street gangs also were involved in street-level robbery and extortion. The youth street gangs or crews often paid homage to Mafia members known as "wiseguys."

Other key connections between youth street gangs and organized crime include gang members running errands for adult Mafia members. The Mafia also recruits street gang youth into its organization. The Mafia "calls up," or "makes" promising youth gang members into regular members. It is noteworthy that historically many Sicilian and Italian organized crime leaders in the United States, such as Johnny Torrio, Alphonse Capone, Lucky Luciano, and Paolo Antonio Vaccavelli (Paul Kelly), followed this same pattern of belonging in youth street gangs before entering the ranks of organized crime. Street gang membership is exclusively male and there are strong ethnic loyalties to regions of Sicily and Italy. Victims of street gangs were drawn from the poor merchants and residents of the areas where the street gangs resided.

STREET GANGS IN EASTERN EUROPE

With the major social, political, and economic changes that have occurred over the past decade and half, it should come as no surprise that street gangs have and are developing in some eastern European and former Soviet block countries. Some would attribute the rise of crime, organized crime, and street gangs to the westernization of these countries, decline of social control, and failure of the infrastructure to address social issues, such as high unemployment and crime. Little has been reported on street gangs in these countries but there are signs that they may be forming.

Street Gangs in Hungary

Grennan et al. (2000) reported that street gangs operate in Hungary. Some Hungarian youth join street gangs that hold similar views as skinheads and neo-fascists in other countries. These street gangs committed crimes against certain racial and ethnic groups, such as Arab, Turkish, and other non-Hungarian peoples. The gangs were involved in drug trafficking, vandalism, assault, and illegal drug use. Gang members wore black clothing, shaved their heads, and pierced their bodies. Grennan et al. provided the following sketch of street gangs in Hungary:

> In Hungary, the enormous increase in the number of crimes since 1991 is due to the involvement of juveniles. Many of the gangs have the same ideology as their American counterparts, the skinhead gangs. The skinheads commit crimes primarily aimed at certain racial or ethnic groups. These gang robberies, assaults, or other encounters are against Arab, Turkish, or non-Hungarian people. These street gangs have also become heavily involved in street-level drug trafficking. Fun for gang members involves entering cemeteries at night, drinking or using drugs, and then vandalizing the graves and mausoleums. In many cases, the gang members wear black clothing, shaved heads, and have both their lips and cheeks pierced with metal objects. (Grennan et al. 2000: 398)

Hungarian communities and officials have been relatively idle in responding to street gangs, including skinheads. Hungarian authorities have taken steps to curb the growth of skinhead violence, such as limiting demonstrations and arresting skinhead and neo-Nazi leaders. Large antiracist protests and rallies have been held in some Hungarian communities to curb the growth of skinhead groups and gangs (Anonymous, 1999).

Street Gangs in Slovenia

Bojan Dekleva (2001) noted that studying gangs in Slovenia was difficult because there has not been a lot of research on the subject and the term gang has not been used much by the media or scholars. Street gangs do not appear to be prominent in Slovenia. In earlier research, Dekleva found no evidence of street gangs in Slovenia, but this may be changing with the development of *Chefoors*. The term *Chefoor* refers to something very offensive, someone who is quick to fight, a person not of Slovenian origin, and someone with a specific style of dress. It is used more specifically to refer to Bosnians but includes other immigrants to Slovenia. Dekleva cited research by Samo Lesar on the *Chefoors* in Ljubljana, the capital city, that found the groups were similar to American street gangs. *Chefoor* groups typically had about 20 members, were age-graded, engaged in crime, and carried a public image of being gangs, which they embraced. If the *Chefoors* continue to develop in Slovenia, Dekleva suggests they will eventually evolve into full-blown street gangs.

Street Gangs in the Czech Republic and Slovakia

Skinhead gangs have received considerable media attention following the split of Czechoslovakia in 1989 into the Czech Republic and Slovakia. Observers have made references to Czech skinhead gangs. These gangs dressed along the same lines as their western European counterparts by cropping their hair, wearing black boots, bomber jackets, and other clothing symbolic of skinheads. According to the Anti-Defamation League (1995), Czech skinheads target Gypsy (Roma), Arab, and African peoples. A media report (Horvath, 1997) disclosed skinhead gang attacks on Romanies and Gypsies in both the Czech and Slovak Republics.

Whether due to socioeconomic barriers and discrimination they faced upon their arrival or prior criminal backgrounds, ethnic minority street gangs have emerged in the Czech Republic. These ethnic street gangs are highly mobile and well organized. They adopt names such as the Flying Dragons and Japanese Red Army. They all appear to have firm ties to organized crime and strong business orientations. Criminally oriented Vietnamese street gangs have been described in the Czech Republic (Nozina, n.d.). These street gangs are involved in extortion, theft, contract killing, violent crime, smuggling people, drug distribution, prostitution, and black market goods. Gang members ranged from aged 14 to 35 years. Membership of the street gangs was mostly immigrant Vietnamese and recent immigrants to the Czech Republic. Many were originally from Vietnam because to pay off war debts, the Vietnamese and Czech governments agreed to send Vietnamese immigrants to the Republic to provide a cheap labor pool.

It was from this immigrant pool and from recent immigrants from other post-communist countries that street gangs arose. These gangs modeled themselves after street gangs in the United States and Vietnam.

The Czech Republic government has moved to curb skinhead activity by banning demonstrations and arresting known leaders of skinhead gangs and organizations, such as the British based Blood and Honor. Authorities have also confiscated neo-Nazi propaganda to hamper the group's efforts (Anonymous, 1999). Some communities have held anti-skinhead and neo-Nazi demonstrations with much popular support.

Many of the patterns present in the Czech Republic are also true of Slovakia. Skinhead gangs and groups are very pronounced in Slovakia (Bollag, 1999; Hufford, 2001). According to David Hufford (2001), skinheads in Slovakia have a Nazi orientation, shaved heads, pierced bodies, and wear other skinhead attire. They are typically male, white, young, and are abusive of Gypsy, Turkish, Black, Asian, Hungarian, and Jewish peoples (Anonymous, 1999; Bollag, 1999). Slovakian skinheads use graffiti to identify territory and convey politically motivated messages of hate and racism.

Slovakian skinheads have been known to gather in large numbers for political demonstrations. In March 12, 2000, a large group of skinheads was able to halt and force a convention of Rabbis to meet in a different location. Slovakian skinheads are known to assault their victims on public transportation. Gang assaults on foreign students from South America and other third-world countries have been reported. Consequently, student enrollments of African, Middle-eastern, and other countries have declined in recent years in response to skinhead attacks. This has led some higher education officials to put pressure on the Slovakian police to take action.

According to Hufford (2001), Slovakian citizens typically do not intervene to stop these assaults. Similar to Germany, citizens often choose to not intervene during attacks. In addition, police responses to skinhead violence in Slovakia are known to be slow in spite of heavy media attention to skinhead activities. Time will tell whether Slovakia begins to respond to street gang violence in a meaningful and effective manner.

ADDITIONAL REFERENCES TO STREET GANGS IN EUROPE

Short and Strodtbeck (1974) noted the existence of the *Tap-Karoschi* in the old Yugoslavia. With all of the turmoil and disruption of recent civil wars and the breakup of Yugoslavia, it is unclear of the extent of street gangs in this region. Reports of small gangs of Albanian men raiding Kosovo have been made by the media (Hedges, 1999). Known as *halabaket*, these gangs of Albanian men cross the border with Kosovo and plunder citizens. These gangs commit auto thefts, armed robberies, homicides, thefts, rapes, and kidnappings. Kosovo's officials and United Nations peacekeeping forces appear to be helpless in stopping these forays into Kosovo. Little else is known about these groups, which may be but are probably not true street gangs. Spain has little more than sports hooliganism. Zurich, Switzerland, appears to follow a pattern similar to the German cities, with Turkish, Yugoslav, Albanian, Lebanese, and Chilean minorities forming ethnic gangs. In Zurich, police refer to youth preparing to develop gangs as "toys" for toy gangsters. Gypsy youth gangs are known to operate throughout major European cities such as Paris and Rome. In general, gangs appear to be active throughout much of Europe.

Romania began its political and economic reforms in 1989. One of the unintended products of reform has been the rise in the numbers of street children. Alexandrescu (1996) provided a brief glimpse of Romanian street children and youth street gangs. The street youth in her study were aged between five and 20 years, with about half coming from single parent families. She concluded that street gangs offered some youth the only viable means to live on the streets. The gangs offered protection and provided food, shelter, and goods to members.

The Romanian street gangs assigned roles to members according to the member's ability to acquire money. The street gangs had leaders who were typically older, stronger, and persuasive. Gang members begged and turned over their earnings from crimes to the leaders for distribution. Gang members committed larceny to make money. Gang members protected each other and slept in small groups for protection. Gang members would come to the rescue of other members who were assaulted by outsiders and other gangs.

In Portugal, racial tensions are reportedly building and a new generation of immigrant youth from Africa may be adopting American street gang styles. McDougall (1994) made a news report on African immigrant youth that were forming criminal street gangs in Portugal. McDougall notes that the police claim gang-related crimes were still rare, nevertheless there was gang crime in Lisbon. According to McDougall, gang members were poor and resided in the shanties of Lisbon. Gang members modeled themselves after American gangs. They identified with the African American street gangs because they viewed all African immigrants, regardless of country, as being part of a larger cultural struggle.

CLOSING OBSERVATIONS ABOUT STREET GANGS IN EUROPE

Evidence seems to point to a rise in street gangs in some but not necessarily all European countries. What is evident is that Europe is not currently overwhelmed with street gangs nor do European cities have the presence of street gangs to the extent or degree of seriousness of American cities (Huizinga & Schumann, 2001; Weitekamp, 2001). Not everyone would agree and scholars continue to debate the presence of street gangs in Europe. For example, Huizinga and Schumann (2001), Dekleva (2001), and Vercaigne (1997) found mixed evidence on the presence of street gangs in Europe. Many scholars and officials seem to deny that street gangs are present (Klein, 1996). Malcolm Klein (2001) referred to this situation as the "Euro-gang paradox." The Euro-gang paradox is based on the notion that because many of Europe's street gangs do not conform to distorted and stereotypical media images of what street gangs are like, they are not gangs. These distortions include misperceptions that gangs are highly organized, cohesive, and violent endeavors. Based on what is reported by the scholars in this chapter and others, it cannot be denied many European cities have street gangs or gang-like groups (Weitekamp, 2001). It appears that law violating youth groups, some evolving into gangs, are increasingly evident as a feature of European societies. Europe needs to move away from the denial stage regarding street gangs. The prospect for the development and growth of street gangs in Europe is clear, Europe can expect to experience a rise in street gangs. This concern has been raised by Malcolm Klein (2001) and many of his associates and is echoed here.

Malcolm Klein (2001) identified four major themes that run through discussions on street gangs in Europe: the youth group context, role of marginalized populations, role of community, and the range and questionable effectiveness of policies. These and other themes surface in some of the studies on European street gangs. For example, Weitekamp (2001) reported that European street gangs share many characteristics, including gangs: exist in deprived communities; often consist of minority or immigrant members of society either by race, nationality, or ethnicity; are predominantly male; have members who are almost always alienated and marginalized youth whose opportunities are blocked; have members who are usually young and typically adolescents or young adults; have members who are involved in all sorts of criminal activities with quite a range in the level of delinquent and criminal behavior; and are stable and can exist over long periods of time.

In Europe, the immigration of people has created fertile ground for the formation of "native" and immigrant street gangs. In all of the countries reporting the presence of street gangs, the ethnic backgrounds or more specifically minority group status of subgroups plays a major role in the establishment of street gangs. For example, in Great Britain, the white reaction to immigrants fuelled the development of various racist and skinhead gangs that targeted these groups. Consequently, some immigrant youth formed self-defense street gangs that reacted to these attacks and the general lack of economic opportunity. These gangs eventually evolved into criminal activities. In Germany, the pattern was the same, as immigrants from Pakistan, Vietnam, India, China, Jamaica, Turkey, Greece, and North Africa all have faced marginalization and racist attacks from German neo-Nazi and skinhead groups. It is not so much ethnicity but the multiple marginalization and alienation of youth that lead to street gang formation in many European countries.

Chapter 4

STREET GANGS IN THE WESTERN HEMISPHERE: CANADA, CENTRAL, AND SOUTH AMERICA

The United States has tremendous socioeconomic influence throughout the world, especially in the Western Hemisphere. Street gangs in the United States have great influence street gangs in other countries in the Western Hemisphere. Even with this influence, it is important to review what is unique to street gangs in the region. Given the pervasiveness of American gangs, it is easy to overlook the fact that street gangs are present in other countries in the hemisphere. This chapter reviews street gangs in other Western Hemisphere countries beginning with neighboring Canada.

It is important to note that the United States policy of deportation of convicted criminals including street gang members to their countries of origin has had a profound impact on street gangs in the Western Hemisphere. While the program was designed to lower crime rates in the US, which it likely has, it has also resulted in the exportation of American street gang "know how" to a variety of countries. This policy poses major problems for the receiving countries that are typically ill equipped to deal effectively with American-style street gangs.

There are other consequences resulting from this policy worth noting. First, American officials are increasingly concerned about what they call the "boomerang effect." That is, deported gang members and criminals form new alliances with their home countries and use these to expand their illegal activities in the United States. For example, journalist L. Rohter (1997) was told deported gang members have been involved in bootlegging weapons left over from the civil wars back to the United States. Second, gang-related violence has replaced the bloody civil wars in some countries, thus disrupting the economies of impoverished countries. In addition, during civil wars, numerous youth were trained in the use of firearms, weapons, and combat. This prepared some youth for the streets and gangs. For instance, in Columbia, children were trained as rebel soldiers and were known as "Little Bees." These youth are well equipped for the demands of street gangs. Third, Rohter (1997) noted that an underground railroad for American gang members avoiding prosecution operates with gang members finding asylum from US authorities.

CANADIAN STREET GANGS

Canada has had a history of street gangs. Ethnic differences, similar to the United States, have served as a key factor in street gang membership in Canada. Gangs generally segregate along ethnic lines, and ethnic differences help account for the wide variation in the form and nature of Canadian gangs. Non-Asian gangs, such as Montreal's Haitian street gang "Public Enemy Number One," and Toronto's "Untouchables," "Goofs," and "Jungle Posse" have received considerable attention from the Canadian press. The Canadian Press (1995) observed that ethnic affiliation continued to form the basis of street gangs. The Canadian Press identified aboriginal street gangs, such as the Indian Posse, present in Winnipeg.

Academic research has also found Jamaican posses present in major Canadian cities such as Toronto (Gay & Marquart, 1993). Klein (2002), summarizing the limited scholarly literature on gangs, noted the presence of Caucasian, Aborigine, Vietnamese, Chinese, and Haitian gangs in the larger Canadian cities such as Montreal, Vancouver, Toronto, and Winnipeg. An all female violent street gang was also found in Toronto (Chapman, 1998).

In the late 1980s, Canadian street gangs started to receive increased attention from the mass media, parallel to the increased interest in the United States (Came et al., 1989a, 1989b). In Montreal, street gangs came to the attention of the police as early as 1985 (The Canadian Press, 1995). In Vancouver, police have had a gang squad since the early 1990s. Canadian mass media described the immigration of gangs, such as the "Red Eagles," "Viet Ching," and "Lotus" to Canadian cities from Asia. This rise of street gangs in Canada was viewed as a product of the failure of Vietnamese, Laotian, Cambodian, and other Asian immigrants to adjust to Canadian culture. Similar to immigrant youth in other countries, their failure to adapt to the host culture and limited opportunities for them in Canadian society were forces that contributed to the formation of street gangs. These gangs were characterized as being violent and having strong economic motives (Bruman, 1983; English, 1995). Their principal criminal activities appeared to be extortion, drugs, and gambling. They tended to target immigrants with similar backgrounds. The ages of gang members ranged from 14 to 25 years of age (Banks, 1985).

Stephen Bindman (1991) summarized the highlights of a Royal Canadian Mounted Police Report released in 1990 that characterized street gangs as a major problem. According to Bindman, the report indicated that street gangs are not a passing fad in Canada and were likely to persist. The report noted that gang members come from a variety of socio economic backgrounds and could be as young as eight years old but typically ranged from 12 to the early 20s. The gangs reportedly recruited members from the school systems. The report noted that American gang culture influenced these Canadian street gangs.

The gangs were involved in a variety of crimes including drug sales, assaults, extortion, and prostitution. Runaway girls were controlled by the gangs to be prostitutes. The pattern of street gangs forcing runaway girls into prostitution has been noted by others (Gordon, 2002a). Besides making money from prostitution, the gangs use prostitutes to lure rival gang members into traps and use the females for trading, and carrying drugs and weapons. Gang members were known to "swarm" victims, which meant to assault victims as a group. Ethnicity was an important factor in gang formation but the report noted links between Asian and non-Asian gangs were developing in British Columbia.

Le Blanc and Lanctôt (1994) conducted a comprehensive study of street gangs in Montreal. They interviewed 506 adjudicated street gang or nongang individuals. The study compared gang and nongang delinquent youth and different types of gangs on a number of dimensions. The results found little difference between gang and non-gang members regarding age, family, and social status. Both groups came from disadvantaged backgrounds and disorganized families. However, Le Blanc and Lanctôt found significant differences between the two groups regarding social control and deviant behaviors. Nongang individuals reported less deviant attitudes, less stress in school, better parental supervision, and fewer opportunities for deviance than street gang members. In addition, nongang individuals were more likely to adhere to conventional norms when compared to street gang members. In contrast, gang members were more socially and emotionally troubled youth.

Le Blanc and Lanctôt (1994) also included questions on the organizational characteristics of the street gangs. They found that most youth described their gangs as having defined structures, including well-defined leaders, a sense of territory, gang identities, continual association among members, and gang names. Other gang members in the study reported their gangs had only a few of the structural characteristics of organized gangs, such as well-defined leaders. The study also looked at other dimensions of gangs, such as those associated with the "punk" subculture, skinheads, and the more structured criminal gangs. The results suggest the retreatist punk gang members had more family and drug problems than other gang members. Their study found that criminal gangs recruited more often from recent immigrants to Canada and the violent gang members (skins) had parents with more deviant attitudes.

Le Banc and Lanctôt (1994) made comparisons between Haitian and white French Canadian gang members. They found that Haitian gang members were younger, more likely to have divorced parents, come from larger families, and have fewer contacts with social service agencies. The Haitian gang members did stay in school longer and favored delinquent rather than general problem behaviors when compared to their white French Canadian gang counterparts. Le Banc and Lanctôt's (1994) results suggest that delinquent youth with lower self and social control join gangs that eventually activate offending patterns. They concluded that the Canadian gang members are significantly different from nongang members on a number of factors but not in terms of characteristics of their gangs, such as the degree of structure or subcultural orientation.

In another study, Robert Gordon (1998) conducted extensive interviews with incarcerated males regarding street gangs in the Vancouver area. His interviews revealed that street gangs were involved in a variety of criminal activities, such as theft and burglary. Interviewees also indicated that conflicts, including drive-bys, with rival gangs occurred. These Canadian gangs copied American style gangs in dress, colors, and rituals, such as jumping in for initiation. Gang members were mostly male and older adolescents with an average age of 19, with 90 percent being aged 25 or younger.

The street gangs were about 40 percent Caucasian, 34 percent Asian, and the remainder being other recent immigrants to Canada. Gordon concluded that ethnicity once mattered but was declining in importance to the gangs, as more ethnically mixed gangs were forming. Some of the interviewees reported gangs comprised of diverse ethnic members as being very common. The street gangs drew membership mostly from recent immigrants from Africa, China, Iran, Europe, and Fiji. Ethnicity, immigrant status, limited language skills, and poor marketable skills all combined to produce economic vulnerability, poverty, and family disruption for gang members. Gordon judged all of these factors as contributing to the formation of street gangs. This is supported by the fact that interviewees reported they joined gangs for money and to maintain peer friendships, goals consistent with poverty and ethnic marginalization. Many of the gang members also reported problems with schools and their families. However, not all gangs fit this model and some interviewers described one gang, the "Los Diablos," as coming from middle-class backgrounds and living in single-family homes.

Other Canadian street gangs characteristics include their marking territory with graffiti and wearing specific colors to represent their gang allegiances. Some gangs were large and could have as many as 60 to 75 members. Interviewees indicated that joining gangs was typically a gradual process and leaving the gang was not difficult. The geographical mobility of gang members coupled with other social contextual factors, such as community repression and fluctuating economic prosperity, contributed to the cyclical nature of gang activities in Vancouver. The gangs seemed to periodically surface and then recede. Malcolm Klein (1995a) has noted a similar cyclical nature with American street gangs. Gordon (1998) also noted a transient quality to these street gangs.

Gordon (2000) also conducted another extensive study of street gangs in the greater Vancouver area. The study compared organized crime, criminal business organizations, to street gangs and "wanna be" groups. Gordon (2000) concluded that individuals joined these groups for numerous reasons including economic and ethnic marginality, financial gain, peer support, and avoidance of abusive families. Gordon recommended that to have successful interventions with these different groups, authorities must consider organizational differences among gangs.

Leslie Kennedy and Stephen Barron (1993) conducted an interview and observation study of Canadian youth involved in street violence in a middle-sized, western Canadian city. They did not identify the delinquent group they studied as a gang, but it took on many characteristics common to a street gang. They studied a group of punk rockers known for their violent street behavior. The group, similar to a street gang, had a sense of membership as to who was in or out and a sense of territory. Relationships were maintained as a network of those that were considered in the group and those outside were labeled "posuers." Group members maintained almost daily face-to-face relationships with each other. The group members wore distinctive clothing that separated them from the mainstream and other youth groups. Male and female members were aged from 14 to 29 years, with the median and mean age being 17 years. Most members lived on their own, but a few lived at home with parents.

There were about 35 members of the group. Much of the group's time was spent, similar to many American street gangs, in simply hanging out. As Kennedy and Barron (1993) observed, much of the time was spent killing time, talking, and waiting for something to happen. Members had specific street corners that they staked out as their own that served as focal points for group interaction.

Group members carried weapons, which were usually knives or canes but not guns. Theft, assault, robbery, and drug use were the crimes of choice of the members. Mugging easy targets was an important source of income for the group. Individual victims would typically be robbed of jackets, money, t-shirts, skateboards, and other desired items. Study participants identified members who were considered to be "hard core" or "tough" and were the most likely to commit crimes. They referred to their victims as "geeks" because they were not respected, seen as likely to resist, and would not report crimes to the police. Their referring to victims as geeks also dehumanized and made them easier targets. One of the group's functions was to protect members from street victimizations. When outsiders attacked group members, other members were quick to come to their aid. Although not a street gang per se, there is enough evidence presented that suggests this group and other similar groups could be considered gangs. The sense of identity, membership, involvement in crime, on-going face-to-face relationships, and rudimentary organizational structure suggest street gang or at least gang-like behavior.

Stephen Barron and David Tindall (1993) conducted an interview and participant observation study of delinquent gangs in a midwestern Canadian city. They found street gang participants dressed in black clothing, such as jeans, t-shirts, heavy boots, and jackets. They also dyed their hair black. While they did not describe all of the characteristics of the youth involved in these street gangs, Barron and Tindall concluded that member participation was best described by Control Theory. They reported those youth with weakened social bonds were the most likely to be involved with the street gangs. They also found little support for subcultural explanations for gang involvement. The gangs were not cohesive units instilling rigid values, norms, and attitudes, but fluid structures for youth with weak social bonds to conventional Canadian social networks.

The Canadian media have paid considerable attention to Tamil street gangs. In Toronto, Tamil refugees reside in the Little India section of the city. These street gangs are involved in crimes of extortion, home invasions, and have territorial wars with rival gangs. The reported ages of Tamil gang members range from 15 to 26 years. The Canadian media speculate that gang members come from homes where there is little to no parental control. Tamil immigrant youth find Canadian society full of new freedoms, which the youth are willing to exploit at the community's expense. This pattern is common to immigrant youth moving from traditional to more open societies. Tamil street gangs in Toronto and Montreal are known to help fund Tamil rebels in Sri Lanka's civil war. The community response to Tamil street gangs has been mostly fear. The community fears retaliation from the gangs and distrusts the Canadian authorities' ability to cope with and control the gangs. Community fear and distrust create an ideal climate for Tamil street gang crime.

Canada's street gangs are not restricted to immigrants or whites. Native (indigenous) populations have also been involved in street gangs. The Indian Posse is an example of Canadian indigenous youth that formed a street gang. Gang members were indigenous youth who came from low-income families where drug abuse was common. Gang members resided in low-income housing areas of Winnipeg. The Indian Posse located in Winnipeg is a violent street gang (Bergman, 1995). According to Bergman, the Indian Posse and similar street gangs have been involved in a number of auto thefts, drug sales, assaults, and breaking and entering crimes. There also have been violent gang rivalries among indigenous gangs in Winnipeg. In response to these gang wars, the Winnipeg police Department established a street gang unit. In addition, sentences have been extended for gang-related crimes.

Recently reports of street gangs patterned after American Bloods and Crips have been made. Sean Gordon (2002b) describes two prominent street gangs named the Bo Gars and Crack Down Posse, modeled after the Bloods and the Crips, that respectively had taken up the appropriate gang colors. Gordon also observed that syndicates are developing where street gangs are recruiting members outside of their ethnic groups and from different ethnic groups for their expertise.

Canadian Skinhead Gangs

According to Young and Craig (1997), skinheads began to appear in Canada in the late 1970s. Young and Craig found that skinheads are present in several Canadian cities, including Vancouver, Calgary, Montreal, Edmonton, and Toronto. Violent skinhead gangs can also be found in other major Canadian cities (Came et al., 1989a, 1989b). The Canadian skinheads are increasingly being associated with racism. In his book *Web of Hate*, Kinsella (1994) suggests that changing immigration patterns and the harsh economic realities of Canada have increased the appeal of neo-Nazi groups of youth. These neo-Nazi groups target immigrants, whom they blame for their economic hardship. The rise of skinhead groups and gangs in Canada provides evidence of this pattern. Some of these gangs parallel the behaviors and activities of skinhead gangs found in Great Britain and the United States. Their style was distinctively unique but also borrows from the English skinheads. They wore cropped hair, suspenders (braces), and cherry red boots similar to the English. Bootlaces and suspenders were color coded by region and purpose. The youth also wear Canadian symbols and bomber jackets.

Young and Craig (1997) suggest that stereotypic views of Canadian skinheads as racist are inappropriate. For example, they argue that skinheads are not entirely homogenous in their values, goals, or practices. They cite the example of Canadian SHARP (Skinheads Against Racial Prejudice), skinheads that are opposed to racism. Young and Craig also found that all members of skinhead crews (gangs) had been members of other youth subcultures, such as the punks or skaters. Skinhead crews met collectively twice a month with drinking and drug use being the most common shared activities. Skinhead members were mostly working-class, had different educational levels, and came from different ethnic backgrounds, including British, Scandinavian, Dutch, and German.

Canadian skinhead gangs reportedly have been known to "swarm" victims by surrounding and then assaulting them. Gangs swarmed to steal clothing such as jackets or boots (Webber, 1991). How often this activity occurs is unknown and may be exaggerated by accounts in the mass media (Webber, 1991). Deviant behavior may be more typical than criminal activity for Canadian skinheads. For example, a particular type of skinhead known as Oi-skinheads were more deviant than criminal.

Canadian Community Reactions to Street Gangs

Canadian authorities have cracked down on street gangs. Authorities have turned to deportation of known gang members as one response. For example, the city of Montreal deported 200 immigrants known to have gang involvement from 1992 to 1997 (Johnston, 1997). The Canadian Immigration Act allows for the deportation of any landed immigrant convicted of a crime committed by organized gangs. Pierre Tremblay, a criminologist, believes deportation represents a serious threat to the street gangs (Johnson, 1997). In addition, Montreal's police gang unit has formed smaller units that specialize in specific ethnic groups including Haitian, Jamaican, Latin, Asian, Sri Lankan, Russian, and Cambodian cultures.

Canadian law enforcement agencies have used a variety of other approaches in dealing with street gangs, such as the city of Winnipeg establishing a street gang unit. In the Waterloo region of Toronto, the police are active in the schools trying to dissuade teens out of joining gangs by convincing them that gangs do not provide true protection and sense of belonging. They police also promote the prohibition of wearing gang clothing and colors (Ash, 2002).

In addition, the Canadian media have paid attention to gangs. The media, according to some scholars (Fasilio & Leckie, 1993; Schissel, 1997), tend to exaggerate street gangs, gang violence, and stereotypes about minority youth and street youth. The media generally depict gangs as widespread and a threat to Canadian society. Some of the media alarm over violent street gangs such as the Jamaican posses seems to have diminished in recent years.

Whether the street gang situation is as serious as the Canadian media would lead us to believe remains to be seen. It is clear that street gangs, although not the issue they are in the United States, are still present in many Canadian cities. Even though they are less prevalent, Canadian authorities have attempted to curb their activities. In some regions of Canada, there is recent evidence that law enforcement interventions, the high risk of drug trafficking, and other factors have lead to decreases in illegal biker gang activity (Alain, 1995).

SOUTH AND CENTRAL AMERICAN GANGS

South and Central American countries are characterized by millions of unsupervised, unprotected, and homeless street children. In Brazil alone, there may be as many as 7 to 8 million children at risk because they live on the streets and similar numbers are present for Mexico. The high incidence of poverty, booming and uncontrolled population, malnutrition, unstable governments, poor health, lack of education, and absence of economic opportunity have created a climate in which many youth turn to the streets to survive. Some of their criminal activities are group delinquency that may be rapidly evolving into true street gang crime. Street gang activity is occurring in some countries, although authorities fail to recognize it as such.

Authorities and the media have reported that street gangs exist or have existed in Mexico (Collins, 1979), Puerto Rico (Ferracuti et al., 1975), Argentina (DeFleur, 1967b), Belize (Miller-Mattei & Smith, 1998), Brazil (Anonymous, 1995; Came et al., 1989b; World Press Review, 1995), El Salvador (Jones, 2000; Munoz, 1996; Rohter, 1997),

Jamaica (Gunst, 1989; 1995), Colombia (Salazar, 1992, 1994), and elsewhere in South and Central America. There is considerable variety in Central and South American street gangs. Some of these street gangs appear to differ substantially from their North American counterparts. However, Klein (1995a) reported the existence in some countries of street gangs similar to the Chicano street gangs found in the United States.

STREET GANGS IN MEXICO

Mexico has a sizable population of youth living on its streets. Many of these youth have developed cohesive groups and support systems to cope with the hardships of poverty and homelessness. Trust and sharing are common values to these groups, that in some case represent law violating youth groups and in others true street gangs. Nearly four decades ago Cavan and Cavan (1968) reported that urban fighting gangs were largely absent in Mexico City, but existed in rural areas of Mexico. References to street gangs and related groups are found in current Mexican gang literature (Marcial, 1998; Portugal & Urteaga, 1998). For example, Marcial (1998) covered street gangs and taggers operating in Guadalajara that were involved with graffiti. Carles Feixa (1995) compared a Spanish gang to a gang operating in Mexico City. The Spanish street gang was smaller and more localized than its Mexico City counterpart. Both street gangs shared common characteristics and embraced the same perception that they were marginalized from mainstream Mexican society.

Jose Manuel Valenzuela (1988) studied Mexican border-town street gangs. The Mexican border areas and towns have been experiencing the greatest population growth and the lowest unemployment figures. Correspondingly, these areas have experienced dramatic growth of youth street gangs, uncommon in other areas of Mexico. Valenzuela contrasted the influences of American pop culture with traditional Mexican culture to understand the development of Mexican street gangs (*la banda*) along the United States and Mexican border. He viewed the youth living along the US border as desiring the American way of life but lacking the legitimate means of obtaining that lifestyle. Border town youth lack the social-economic standing to obtain wealth and American goods. These border town youth have suffered from drug addiction, alcohol abuse, discrimination, poor education, dysfunctional families, and other obstacles to goals. The situation is further confounded by the influence of traditional Mexican culture and values on the youth. Traditional Mexican culture and values are relatively conservative compared to those of contemporary American society. Mexican youth are thus marginalized by both American and Mexican cultures (Vigil & Yun, 2002). These marginalized youth attempt to put on the facade of being participants in the American lifestyle, but with limited socioeconomic opportunities, turn to street gangs to obtain the things they want.

Robert Trussell (1999) conducted another study of Mexican street gangs. Trussell conducted an ethnographic study that found street gangs or possibly law-violating youth groups in Mexico were involved in robbery and theft. These loosely organized street gangs were territorial and had members that sought protection from other street gangs. Trussell discovered that little street gangs (*pandillita*) were formed for protection from other more organized gangs that were known to prey on street children. Community perception of these gangs was that they were rude and aggressive but particularly a community problem. The Mexican communities were tolerant of these street gangs, as they generally had a distrust of the local police.

Females in Mexican Street Gangs

Very few studies have been conducted on female participation in Mexican street gangs. One exception is Ines Cornejo Portugal and Maritza Urteaga's (1998) study that described the influence of punk rock on female participation in street gangs in Mexico. Noting that females historically took subordinate roles in Mexican gangs, Portugal and Urteaga found female gang members were starting up their own gangs. These gangs had horizontal structures and operated without recognized leaders. Gang members dressed in ways that identified themselves as gang members.

Cummings (1994) conducted a study of the rules of fighting among females in Chihuahua, Mexico. Although not focused on street gangs per se, the study sheds light on how individuals and groups of females street fight. Cummings found that females between the ages of 17 and

22 fought by sets of rules. Some of the fights were labeled clean, which meant one-on-one with equal opponents. Others were called *bolas*, which were free-for-alls, or *cinchos*, which were unfair fights, such as when one opponent used a knife. Nothing in Cummings' work suggests street gangs. However, with American influences so strong in the area and plenty of Hispanic gangs in the United States serving as role models, it is easy to speculate that American style street gangs are not far off in the future for Chihuahua's youth.

THE STREET GANGS OF EL SALVADOR

Some have proposed that the street gang problems in Central America are the worst in El Salvador (Elton, 2001). The conditions in El Salvador are ripe for the development of street gangs. The civil war in El Salvador resulted in at least 75,000 deaths and considerable disruption in the country. Violence became increased and more tolerated each year. According to the Pan American Health Organization, El Salvador has the highest per capita homicide rate of around 150 per 100,000 population in the Western Hemisphere (DeCesare, 1998).

Journalists Lucy Jones (2000) and Donna DeCesare (1998, 1999) recently described Salvadorian street gangs. While Jones noted these street gangs gave youth something to do and a sense of belonging, they were also heavily involved in crimes such as auto theft, kidnap, murder, extortion, drug dealing (cocaine), and other crimes. Street gang membership was drawn from the very poor slums of El Salvador. The age of gang members ranged from 14 years to young adulthood. Some gang members had been deported from the United States back to El Salvador following the civil war that ended in 1992. Many had criminal records in the United States and undoubtedly learned much about street gangs from their American stay (Jones, 2000).

Similar to Mexico, the Central American country of El Salvador is importing American style street gangs (Anonymous, 1994; Rohter, 1997). DeCesare (1998; 1999) found numerous examples of gang members moving to El Salvador to avoid prosecution, gang fights, and conflicts in Los Angeles. These migrating youth brought to El Salvador their gangster lifestyles. Munoz (1996) and Banks (2000) describe the involuntary repatriation of Salvadoran refugees, including individuals who became street gang members in the United States, to El Salvador. During the early 1990s, the United States INS deported convicted gang members back to El Salvador. In 1992, nearly 1,000 Salvadorian youth were rounded up in Los Angeles alone and deported to El Salvador (DeCesare, 1998). The program strove to free up prison space and lower crime rates by deporting people who were not US citizens back to their countries of origin. According to Salvadoran officials, this has either created a gang problem in El Salvador or perhaps exacerbated an existing problem. The immigrant street gangs introduced drug trafficking as part of the criminal repertoire of the existing Salvadoran street gangs.

Without question, the deportation of youth back to El Salvador swelled the ranks of street gangs and violence in an already violent country. This migration cannot account for all of the country's gang problems. The civil war, bandits, poverty, crime rings, powerful drug syndicates, and inept law enforcement also contributed to the rise in street gangs in El Salvador. Rohter (1997) also suggests that out-manned and gunned police are contributing factors to the spread of street gangs in El Salvador.

During their stay in the United States, Salvadorans learned much about American street gangs. Salvadorian youth lived in broken families or families lacking parental supervision. Faced with the dangers of the streets and street gangs, Salvadorian youth formed or joined existing gangs for protection and good times. Many adopted the cholo style of dress and gang involvement and became involved in drugs, weapons, and the gang lifestyle. These insights about gangs were carried back to El Salvador.

El Salvador's culture is dramatically different that Southern California and deported youth became social outcasts in El Salvador, sometimes being killed by right-wing vigilante groups (DeCesare, 1999). In addition, right-wing death squads, such as the *La Sombra Negra* (Black Shadow) and the Lightening Command, patrolled the streets looking for gang members and at-risk youth to exterminate. Ex-gang members who immigrated from the United States with their gang tattoos and appearance were ideal targets for these squads. Salvadorian culture looks unfavorably on tattoos. Communities tired of gang-related crime have generally been supportive of these death squads (Rohter, 1997).

The real threat of Black Shadow and other death squads has reportedly led some Salvadoran youth to move to the United States and take their chances with American street gangs (Sanchez, 1995). Others, according to Sanchez (1995), have used acid and cheese graters to remove gang-related tattoos to avoid the death squads. For protection, some youth formed street gangs to counteract these death squads. Some street gang members reunited with gang youth they associated with in the United States (Anonymous, 1994; Banks, 2000). These youth reportedly established gangs that eventually developed rivalries with other gangs for territory and respect (Anonymous, 1994).

Regardless of whether the problem was home grown or made in the U.S.A., Munoz's description of Salvadoran gangs suggested parallels with American drug dealing gangs. An important difference between the two was that the Salvadoran gangs attempted to keep a lower profile (in this respect, more like Asian than Hispanic gangs in the United States) for fear of assassination by Salvadoran "death squads." The Salvadorian gangs established auto theft and arms sales rings to support themselves (Anonymous, 1994).

Salvadorian street gangs were comprised of mostly males but included some females. Gang members were called *pandilleros* (gangsters). Gangs often took their names from locations, such as 18th street. The street gangs marked their territories with graffiti, similar to American street gangs. Although not culturally correct, gang members had gang-identifying tattoos. The street gangs were known to have violent conflicts with rival gangs (Banks, 2000). The gangs also were involved in illegal drug distribution, especially crack cocaine.

Freelance writer and photographer Donna DeCesare's (1998) depiction of street gangs in El Salvador mirrors other descriptions of street gangs. Her work noted that most of the gang members were between 15 to 16 years old. Gangs beat members into membership, similar to the practice with some gangs in the United States. Membership was mainly drawn from youth deported from the United States. Gang members flashed gang signs, carried gang symbols, and had defined leaders (chieftains). The gangs were heavy users of drugs, especially cocaine and alcohol. Gang members were known to get tattoos of teardrops symbolizing the death of homeboys or years of being locked-up for crimes (DeCesare, 1999).

Gang members broke into small subgroups at night and patrolled their barrios. Gang barrios or territories were marked with gang graffiti. These patrols were conducted to identify intruders from other barrios who might be stealing or robbing local residents. The gangs had codes of conduct that dictated that it was okay to victimize residents of other barrios but not their own. Hence it was necessary for gangs to raid other neighborhoods to commit crimes.

In El Salvador, the large and flourishing Mara Salvatrucha and 18th Street gangs are present (Rohter, 1997; Sanchez, 1995). Both gangs are named after the Los Angeles street gangs for which they are linked, modeled, or at least named. These gangs and others Los Angeles-style street gangs, such as White Fence, Crazy, and Mau-Mau, have branched out into the villages of El Salvador. Gang members adopted many American gang practices such as wearing baggy jeans, getting gang-related tattoos, making graffiti, adopting gang names based on territory, and marking territories. The returning youth had comparatively nice clothing, money, and the romantic gang trappings that proved attractive to the less fortunate youth of El Salvador. In addition, the civil war in El Salvador made people more tolerant of violence and its use to resolve disputes. This tolerance of violence, coupled with American street gang know how, contributed to the establishment of violent street gangs in El Salvador.

Community Responses to Street Gangs

Local residents were openly supportive of their street gangs because of the protection from intruder street gangs (DeCesare, 1999). The gangs served as vigilante police forces for some communities. In response to the formation of these "Americanized" street gangs, some native born Salvadorian youth have formed defense gangs to protect themselves from what they saw as a threat (Anonymous, 1994). The police have also taken to the streets to address the gang issue through greater enforcement (Garvin, 2000).

In addition to the death squads, some communities and officials in El Salvador implemented gang prevention programs. One of the largest was the *Homies Unidos* organization that focused on stopping street violence and urban gang warfare. *Homies Unidos* was comprised of ex-gang members and nongovernmental organizations. The organization offered a variety of services and pro-social activities for at-risk youth (Banks, 2000). The organization conducted research on street gangs and offered a safe haven for Salvadorian gang youth. Among its offerings were classes in English language, trades, arts, crafts, computers, and other pro-social activities.

Another reportedly successful anti-gang program was the Poligono Don Bosco Industrial Park in San Salvador (Elton, 2001). The program was a private residential facility and day treatment center where the courts sent youth offenders. The program had about 45 residents and 400 day-participants. Founded by a Catholic priest, the program worked with street youth and convicted offenders. It combined work for pay with occupational training. Youth in the program were trained and paid to work for small businesses operated by the program. The program went beyond work training in that it trained youth to operate and manage their businesses. Youth worked up the occupational ladder from apprentice, worker, manager, and partner. The program established a personal bank account for all of its participants. The program claimed about 70 percent of its graduates had and maintained jobs (Elton, 2001). Parents of youth were expected to pay a small fee to help cover costs. Program staff saw this fee as a way to get emotional support and participation of the parents into the program.

Finally, at least one community, Mejicanos, is trying a different approach to street gangs. Mejicanos is a suburb of San Salvador that according to police had a major street gang problem. With $2.5 million support from the United States Department of Justice, officials decided to implement a community policing approach to control street gangs and crime. Police in Mejicanos now walk the streets and have increased contact with the general public. Early results suggest that it may be working (Garvin, 2000). Police report homicide is down by 67 percent, carjacking down by 42 percent, and robbery down 22 percent since the program was implemented. Based on the success of community policing in Mejicanos, three other cities are implementing similar programs.

JAMAICAN POSSES AND DRUG GANGS

Jamaica is a third world country of extreme poverty for the vast majority of its population. About 50 percent of the population is functionally illiterate. The country has a steadily deteriorating economy coupled with a rapidly growing population that taps into already limited wealth and resources. In Jamaica the number of youth in or wanting to join the labor market is exploding without parallel growth in employment opportunities (Drori & Gayle, 1990). The United States has deported almost 4,200 Jamaican criminals back to Jamaica from 1996 to 2001, which likely affected the country's gang problems (Erlich, 2001). The deportation of criminals from the US, Britain, and Canada added to the Jamaican problem (Borger, 1999). These and other conditions contribute to the creation of street gangs.

During the 1960s, groups of Jamaican youth, referred to as "rude boys," turned to crime for survival and as an act of rebellion against the established order. The rude boys represented not only a subcultural movement but in some instances street gangs. The rude boys participated in rival gang warfare, adopted a specific style of music known as Ska, which was adopted by early skinhead groups in England and Europe. These youth were from impoverished backgrounds, were male, unemployed, and patterned themselves after the Rastafarians (Rastas). The Rastas were known for their dreadlocks, religious beliefs, rejection of the dominant social order, use of marijuana (ganga), and adoption of selected traditional African cultural values. Rastafarians were rebels against the system and rejected much of traditional Jamaican society.

Drori and Gayle (1990) discovered numerous informal youth gangs in Jamaica. Most members of the gangs were unemployed or looking for work. Youth who were disenchanted with the prospects of employment or low wages were attracted to the gangs. These gangs had well-defined hierarchies and territories. Political groups mobilized these gangs with payments of food or cash. It is important to note that the gangs Drori and Gayle were describing were not identified as posses or crews by the authors, suggesting a variation from the traditional Jamaican posse.

Laurie Gunst (1989, 1995) and Janice Joseph (1999) conducted ethnographic studies of Jamaican "posses" in Jamaica and the United States. Because initial gang founders were intrigued with Hollywood westerns and cowboys, they took to calling themselves posses (Joseph, 1999). In England, Jamaican posse equivalents were referred to as "Yardies" and were known for their involvement in drug sales and distribution (Grennan et al., 2000). The Jamaican posses (Gunst, 1989, 1995) appeared to be political, violent, and involved with illegal drug sales, especially marijuana (ganga), crack, and cocaine. Some posses operating in the United States and Canada were linked to stash houses where drugs were stored and distributed (Grennan et al., 2000). Gay and Marquart (1993), along with numerous media reports, observe that the posses' propensity toward extreme violence was a key characteristic of the gangs.

The posses in Jamaica have a long history of being associated with political parties and have had unofficial ties with elected officials. Posses are thought to have grown out of the politically affiliated street gangs that arose during the period of violent confrontation between Jamaica's two main political parties. The two main political factions in Jamaica were the Jamaican Labor Party (JLP) and the Peoples National Party (PNP). Posses worked for politicians by using violence to control the polls during elections and intimidate or murder political rivals. In return for posse monetary and criminal support, political parties granted posse members favors such as public works projects and asylum from persecution.

Over the course of recent years, sociopolitical change has occurred in Jamaica that has diminished the political links of the posses. During the 1980s, government budgets were reduced resulting in less money for ruling political parties to pay armed supporters (gangs). These supporters (gangs) therefore turned to drug sales and smuggling for income (Erlich, 2001). The posses became less political and more drug sales oriented. However, incidents of gang warfare along political lines continued in Jamaica in 2001 (Deziel, 2001). Jamaican politicians now exercise less control of the posses than they had in the past, and the posses act autonomously.

Posses were territorial for drug distribution as well as for political reasons. The organizational structure of posses usually consisted of gunmen, leaders, enforcers, "dons," and "don-gaddas" (gods of the streets). Some posses had multitiered structures stemming down from a top leader to a second tier or subleaders who transport drugs, guns, and money for the leader. A third tier were the street-level dealers, who also were involved in violent activities for the posse. "Mules" were posse associates who carried drugs or weapons for the posses across international borders. Jamaican posses have been involved with organized crime activities since the 1960s (Grennan et al., 2000). Occasionally, posses were known to fractionalize into splinter groups as economic or political needs arose.

Whether posses represent organized crime syndicates can be debated. A strong case can be made that posses are more similar to organized crime than street gangs. Posses clearly have more sophistication than the typical street gang does. It should be noted that some of what they do and how they operate resembles street gangs. Gay and Marquart (1993) contend they may be locally organized organizations with affiliations that allow them to expand their drug distribution networks. According to Gay and Marquart (1993), posses differ from organized crime in three important ways. First, each posse has a boss and operates fairly autonomously. Second, posses are less cooperative and more competitive with each other for control of drug trade. They tend to have violent conflicts over the drug trade. Third, unlike organized crime, they have not had much involvement in legitimate businesses.

Gunst (1995) did not elaborate on the characteristics of the posse members other than they tended to have a fatalistic outlook on life and came from very extreme poverty. Grennan et al. (2000) elaborated on some posse member characteristics. For example, posse members made little or no effort to hide their posse (gang) affiliations, although as they have become more sophisticated, this may be changing. Most posse members were male and identified with specific neighborhoods in Jamaica. Often posse names were linked to local districts. Posse members maintained social links with their neighborhoods, as they shared wealth with neighborhood friends and family.

Youth belonging to posses frequently migrated to the United States, mostly New York and Miami, to make their fortunes selling drugs. The United States was viewed as an opportunity to improve one's status in the gang and community (Grennan et al., 2000). Gunst (1995) described the Jamaican posses as being violent and capable of torturing victims to gain control over drug sales. Gunst reported the practice of shooting victims in their legs as common. Violence was instrumental in gaining control of territory for the drug trafficking. Recent reports of posse violence indicate it remains a problem in Jamaica, as gang warfare is commonplace (Anonymous, 1998).

Jamaican posses have been operating in the United States since the mid-1970s (Gay & Marquart, 1993). Gunst (1995) reported that members of posses operating in the United States often send money back to their families in Jamaica. The life of the posses was seen by some Jamaican youth as an attractive alternative to the slums of Jamaica. Community response in Jamaica has been fairly tolerant, as gangs represented a source of wealth from the United States for low-income families. A measure of community tolerance was the fact that gang allegiances were publicly known and declared openly in Jamaica. United States authorities obviously have a different view of the posses, given their violence and role in the distribution of drugs. Under pressure from the United States, Jamaican authorities have implemented local measures to control posse drug distribution (Joseph, 1999).

Street gang violence and homicide rates in West Kingston (Craig Town) have been high for years, but there have been media reports of recent declines. The decline in street gang violence was attributed to community initiatives for local gangs to halt the violence (Erlich, 2001). The Craig Town area became weary of the high number of youth being killed by gang violence. Under a high level of grassroot pressure, street gangs formed peace pacts to help reduce violence. This community effort may be expanding to other areas of Jamaica. In 1999, the Jamaican Prime Minister deployed troops to control gang wars in Jamaica. Armed troops patrolled Kingston as well as operated anti-gang checkpoints to limit the violence. Jamaican street gangs persist. In 2002, Jamaican authorities were compelled to provide extensive security for the Queen of England's visit. Gang members known as Yardies were viewed as a significant threat to the Queen's safety as she visited Trench Town, an area of urban poverty known for Yardie gangs. The gangs are labeled Yardies after government yards of two-story concrete homes with shared cooking facilities (Womersley, 2002).

BRAZILIAN STREET GANGS

Brazil's urban areas have literally millions of homeless street children, sometimes labeled *moleques* (scamps or rascals). According to a *Save the Children Report* (1992), there were an estimated 8 million children on the streets of Brazil. The report noted most of these street children hand over a portion of their earnings to their parents, but others have no homes. They sleep on the streets and participate in street gangs for protection. These youth were generally viewed as a public nuisance (Scheper-Hughes & Hoffman, 1994). These youth suffered from parental loss, became involved in substance abuse on a grand scale, became victims of sexual abuse and exploitation, had early onsets of sexual activities, were exposed to the HIV virus, and became involved in several forms of at-risk behavior (Campos et al., 1994; Inciardi & Surratt, 1998; Scheper-Hughes & Hoffman, 1994). Often these youth were ideal targets for adult death squads, exploitation, and violence.

The lure of the streets to youth in major Brazilian cities, such as Sao Paulo, has been noted by researchers (Sposito, 1994). Sposito (1994) viewed the streets of Sao Paulo as having the right conditions for the formation of street gangs, mobs, and racist groups, such as the skinheads. The prospect of joining a street gang or law-violating youth group is an attractive means of survival for some of these youth. Many young males see life on the streets as the only option available (Scheper-Hughes & Hoffman, 1994).

In Rio de Janeiro, there are about 600 slums known as *favela*. The *favela* hosted a variety of organized crime organizations and street gangs. The youth street gangs sometimes work for the more organized criminal groups. Youth followed the dictates of the organized crime groups and viewed the leaders as role models. Gangsters were viewed by youth as men with money and power. The adult residents of the *favela* disliked the gangs, as they preyed on the community, but had a law of silence (*lei do silencio*) which meant they did not cooperate with the police in responding to gang violence and crime (Lamm, 1993).

The increase of involvement of gangs in the drug trade resulted in high rates of violence in some of Brazil's major cities. The violence was so high that the homicide rate for Rio de Janeiro is 68 per 100,000 compared to New York with 30, Sao Paulo Brazil with 28, and 78 for Washington D.C. (Anonymous, 1995a). Violence between rival gangs reached the point in 1995 that some elected officials called for military intervention (Anonymous, 1995a).

In Sao Paulo, youth street gangs known as *Trombadinhas* (little crunchers) commit robberies of unsuspecting adults. Dimenstein (1991) provided one description of the treatment of Brazil's street children that referred briefly to youth gangs. Dimenstein reported that the lure of the streets was an attractive option for children growing up in the slums of Brazil. According Dimenstein, street gangs recruited children because the criminal justice system did not hold children responsible for criminal acts. Most of the crime committed by Brazilian adolescents was property crime. Most of the children on the streets were males. Dimenstein noted that girls not able to cope with prostitution sometimes turned to gangs to support themselves. Youth also joined gangs during their stays in state institutions. Dimenstein (1991) referred to gangs of youth called *galeras* in the city of Manaus that have taken over control of neighborhoods.

Youth in gangs and alone on the streets faced the constant threat of being murdered by the police, rival youths, rival gangs, or death squads hired by business people and the middle class to control crime on the streets. They were judged to be expendable because they had no futures. Extermination gangs operated in Sao Paulo and Rio de Janeiro to kill youth, young adults, and gang members with the indirect or direct support of the police (Veash, 2000a, 2000b).

In journalistic reports by Rocha (1991) and Isabel Vincent (1992) and supplemental academic work on Brazilian street gangs. Rocha, (1991) noted that Brazil youth join teenage-armed groups and enter the drug trade as street gangs. Accounts of drug use and abuse among Brazilian youth are commonplace (Inciardi & Surratt, 1998). Street gangs played an important role in the distribution of drugs to these Brazilian youth. The market was strong and competitive enough that turf wars between rival gangs have been noted in Rio de Janeiro (Anonymous, 1989-90). Besides drug distribution, these street gangs committed armed robbery and theft.

Vincent (1992) found Brazilian skinhead gangs in some of the urban areas. These gangs were remarkably similar to skinhead gangs found in other countries. The gangs were racist and ethnocentric and were involved in assaults and beatings of immigrants, Jewish people, non-whites, homosexuals, and racially-mixed migrant workers. A major theme of Brazilian skins was their hatred of *Nordestinos* (Northeastern Brazilians), which they viewed as subhuman. The *Nordestinos* were from the impoverished northeastern states who moved to the larger cities in the south for a better life (Anti-Defamation League, 1995).

Similar to other skinhead gangs, they were not ideologically sophisticated when being violent. They tended to be very nationalistic and white power oriented. They, like their German and English counterparts, were concerned with foreigners taking away their jobs and the maintenance of racial purity. At the time of Vincent's report, the Brazilian economy had been undergoing major crises such as inflation, unemployment, and a series of political upheavals, conditions that some authorities would find conducive to the development of skinhead type groups.

Characteristics of skinhead gang members were similar to other skinhead groups, as members came from middle class or working class backgrounds, were white, male, anti-drugs and alcohol, and militant. The *Carecas do Suburbio* (skinheads of the Suburbs) reflected the suburban backgrounds of some of the youth attracted to the skins. Brazilian skins shaved their heads, had tattoos, and developed skinhead and racist graffiti. Some communities responded to these gangs by forming self-defense groups to protect citizens from skinhead attacks.

Another journalistic account of street gangs of Rio de Janeiro described teenage residents of Rio's slums operating as street gangs that frequent the city's dance clubs to fight with rival gangs. Adam Brown (1994) reported that street gang youth worked menial jobs throughout the week and occasionally sold drugs. After dressing up on Friday nights, the gangs traveled in mass to funk dance clubs. The youth are called *funkeiros* because of their love for American funk music. At the clubs, the gangs confront other rival gangs with assaults and sometimes homicide being the result. Occasionally, large groups of gangs go on rampages vandalizing sections of the city. The gangs, according to Brown, provide poor youth with a sense of self-worth.

Not all of the street gangs in Brazil necessarily have roots in the impoverished social classes. The media have noted the existence of wealthy Brazilian youth participating in what has been labeled "silver spoon gangs" (Veash, 2000b). Brazil's silver spoon gangs were the children of the wealthy elite of Brazil. They were known for targeting other wealthy Brazilians. Their crimes of choice were property crimes, such as auto theft and burglary. Members were characterized as having expensive drug habits and the desire to impress girlfriends by their participation in gangs. The gangs were known to use violence when committing robberies of homes. They tortured and murdered some homeowners and may have been responsible, according to the police, for half of the auto thefts in Rio de Janeiro (Veash, 2000b).

THE STREET GANGS OF TRINIDAD AND TOBAGO

Off the coast of Brazil are the islands of Trinidad and Tobago. Street gangs have been reported on the two islands since the 1950s. In Port-of-Spain, Trinidad, during the 1950s, gangs of criminals known as *marabuntas* and desperadoes were involved in petty street crimes such as robbery. Some steel bands also operated as gangs. Steel band rivalries sometimes led to the formation of corresponding violent gangs that attacked other steel bands and their respective gangs (Mahabir, 1988).

In mid-1980s, Cynthia Mahabir (1988) conducted a study of urban gangs on these two islands. She found that impoverished and unemployed male youth sometimes joined street gangs. Mahabir suggested that urban gangs formed out of confrontations with authorities, awareness of their economic exploitation, and a redefinition of illegal activities by officials. Mahabir (1988) rejected the notion that crime in developing countries, such as Trinidad and Tobago, was an inevitable by-product of economic growth. The economic exploitation by the United States and other neighboring countries of Trinidad and Tobago was thought to promote the creation of these gangs. Gang members were trapped in their respective slums and attempted to defy psychological, economic, and political repression. Mahabir (1988:328) wrote, "The extent to which the activities of the poor are in response to either direct or indirect exploitation is a critical dimension of urban criminality missed by the urbanization hypothesis." The gangs also picked up much of their style and philosophy from the Rastafarians because both shared common backgrounds and rejected the established socioeconomic order. The gangs had names, such as the Red Army, Tokyo, and Invaders.

According to Roy McCree (1998), both of these islands had street gangs that reportedly represented about 10 percent of the male adolescent population. According to McCree, who conducted a random survey of 400 households, the types of street gangs found on these islands included "soft" gangs comprised of teenagers involved in petty theft, such as stealing fruits. These "soft" gangs were not violent and did not carry weapons. A more serious form of gang was the "semi-hardcore" gangs comprised of unemployed youths and adults who were involved in larceny, assaults, minor robberies, and more serious crimes. These street gangs carried weapons used to support their criminal activities. A third form of street gang was the "posh" gang, which drew membership from middle- and upper-class families. Some posh gang members were employed. These gangs were involved in drug-related offenses and were not violent. The final and most serious form of street gang was the "hardcore" gang. These gangs were involved in all types of crimes, such as murder, drug sales, contract killing, drive-by shootings, kidnapping, and rape. Members of the hardcore gangs were drawn from working class, lower income, and unemployed sectors of society.

McCree (1998) did not elaborate on the organizational structures of these different forms of street gangs. However, he did find some community support for their existence. Noting the criminal element was an economic force in the community, gangs were sometimes viewed as sources of financial support for the communities. They victimized outsiders and shared wealth with their respective neighborhoods. This was not to suggest that antigang efforts did not exist on the islands. McCree described a Youth Training and Apprenticeship Program that operated to help gang-inclined youth develop economic skills.

COLOMBIAN STREET GANGS

Abandoned children are commonplace in the streets of Columbia's cities and have been a problem for decades. In 1968, before Pope Paul's visit, authorities in Bogata rounded up the city's street children and held them in an amphitheater to avoid public embarrassment (Romero, 1991). There are few studies of street gangs in Columbia. Law enforcement in Medellin estimated that in 1994, there were about 200 gangs with 5,000 young members in the city (Salazar, 1994). Most of these gangs were involved in drug trafficking, as Medellin is well known for its involvement in the worldwide drug trade and cartels. The drug cartels and their connected gangs were formed during the late 1970s.

Sociologist Alonzo Salazar (1992) interviewed adolescent gang members in Medellín. According to Salazar, youth are born into a world where death is the only escape from severe poverty. Salazar described the gangs as being extremely violent and comprised of youth ranging from the age of 12 years to the early 20s. He found the average age of gang members to be 16. The gangs were age graded with the two to three older and tougher youth assuming leadership roles. Youth joined the gangs for socialization and identification, but mostly because they faced blocked opportunities to the good life they desired. By joining gangs, they escaped poverty and hunger, but they also guaranteed a certain death. These children, to Salazar, had no escape from their extreme poverty other than death. Street gang youth were a consumable item to be discarded and killed. Some of the Colombian children joined street gangs because they were unable to survive on their own. The youth joining the gangs were from the poorest areas of the city. They came from poor neighborhoods, had dropped out of school, were unemployed, and had been abandoned by their fathers (Salazar, 1994). Regarding violence and gang structure, Salazar (1992:9) stated, "At the bottom of the hierarchy of violence are the *pelados*, the kids, who are already learning the craft at the ages of 12 or 13, secure in the knowledge that few crimes are punished." The structure of the gangs was also influenced by whether the gang specialized in certain types of crime. Specialist gangs tended to be comprised of more successful gang members.

The street gangs participated in a number of predatory crimes, such as extortion (taxes), burglary, robbery, theft, drug sales, and murder. Paid killers were known as *sicario.* To gain membership in some street gangs, youth had to commit a crime (do a job) and or go through an initiation ritual. The gangs formed spontaneously from groups of friends and within neighborhoods. Similar to gangs in the United States, gang cohesion was fueled by external threats to the group.

Violent crime was a preoccupation with the street gang members as well as the acquisition of the material things in life. According to Salazar, gang youth progressed from crude to more sophisticated and expensive weapons as they aged. A motorbike and gun, he states, were viewed as tickets to the good life. Murder for hire was characterized as one crime common to these gangs. Salazar (1992:4) wrote, "Murder is the greatest cause of death among young males in this home to teenage gangs of sicarios and their paymasters, the infamous Medellín cartel." Salazar noted that the gangs were not the products of the drug trade in Colombia, as they existed before it became a growth industry. The gang members did not limit their employers to the cartel and freely worked for whoever would pay them. Gang members did not kill for religious or political reasons, they just killed. Salazar concluded that they had a distorted view of the value of human life. They also killed to protect territory or carry out vendettas. Territory was defended to exercise power and for self-defense.

Salazar made several references to the cultural factors and socioeconomic conditions under which these gangs existed. Some cultural traditions in this region of Colombia that he considered deeply rooted in the gangs included the desire for money (material things), a religious sentiment (God and in particular the Virgin Mary who forgave them for all the bad things they did), and the law of vengeance. Violence was very much a fact of life for these youth. Ever since the colonization of Colombia and more recently the since the period known as *La Violenca,* where as many as 200,000 rural people were killed by conflicting political factions, violence was a fact of life. Unlike adult professional gang members, such as those in the cartel, these youth gang members wanted to be noticed (feared and admired) for their criminal accomplishments.

Community Responses to Street Gangs

Neighborhoods tolerated the gangs and some benefited, as gangs typically expelled outsider thieves. Gangs that were unsuccessful in their criminal ventures would turn on their host neighborhoods. This typically drew negative responses and erosion of community support.

Social responses to the street gangs included "social cleansing," that is, extermination by official agencies, the police, or right-wing forces. However, some communities and youth viewed the crime bosses associated with the organized cartels as heroes because they were anti-establishment. The cartel leaders inspired youth to view criminal activities as a way to gain wealth and rebel against the establishment. Street gangs represented a means for obtaining wealth and rejecting the establishment.

Another Columbian response to gangs included an innovative soccer program designed to provide youth with a pro-social outlet (Lawrence, 1998). Founded by a German graduate student named Jurgen Griesbeck, the program was labeled Soccer for Peace. The program organized teams and soccer games for youth from the poorest sections of Meddelin. Before games, rival gangs met on the field to establish rules of play. Disputes during the game were resolved by teams immediately or an arbitrator from the sideline was called onto the field. A female would have to score the first goal for each team. This helped develop cooperation and a sense of fair play. The teams debriefed after games and discussed what they had learned. According to journalistic sources, the program was embraced by the city of

Meddelin and has been credited for reductions in street gang violence (Lawrence, 1998).

OTHER REFERENCES TO STREET GANGS IN CENTRAL AND SOUTH AMERICAN COUNTIES

Almost 40 years ago, DeFleur (1967b) studied youth street gangs in the slums of Cordoba, Argentina. She found these gangs to be small, with about eight members of similar ages, and comprised entirely of males. Organizational structures varied from gang to gang. Some Cordoban gangs had strong and stable leaders, while others did not. There were no initiation rites, and there was no evidence of age grading, but gang members tended to be comparable in age. These gangs appeared to be very hedonistic, with a "live for today" attitude. The gangs had their own argot. Although drugs were used, they were too expensive at that time for widespread use among gang members, except for alcohol. Illegal activities of the gangs included robbery and theft. There was little fighting, and vandalism was uncommon. Gangs were aware of territory, and fighting sometimes occurred among rival "barras," but territoriality and gang fighting appeared to be less important for Argentine gangs than it is for gangs in North America. More recently, Margulis and Urresti (1998) used an ethnographic approach to describe street gangs in Buenos Aires. They likened these urban gangs to being "tribes." Right-wing death squads and vigilantes patrolled the streets of Buenos Aires targeting youth (Robert & Hermelo, 1992).

Whether the Marielitos of Cuba represent street gangs or organized criminal crime organizations can be debated. In 1980, Castro deported around 25,000 Cubans to the United States during the Mariel Harbor boatlift. Many of these Cubans had criminal records and other issues making them undesirable to Cuban society. Many of them had been imprisoned in Cuba. Cubans referred to them as *guzanos* (worms) or *escoria* (scum). Undoubtedly, some Marielitos operated and continued to function as street gangs in Cuba and the United States.

Marielito street gangs have been involved in drug distribution, homicide, mutilations, burnings, and an assortment of crimes. Colombian drug syndicates hired Marielitos to be drug couriers or hit men. Marielitos acted as street gangs by scarring or tattooing their bodies with signs or symbols of the identity as Marielitos. Some Marielito gangs adhered to specific religious beliefs, such as the belief that everyone has a patron saint. Religious rituals often accompanied criminal acts and some groups raided cemeteries for body parts. Some Marielito groups practiced forms of witchcraft and believed they were invincible.

Dominican Republic street gangs were known for running drugs to New York for distribution. These gang and organized crime groups recruited young and poor youth for membership. Street gang or organized crime membership was attractive to impoverished youth who faced an unemployment rate of 300 to 500 percent higher than in the United States (Grennan et al., 2000).

Street gangs are present in the El Mezquital area of Guatemala City, the capital of Guatemala (Mojica, 2001). El Mezquital is a shanty town of extreme poverty, violence, and crime. A street gang of youth in Guatemala is known as a *mara*. One survey on the *maras* estimated that in 1999, Guatemala City may have had as many as 4,000 members. Gang members were youth from the slum areas who used the gangs to commit crimes. Other references note that *mara* gang members are comprised of street children who live by working at odd jobs, begging, scavenging, and searching the street for money or food (Moorhead, 1990). The mara gangs were involved in drug sales, blackmailing, gun possession, and committing homicides. Moorhead (1990) described the conditions leading to the expansion of Guatemala's population of street children from which the gangs draw their membership. Moorhead observed that civil strife has lead many village residents to move to the cities for protection. These destitute families sometimes dump their children to the street to fend for themselves and in doing so create a pool of ready recruits for the gangs.

Severin Carrell (1998) provides a journalistic account of street gangs in Guatemala City. Carrell identified an El Salvadoran street gang named the MS Gang. Gang members had extensive tattoos proclaiming their gang affiliation. The gang was involved in fights with rival gangs, sometimes resulting in homicides. Comprised of youth, the gang was involved in fights with rival gangs, sometimes leading to homicides. Gang members used crack cocaine and huffed to get high.

Another form of gang was the many death squads that roam the streets looking to kill street children and gang members. Street children and gang members are known to "disappear" at the hands of the death squads. The squads are comprised of plain clothed military officers, police, and private security firms. The squads practice "social cleaning" by murdering undesirable street gang children and gang members (Carrell, 1998). Claudia Mojica (2001) reported that the response to the *mara* street gangs in some neighborhoods was to organize into neighborhood watch programs where residents blew whistles when spotting gangs or suspected criminals. She also noted that other neighborhoods have formed co-ops that work on community projects that improve living conditions for area youth.

Managua Nicaragua has street gangs. Howard La Franchi (1996:1) wrote, "Nicaragua is experiencing what other countries of Central America, especially El Salvador, already know too well: the end of a civil war combines with tough economic conditions, plus the influence of youth-gang movies and exiled adolescents who have imported gang culture from the United States, to spawn a worrisome rise in gang-related crime and violence. In the opinion of authorities and gang members, these street gangs are not imports from the United States but homegrown street gangs simply imitating American gang styles (La Franchi, 1996). In addition, the government has pulled back on public education, thus youth have less opportunity to acquire skills. Schools now charge fees that put education out of reach for many of the country's poor children. In 1996, the Managua police estimated that 71 street gangs operated in the city with about 1,500 members. These gangs were involved in robberies, some drug sales, and an occasional homicide. In addition to law enforcement, the Prison Fellowship International Organization has implemented gang prevention programs on the streets of Managua.

Ferracuti et al.'s (1975) study of Puerto Rican gangs and violence found that violence seemed to be much less prevalent among Puerto Rican gangs in Puerto Rico than among Puerto Rican or other gangs on the U.S. mainland. Gang members were typically 11 to 17 years old. Gang fights, gang identification symbols, and other features of gangs thought to provoke violence were absent. Joining a street gang was viewed by the gang members as means of coping or survival. Studies by Ferracuti et al. (1975) and De Fleur (1967b) emphasized that cultural differences between Anglo and Central America were so great that generalizations from one culture to the other, with respect to youth gangs, were inappropriate.

Haiti, known for its political instability over the years, has experienced a growth of street gangs. The United States has deported many criminals back to Haiti and these criminals have formed or joined gangs called *zenglendo* gangs. These gangs modeled themselves after the American-style gangsters and committed armed robberies against tourists and Haitians (Ridgeway & Jean-Pierre, 1996). They were violent and did not hesitate to kill their victims. Car jacking, kidnapping, armed robbery, and the drug trade were the crimes of choice for these gangs.

The *zenglendo* gangs originated from the slums of Haiti, the poorest country in the Western Hemisphere. The street gangs carry sophisticated automatic weapons and were generally better armed than the Haitian police. Gang members idolized American action film heroes, such as Steven Segal and Arnold Schwartzenegger. Ridgeway and Jean-Pierre (1996) believed that American immigration and deportation policies fuelled the growth of criminal street gangs in Haiti, as many criminals unfamiliar with Haitian culture have been deported to Haiti.

CONCLUSION: STREET GANGS IN THE WESTERN HEMISPHERE – CANADA, CENTRAL AND SOUTH AMERICA

Although there is considerable variation among the street gangs of Canada, Central, and South America, much of what is observed is influenced by the development of street gangs in the United States. This observation is grounded is the patterns of Canadian, Jamaican, Brazilian, Mexican, and other gangs. A good example of how American street gangs have influenced these gangs can be found in the tiny country of Belize. The United States has a strong cultural influence on the small country. Since World War II, the Citizens of Belize have migrated to the United States for work. Some naturalized Americans and others have chosen to return to their native Belize. Through this migration, street gang know-how and culture was transferred to Belize. Belizean youth embraced the California-style of street gangs and brought what they learned back to Belize. According to Miller-Matthei and Smith (1998), Belizean youth imitated Crip and Blood style street gangs. They called themselves Crips or Bloods, carried weapons, had graffiti, used and sold drugs, and otherwise acted as American street gangs. Similar patterns can be observed in El Salvador and border towns of Mexico.

In addition, the United States deportation of criminals back to Central and South American countries has contributed to the rise of American-style street gangs. This deportation is not the sole explanation for the rise of street gangs. Other factors also created fertile ground for the development and expansion of street gangs.

The numerous civil wars, struggles for power, economic woes, growth of the drug trade, political violence, swelling population growth, abject poverty, and general social upheaval have created ripe social conditions for the development of street gangs in Central and South America. Youth in many countries have experienced a great deal of violence and death, which has prepared them well for the violence of street gangs. The prospect for the development of criminal street gangs in this region of the world is great. It is very likely that street gangs will continue to arise and be violent unless major social changes in opportunities for these at-risk youth occur. These changes will likely not occur without a political and social price that many will be unwilling or unable to pay.

Chapter 5

STREET GANGS IN RUSSIA AND ASIA

Increases in juvenile delinquency have been reported in Asian countries such as Hong Kong, Ceylon, Indonesia, Malaysia, Nepal, Pakistan, Philippines, Singapore, Sri Lanka, Taiwan, Thailand, and India since the 1960s and 1970s (Clinard & Abbott, 1973; Francia, 1991; Hotyst, 1982; Kuo, 1973). It is likely that corresponding increases in street gang activity have also occurred. Although we know that street gangs exist in these and other Asian countries, information is limited. There are some exceptions and in some Asian countries and regions, more is known about gangs. For example, we know that street gangs have thrived in Hong Kong and may have found their way to major United States cities (Rice, 1977). We also know that in the 1960s, criminal youth gangs were a problem in Indonesia and Thailand, and two decades later they committed a large proportion of the criminal offenses in these countries (Hotyst, 1982). Although literature is sparse, researchers and journalists have looked into the issue of street gangs in Asia and some of their observations are presented in this chapter.

STREET GANGS IN RUSSIA

Russia is as much a European as Asian country that spans several time zones. Most of the information collected about Russian street gangs comes from the western portion of this vast country. It is safe to assume that street gangs, if they exist at all, do not represent a noticeable problem in most of the country. However, as one moves west towards Europe, they are increasingly part of the Russian social landscape.

135

How far do street gangs go back in Russian history? Alexander Salagaev (2001) traced the appearance of delinquent street gangs in Russia to the Russian Revolution that spanned from 1918 to 1921. In the period just before the Russian Revolution, the government used the term "Hooliganism" to describe rowdy behavior by students and youth groups (Chalidze, 1977). Some of these hooligan groups might have been street gangs or at least acted similar to street gangs.

Following the Russian Revolution, many youth were left homeless and without parental care. According to Binder et al. (1988), the Revolution had left many youths homeless. Some homeless and other youth found it necessary to turn to street gangs and crime to survive the aftermath. This adaptation is similar to what occurred in Europe and Japan following World War II. Binder et al. wrote:

> Large groups of Russian youths, finding themselves in a disorganized society and without adequate adult supervision because of the death of one or both parents or the dislocations of their families, formed marauding bands, housing themselves in cellars and makeshift shelters near large urban centers. These youths were referred to as "*Gezprizornye,*" or the "neglected." (Binder et al. 1988:396)

Following the Russian Revolution, street gang authority Frederick Thrasher also observed that Russian youths joined gangs for survival. He noted:

> Russia's 100,000 neglected children are said to travel in gangs, winning a precarious living by stealing and finding shelter in deserted buildings and in Moscow and other cities in the sewers and catacombs. (Thrasher 1927:40)

Similar street gangs formed decades later in the aftermath of World War II, as homeless and destitute youth banded together to survive the repercussions of war.

Russian Gangs (*Banda*) Since the Russian Revolution

Determining the extent of juvenile delinquency and street gangs in the Soviet Union always has been difficult. It is complicated by the Russian notion of "informal youth groups" (IYGs) that encompass a wide variety of youth subcultures, including street gangs. Separating and identifying street gangs from informal youth groups is difficult. In addition, Binder et al. (1988) concluded that national data on delinquency were absent and only recently have Soviet scholars been able to address these topics openly. In the Soviet Union, officials traditionally regarded delinquency as a problem in Western capitalistic societies but not the Soviet Union. However, evidence suggests that youth gangs and subcultures have been present in the Soviet Union at least since the beginning of the twentieth century and that they are currently active.

Like their counterparts in other countries, Soviet youth tend to commit offenses not as individuals but as members of groups. Connor (1972) estimated that as much as 95 percent of all offenses committed by Soviet youths were done by groups of youths. Others have estimated that 70 to 75 percent of Soviet juvenile delinquency is group delinquency (Binder et al., 1988; Zeldes, 1981). Whether some of these groups represent street gangs or law-violating youth groups is uncertain. Connor (1972) observed that these groups do not resemble the 1950s-style American gangs, and concluded that these groups were spontaneous and temporary. Zeldes (1981) also supported this view of Soviet youth groups. This view holds that the groups were not true street gangs but law-violating youth groups. However, if the 1950s' archetypical traditional gang is the measure of street gang presence, then these observations may not be warranted. Experience suggests that street gangs in many countries, including Russia, take many forms other than that of 1950s' traditional gangs.

During the 1950s, the Soviet government labeled youth with interests in Western dress and ideas as *stilyagi* (Cavan & Cavan, 1968; Fyvel, 1961). The *stilyagi* or *stiliagi* youth culture and its rejection of traditional Soviet values clashed with other youth subcultures that adhered more closely to traditional values (Pilkington, 1994). Whether these groups of nonconformist youth were only subcultures or had factions of youth gangs similar to American youth gangs is questionable. Cavan and Cavan (1968) noted that organized gangs similar to those found in the United States had not developed in the Soviet Union as late as the 1960s.

Beginning in the 1960s, a Soviet youth subculture became more evident. For example, *khippi* (hippies) and *fanaty* (gangs of soccer fans) emerged. Bushnell (1990) likened the *fanaty* to a cross between British soccer fans and American street gangs. The first *fanaty* followed the

Spartak soccer team, which might be considered the New York Yankees of Soviet soccer (Bushnell, 1990). The *fanaty* drew their membership initially from the Soviet middle class but increasingly have drawn more membership from the working class. The *fanaty* fought gangs from rival teams, developed graffiti, stormed through subways, and adopted other gang behaviors similar to street gangs in the United States. Officials estimated the *fanaty* membership associated with one team, the Spartak Team, may have numbered as many as 100,000 (Bushnell, 1990). These 100,000 *fanaty* were broken down into smaller groups at the street level, more closely approaching the size of street gangs.

By the late 1980s, a broad spectrum of Soviet youth subcultures was in evidence. Gangs of punks, *pacifics, rokery* (bikers), and *metallisty* formed (Bushnell, 1990; Pilkington, 1994). The *metallisty* were associated with heavy-metal music and wore leather clothing decorated with metal studs and chains. They developed their own style of street gang graffiti. The *metallisty* adopted gang names after heavy metal bands such as AC/DC and Kiss (Bushnell, 1990). Subgroups of *metallisty* functioned as true street gangs that committed criminal acts and otherwise behaved as gangs did in other countries (Fain, 1990).

Russian Street Gangs After Perestrokia

During the transition from the Soviet Union to Russia, juvenile delinquency in the form of drunkenness, drug crimes, violence, and other forms of youth crime increased (Pridemore, 2002). This might have been expected given the economic difficulties faced by many Russian families. In addition, the failure to develop capable educational institutions and school-related activities for youth contributed to the problem and consequently increased the risk of youth becoming involved in illegal activities. All of this was heightened by high rates of alcohol consumption characteristic of the general population. Furthermore, many Russian youth, disenchanted with the communist way of life, desired western capital goods at a time when economic opportunities too were rare. These factors also led to a high demand for narcotics and other drugs used by youth and adults to escape the harsh realities of Russian life. Divorce rates rose, poverty increased, single parent households increased, youth became less supervised than they had been in the past, and schools weakened, all factors often linked to the rise in crime and street gangs.

At the time of the breakup of the Soviet Union in 1991, the variety of youth groups and subcultures was surprisingly diverse. In Russia, the word *banda* is used to refer to gangs. Russian *banda* included break dancers, new-wavers, punks, rockers, and left-wing extremists (Fain, 1990; Pilkington, 1994). Today in post-revolutionary Russia, they are known as *bezprisornye* (Klein, 1995a). Regarding these groups, the Soviet punks were similar to punks in Western countries and attempted to shock and disgust Soviet citizens by their behavior and appearance. One subgroup, the "Majors" or *pseudiuhniks* were known for their Western style of dress. Another, the Soviet "rockers," like their British counterparts, imitated the American motorcycle gangs of the 1950s.

There are major regional differences regarding the presence of street gangs in Russia. Malcolm Klein (2001) found little evidence of street gangs in Moscow, Kiev, and St. Petersburg except in the Volga (east) region. Klein (1995a) earlier reported the existence of gangs similar to American gangs, plus a wide variety of informal youth groups, some highly cohesive and resistant to intervention. Yet other scholars have observed that street gangs are currently an issue of great concern in Russia (Omel'chenko, 1996).

Examples of Russian Street Gangs

Although rare, there have been scholarly and journalistic references to Russian street gangs. For example, some Russian youth have adopted Nazi clothing and culture, but not necessarily Nazi ideology. According to Fain (1990), these youth wear Nazi symbols to express their group identity, have complex initiation rites, and commit criminal acts. They have organized structures including fuhrers (*fiurery*), chiefs (*shefy*), and other specialized positions. They distribute racist and anti-Semitic literature and seem akin to the skinhead groups of Western countries. The Russian skinheads (*skiny*) emulate western style neo-Nazi dress. They enjoy heavy metal music, see themselves as the children of economic repression, and feel rejected by older Russians. Conflicts between skinhead youth and youth involved with rap music and subculture (rappery) occur in Moscow. Caryl (1998) observed that skinhead conflicts are not decisively linked to street gangs and may simply reflect subcultural activities of youth.

Russian left-wing extremist groups are a reactionary response to other Westernized youth groups. They view themselves as rejecting the liberalization and Westernization of Russian society by other youth subcultures. Youth in these groups train and exercise to prepare for fights with youth from other youth subcultures. They have distinct leaders, a sense of territory, rituals, and characteristics common to street gangs. They are involved in street clashes and fights with other youth subcultures and street gangs (Fain, 1990). Like Los Angeles street gangs, they name themselves after specific locations.

It appears that youth joined these groups between the ages of 13 and 16 years, then departed when the males joined the military. Very few members returned to the groups after military service. Females also participated but in smaller numbers than the males. Females typically left the groups when they got married. Members of these groups often abused alcohol, but this pattern was only reflective of the extensive prevalence of alcoholism in the larger Russian society.

Similar to some street gangs in China, many Russian street gangs and subcultural groups are organized among coworkers who work in the same factories or are formed by individuals coming from the same towns (Stites, 1992). Street gang members generally knew each other from their mutual work settings. Street gang membership represented an after work association and social activity. Stites noted that these work-associated street gangs engage in semiorganized brawls with other street gangs.

It is difficult to know whether these youth groups were true street gangs or more spontaneous gatherings of Russian youth. Russian research on youth subcultures and gangs is still relatively undeveloped, but if current youth trends continue, this research is likely to expand in the future. One reason for its future growth may be the growth of street gang activity in some of the previous Soviet Republics and Moscow. Street gang violence, including rape, robbery, and fighting, have been reported in Moscow and in smaller cities. This represents a dramatic change from the absence of gang activity and violence reported over three decades earlier by Cavan and Cavan (1968).

Over recent years, the provincial city of Kazan has received much attention for its street gangs. For example, the Soviet newspaper *Sovetskaya Rossiaya* reported in 1989 that street gangs in the city of

Kazan had divided the city into "zones of influence," which were controlled by gang violence (Wilson-Smith, 1989). Much of the gang violence observed in Kazan was among rival gangs (Pilkington, 1994; Shabad, 1988). The gangs were stratified according to function and had goals, including the control of specific economic spheres.

Dmitri Likhanov (1991) provided a detailed journalistic look at the street gang activity in Kazan and Tashkent. According to Likhanov, antigang officials in Kazan indicated that street gangs generally were organized along similar age-graded principles. Twelve to 14-year-old boys belonged to what was known as a "husk." As they grew older, they became "supers" and then "juveniles." By age 18 they were known as "elders." All of Kazan's street gangs had defined leaders. The gangs fought with rival gangs for control and committed property offenses to make money. In Tashkent, the leader of one gang reported to Likhanov that his gang was involved in fighting business and government corruption.

The uproar over street violent street gangs in Kazan led to the expression the "Kazan Phenomenon," referring to excessively violent street gangs. The "Kazan" Phenomenon" may, at least in its early phase, be likened to a moral panic but with an editorial twist. The street gang events in Kazan led to intense media attention and sensationalism of the gang phenomenon. The number of Russian street gangs throughout Russia may have increased as a result. The exaggeration of events in Kazan led some Russian youth to find street gangs romantic and appealing. Correspondingly, some youth viewed the Kazan gangs as a fashionable trend and something worthy of their involvement. Kazan-linked gangs reportedly have branches in St. Petersburg and Moscow (Weitekamp, 2001). Alexander Salagaev (2001) studied street gangs in Kazan. From 1970 through the 1980s, Salagaev reported about 100 street gangs formed in Kazan. Today, he estimates there are about 20 large gangs in Kazan. From the 1970s to present, Kazan experienced an evolution of gangs from simple neighborhood peer groups that engaged in occasional criminal activities to youth street gangs that had age-stratified structures and fought for control of territory.

Alexander Salagaev (2001) found Kazan's gangs have a sense of organization uncommon to typical street gangs. The internal organizational structure of the gangs is fluid and changing. The gangs have brigades of members assigned to specific business operations. There are also reserves of youth wanting to join the gang brigades. Members in this latter form of gang have well-defined roles and responsibilities. There were four types of members. Lowest in the organizational structure were the infantry who carried out the tasks of the gang at the street level. They were typically the strongest and youngest of the members. They lacked any decision-making authority in the gang. The second level in the hierarchy was the *razvodyashie* or business stratum of the gangs whose role was to develop the business profits of the gang. The next level was the *artoritety* (authorities) who were a small group of high-ranking members that were typically older (age 25-30 years). They served as a council for the gang in decision-making. The highest level was the gang leader who made the final decisions, when the *artoritety* needed decisions or leadership. These gangs were territorial, had strict norms, and employed strong disciplinary controls over members. The gangs held regular meetings at fixed times. The gangs were involved in robbery, extortion, racketeering, fights, beatings, homicides, and other offenses. These gangs fought with rival gangs but also engaged in other social activities.

The Russian *Liubertsy*

Liubertsy were youth generally from the provinces outside of Moscow. These youth came from blue-collar backgrounds and families that had not shared in the socio-economic benefits of the recent changes in Russian society. They were anti-Western and directed their hate toward groups that they believed were a product of nontraditional influences, such as heavy metal youth, hippies, soccer fans, and punks. They took pride in being physically fit and assaulted youth from other Russian youth subcultures.

Hilary Pilkington (1994) identified the following characteristics of *Liubertsy* street gangs; they: (1) were predominantly male but increasing numbers of females are becoming involved; (2) are involved in gang fights and assaults on targeted Westernized groups, such as punk rockers; (3) have territorial allegiances and conflicts over control of territory for business purposes; (4) are called *gopniki*; (5) wear Soviet tracksuits and trousers as uniforms; (6) are likely to allow members (*Gopniki*) to leave if they make a payment. Gang members violating gang rules are sanctioned. A common gang rule is the prohibition of using alcohol as it interferes with gang business; (7) have internal hierarchies based on the members' ages and criminal experience. Those with more of both typically assume higher positions in the gang. About 60 percent of the gang members were under age 18 and the remaining 40 percent between 18 and 35 years (in the city of Kazan); (8) have one to three leaders (*avtory*) and close reserves of 10 to 25 members; (9) have central funds and dues to support gang activities; (10) are involved in assaults, thefts, robberies, and muggings. Some had links with organized crime in Russia; and (11) are increasingly armed with weapons.

What we can gather from the description of the *Liubertsy* is that they are remarkably similar to the Western skinhead groups. They, like their skinhead counterparts, borrowed from their traditional culture and created an ideological view based on the proud Russian worker taking to the streets against the decadence of foreign cultures (Pilkington, 1994). Although many *Liubertsy* are apolitical, many act in response to what they view as an invading Western foreign culture, which they viewed as weak and decadent. Victims of gang violence are often the Muscovites and other groups associated with the West. A common practice is for gangs (*gopniki*) to take "tours" (*gastroli*) of the large Russian cities to beat-up or steal items from better-off "Westernized" youth.

Russians refer to another form of street gang as the *rokery,* or biker gangs. These street gangs are criminal and involved in gang conflicts with rivals. Minor traffic offenses are typical of these gangs. *Rokery* gang members sometimes have tattoos that reflect their gang membership. Most gang members are male; however, females also are involved or at least try to be involved with the gangs. For example, Hilary Pilkington (1996; 1996a) refers to unsuccessful attempts by females to form their own *rokery* gangs.

Little is known about female participation in Russian youth gangs. One exception is a study conducted by Elena Omel'chenko (1996). Omel'chenko (1996) interviewed street gang members in the Volga city of Ul'ianovsk. Omel'chenko (1996) attributed the emergence of street gangs in Russia to the construction of new housing estates that outpaced the parallel development of cultural infrastructure in a difficult sociopolitical context. Russian society has experienced considerable alienation and a breakdown in social relations and communication. Omel'chenko believes that some youth street gangs became dangerous when they formed alliances with organized crime in Russia. According to Paddy Rawlinson (1998), Russian organized crime syndicates often co-opted youth into criminal activities. This pattern is similar to Sicily, where adult organized crime syndicates, such as Cosa Nostra and Camora, subdue and control brazen youth gangs' criminal activities (Gambetta, 1993; Hazlehurst & Hazlehurst, 1998).

According to Omel'chenko, youth street gangs can be viewed along their territorial dimension. They, in differing degrees, emphasized the defense of their territory. The gang member's age was another important dimension. Similar to *klikas* in the United States, young children were known as *soplivie* (babies) or *melkie* (small-fry). Those aged 11 to 13 were labeled *zelenie* (greens), and those between 11 and 16 *kratie* (toughs) or *normalnie* (sound lads). *Staviki* or super *staviki* (old-timers) were terms for those who had outgrown the gang but continued to associate with gang members.

Youth at risk of being drawn into the gangs of Ul'ianovsk were those from lower income and educational households with single parents. The households had histories of domestic violence, drug abuse, and alcoholism. These factors coupled with the strong presence of gangs in the neighborhoods promoted youth gang participation (Omel'chenko, 1996). There is some evidence that the gangs were so powerful in some areas that youth between the ages of 11 and 12 years were forced into paying fees and attending gang sponsored gatherings called *sbor*. Any noncooperation on the part of youth could result in assaults or shunning by other gang members. Omel'chenko reported that some youth believed it was easier and safer to pay fees than resist the gangs. New gang members were expected to assault outsiders and make payments to the gang. These street gangs were primarily financed by extorting nonmembers and members alike.

Rather than focus on territory as they might have in the past, Ul'chenko's street gangs now operate in spheres of influence with stronger ties to Russian organized crime. Spheres of influence include businesses and activities where organized crime was involved in extortion and other crimes. The street gangs did not organize along ethnic lines and were not known to fight on the basis of ethnicity or nationality. The street gangs were concentrated in schools, sport centers, technical colleges, and other locations with high concentrations of youth. The gangs valued strength and fighting ability and youth possessing these skills were actively recruited. Young male adults aged between 21 to 24 years generally served as bossmen for the gangs. These bosses often had prison time in their backgrounds.

Given the degree of organization, it would be wrong to conclude that Omel'chenko was simply describing organized crime groups rather than street gangs. Omel'chenko (1996:224) stated, "The youth gang is not simply a subordinate element of the Mafia, it is an organization in itself." The Russian Mafia used the youth gangs as low cost and safe means of intimidation. The street gangs were responsive and highly mobile groups called upon to carry out tasks for the Mafia. Although there was no "fusion" of Mafia with youth gangs, Omel'chenko (1996) believes the gangs were beginning to adopt Mafia practices.

Russian gangs can be exclusively all male, female, or mixed gender. Omel'chenko (1996) provided a description of female street gangs. Omel'chenko reported that female gangs in Ul'janovsk assaulted male students at a local military communications college. Their unique gang dress included wearing bows in their hair, wide pants, and gaudy makeup. Gang size ranged from 15 to 20 members. The street gangs had few organizational levels but had a well-defined leadership. All female gangs, according to Omel'chenko, disappeared by 1993 and now females only participate in mixed gender gangs.

Omel'chenko (1996) studied the positions held by females in mixed gender Russian street gangs. Females generally joined gangs for protection, money, and defense from others. In general, female positions in mixed gender gangs mirrored those of the males. A primary factor affecting female roles in the gang was their age. The oldest females were called "wives," who were usually between 18 to 22 years old. Wives were always attached to male gang members. Wives made a special point of extravagant dressing to convey their mates' high status in the gang. The second level in the hierarchy were the "prestigious girls," aged between 15 to 18 years. The prestigious girls often were asked to carry out crimes on the behalf of the gang. Males in the gang did not generally touch the prestigious girls. "Girl fighters" (*boitsy*) were the next level, aged between 16 to 17 years but seldom older. They participated in gang crimes and took care of the males. Other females played different roles in the gang, such as the "common girls," who were used by gang members for sex, and "attached girls," who were also used for sex and prostitution. Females left the gang upon marriage or when they became self-employed as prostitutes.

The theme of females as sex objects of the male gang members is consistent in Omel'chenko (1996) and other gang research in Russia (Attwood, 1996; Pilkington, 1996, 1996a, 1996b). Females joined street gangs for physical and sexual protection from other males in the community. In return for this protection, they were expected to provide sexual favors to males in the gang and were often passed from one male to the next and in effect becoming the very victims they were trying to avoid.

Omel'chenko (1996:234) identified three specifics to Russian gang culture: (1) the absence of ethnic origin as a basis for the formation of gangs; (2) the significance of an almost complete lack of urban cultural infrastructure in the cities in which gangs thrive (there is not even elementary provision of bars, pubs, or cafes); and (3) the absence of the concept of "social work" with difficult teenagers in Russia. This means that the only people working with these kinds of young people are the police, drug specialists, and lawyers (which explains why the literature on gangs focuses on "the struggle against deviance"). Given these observations, Omel'chenko (1996:235) concluded, "Youth gangs in Russia are thus unlikely to become gangs (*bandy*) of the Western type."

Community Responses to Russian Street Gangs

The Russian mass media sensationalized the *Liubertsy*. At times, the Russian press promotes a moral panic regarding any youth diversion from traditional culture. Pilkington (1994) suggests that the Russian media may have created a self-fulfilling prophecy by promoting the tough and unruly image of the street gangs. Similar to reactions in Japan, Russians viewed youth involved in subcultures (noncriminal and criminal alike) and street gangs as a social control problem. Many older citizens yearned for the pre-perestrokia days of the Soviet Union.

In response to youth subcultures and street gangs, the Russian government promoted an organization of youth called the *komsomol*. The basic goal of the *komsomol* was to maintain order by forming defensive groups to combat negative Western and social influences. The *komsomol* viewed decadence as a larger power struggle against the West and blamed society and not gangs for street crime. The negative reaction of the *komsomol* to street gangs may have indirectly added to street gang cohesion, as the *komsomol* represented an outside threat (Pilkington, 1994). The youth faced with this outside threat simply banded together even more tightly. This pattern is similar to street gang responses to external threats, such as the police, in the United States (Klein, 1996).

In Ul'ianovsk, authorities have attempted to get at-risk youth away from the street gangs by promoting teen clubs (Pilkington, 1996). These efforts failed and street gangs continued to thrive in the area. Undoubtedly, other measures such as police crackdowns on street gangs have been attempted throughout Russia.

STREET GANGS IN INDIA

Historically, India is no stranger to street gangs. During the 19th and early 20th centuries, groups of professional stranglers preyed on travelers (never the English). Known as Thugees, they were dedicated to the God of Kali, and operated throughout India (Roy, 1996). The Thugees were a secretive group of criminals involved in robbery, extortion, and murder. They were known to groom their victims by earning their trust and then victimizing them. The Thugees represented a community apart from the host mainstream Indian society and presented themselves as a religious sect. Following the Thugees, in the mid-19th century, criminal gangs operated in India, including the Goondas.

In a study of Bombay gangs, Srivastava (1955) concluded that street gang participation and membership was based on caste, with members only joining gangs within their caste. According to Srivastava, gang membership was very small. The street gangs were loosely defined affiliations, sometimes headed by adults. The gangs were temporary and arose spontaneously to commit criminal acts, mostly property crimes. Over time, these groups might evolve into more lasting gangs. The average age of members of the more transient gangs, which may be nothing more than law-violating youth groups, was 14 years, but more permanent gang members averaged 16 years.

Examples of Street Gangs in India After the 1950s

Clinard and Abbott (1973), citing existing research by Sheth (1961) and others, report that gangs in Benares were transitory in nature. Street gang members had weak loyalties to the gang and each other. The gangs did not form for long periods of time. Adult organized criminals sometimes supported these street gangs. Similar to street gangs in other developing countries, street gang youth performed criminal tasks for adult gangs and adult leaders. Clinard and Abbott stated that youth gangs were loosely organized and criminal in focus.

Street gangs during the 1950s and 1960s were of two general types. Gangs with only juvenile members lacked discipline, had no social hierarchy, were loosely structured, and acted impulsively. Gangs with members of mixed ages, including adults or older youths, had hierarchies, well-defined leadership based on ability, and implemented strategies for recruiting members to perpetuate the gang. These latter street gangs committed shoplifting, sexual crimes, and smuggled drugs and alcohol into areas where they were prohibited. The street gangs in Bombay were viewed as substitutes for other social organizations, such as schools and family, which failed to meet the needs of youth (Cavan & Cavan, 1968; Srivastava, 1955).

Indra Singh (1969) identified roughly 40 street gangs operating in the 1960s in the city of Varanasi. Varanasi is a city of many upwardly mobile families who are supportive of the city's poor. Varanasi is a city that is known also for its permissive atmosphere, tolerance, and lack of control over its youth. In addition, the city had an active adult organized crime network. Dada or gurus operated, with the cooperation of the police, numerous criminal enterprises, such as extortion and political corruption. These adult criminal organizations often contracted with youth street gangs for criminal activities. Singh suggested that the city was ripe for the development of youth street gangs.

Singh discovered that Varanasi's street gangs were mostly comprised of adolescent males who operated under the direction of adult gang members. There were some mixed gender gangs, but most participants were male. Singh (1969) concluded that some of the gangs she studied were not true street gangs but other criminal and delinquent associations. Singh classified them as *muhalla* groups, which refers to criminal groups of friends or siblings, causal delinquent associations, and what could be labeled law-violating youth groups. The street gangs, as well as these other groups, were involved in theft and minor robberies. She also found that gangs fought each other over turf and business-related issues.

K.S. Shukla (1981-82) conducted a case study that included interviews with 200 street gang members in India. Shukla discovered criminal street gangs were involved in property crimes and occasional acts of violence against rival street gangs. Motivated mostly by economic gain, the street gangs committed theft, burglary, pick-pocketing, and assaults on rival gangs. Gang members achieved status not solely by age, but by demonstrated success in criminal activities.

Typical gang members were male, aged 16-21 years, and lived in urban settings. India's caste system played a role in gang member mobility, recruitment, and victims, as gang members were drawn from and victimized people of similar castes. Gang members were expected to be loyal to the gang and not cooperate with authorities, but Shukla observed that if a gang was going through economic hard times, members simply moved to other more successful gangs. Street gang loyalty was contingent upon earnings, and spin-off gangs were common when economic success was strained.

Shulka (1981-82) found that two types of gang structures existed, one informal and the other compact and more organized. Gang members from both types had heavy face-to-face contact. Gangs had different types of members including leader-core, peripheral, and fringe or associate members. The cores of the gangs were usually comprised of a small group of the more committed members. Leaders were always drawn from this core group. Leaders were expected to distribute wealth to members, and have professional integrity, tolerance, and loyalty to the gang. Leaders were typically the most skilled criminals with the fewest arrests. They were expected to be authority figures who planned all operations of the gang. The members' complete obedience to the gang leaders was expected.

Peripheral (*Salaibasz*) and fringe members were less involved in the operations of the gang but did perform certain functions. These members also received benefits from their street gang membership, such as a share of the wealth acquired through criminal activities. Those members not following gang rules did not receive their shares of the wealth. Somewhat unique to the street gangs was the role of "prompter," a member who attracted groups of potential victims to areas where the gang operated. Prompters also helped with recruiting new members by distributing wealth (money) to prospective gang members. Recruits were typically drawn from poor and criminally inclined youth.

Rivalries existed among street gangs over control of territories. Gangs sometimes paid fees to rival gangs when working in the other gang's territory. These street gangs were known to cooperate and share information with rival gangs when common enemies, such as the police, tried to suppress gang activity.

Other more contemporary references to Indian gangs are made in the literature. References are made to India's Youth Congress and groups of the party's youth wing being involved in criminal acts such as rape, murder, and political reprisals. There is a high probability that these "gangs" are really criminal factions of organized political action groups. Although they are referred to as gangs, they are most likely not true street gangs, even though they are involved in street crimes.

Shivaz Sidhva (1997) provided a report of youth gangs in Bombay. These gangs appeared to be more organized than the typical street gangs. According to Sidhva, the street gangs had political support from high places and ties to the police. The victims of these groups were businesses and political organizations or figureheads. These groups hired themselves out to real estate developers, politicians, industrialists, and trade unions to carry out crimes.

Grennan et al.'s (2000) description of Indian street gangs conforms with other academic accounts. They reported individuals joined gangs between 16 and 18 years of age, were unemployed, and had prior criminal involvement. Once they joined a *Goonda* gang, they became very loyal to the gang and its leader known as the *dada*. The *dada* normally was an older male who has great business skills and used them to lead the street gang. *Dadas* were often middle-class. When *Goonda* gang members became prosperous, they were free to leave the gang and start their own gangs. Indian political parties were known to hire *Goonda* gangs to influence voters during elections. *Goonda* gangs were also involved in controlling labor unions and business competitors, but most of their activities were with street-level crimes.

STREET GANGS IN PAKISTAN

Similar to the groups described as operating in India were those in Pakistan. Salamat Ali (1989) provided evidence of street gangs or groups involved in criminal abductions of wealthy Karachi residents who were of non-Sindhis backgrounds. Motorists, middle-class, and mostly the wealthy individuals served as targets for these groups. These groups might be simply sophisticated criminal gangs or organized crime groups rather than street gangs. The planning and organization required to carry out some of the abductions suggested more know-how and organization than most street gangs possess. The opposite might also be the case and these groups were simply law-violating groups of students, professional criminals, or others pulled together for the simple act of committing a crime.

CHINESE STREET GANGS

China has a long history of secret societies, possibly dating back as far as 1500 BC (Matheron, 1988). These societies were principally composed of Chinese men and were called "triads." Traditional Chinese triads include the "Yellow Turbans," "Green Gloves," "Copper Horses," and "Big Spears." The triad is an equilateral triangle symbolizing the three concepts of heaven, earth, and man. The Chinese Code of Confucius serves as a guide to the triads. The Code indicates that if all persons fulfilled their duties toward themselves, their families, states, and the world, a "great harmony" would prevail. This Confucian philosophy underscores much of the Chinese way of life, including triads and gangs.

In the late 17th century, Buddhist monks founded triads as a nationalistic rather than criminal groups (Posner, 1991). These triads sought to overthrow the Ming dynasty, which had assistance from the Manchus, who were viewed as Northern barbarian and oppressive invaders of China. The triads represented pockets of resistance to the Manchus. The most notable monastery was the Shaolin monastery in Foochow (Grennan et. al., 2000). The Manchus were successful in overtaking the Shaolin monastery and killing most of the monks, but legend has it that five monks escaped and formed the first triad. Eventually, the triads became quasi-governmental organizations performing administrative functions for regions in China. In the mid-1800s, triads made significant attempts at overthrowing the Manchus, such as the Taiping and Boxer Rebellions. With the communist revolution, the triads became less political and more criminal in orientation.

The triads have been romanticized by the Chinese for centuries and provide a cultural role model for Chinese street gangs. Chinese triads are not restricted to mainland China; triad members have been arrested in Hong Kong and the United States (*Far Eastern Economic Review,* 1989; Matheron, 1988; Posner, 1991). Although triads are primarily adult organizations, the triads recruit new members from youth street gangs. Modern triads, some have suggested, are made up of individual entrepreneurs who use the power of the triad for unlawful gain. Modern triads are more like social networks where individuals can pull together resources for criminal activities (Chu, 1994). They are not organized similarly to the Mafia with strict hierarchical-controlled organizations.

According to Main (1991), modern triad societies vary from highly organized gangs to loosely organized street gangs. Triads sometimes work with and provide directions to street gangs. Main (1991) observed that triad leaders did not control or dictate to subordinates what crimes they undertook. For example, the Big Circle Boys (BCB) is only a loosely affiliated group of street gangs that operates independently in Hong Kong. In a similar vein, Chu's (2000) representation of a triad society depicted youth and street gangs as members at the bottom of the organizational structure. Street gang leaders were at the next highest level and even higher were the area bosses. Above the area bosses were the treasurers and chairmen who directed the bosses' activities. Chu noted the street gangs were where the highest degree of organizational structure existed in the triad, a conclusion different from Main (1991).

Jon Vagg summarized his view of the relationship between triads and street gangs:

> Although triads are in essence secret societies with a hierarchical structure, they shade at the bottom end into juvenile street gangs. Most gang members are not, properly speaking, triads; but it is common for one or two of the core members to have been initiated into the lowest level of the formal triad ranking. (Vagg 1997: 56)

Vagg added:

> However, it is widely accepted that while these juvenile or youth gangs spend much time "hanging around" in ways familiar in Western societies, they are also a resource that can be used for communication and deliveries (running messages, delivering drugs, and so on). (Vagg 1997: 56-57)

Over 20 years ago, Brady (1983) found that police in the People's Republic of China believed that urban crime had become increasingly a gang-related phenomenon. Without defining the term gang, Guo Xiang (1999) summarized that delinquency studies in China showed that about 7 percent of delinquency was gang-related. The increase in youth gangs in China paralleled other trends, including increases in juvenile offending, violent crimes, and female delinquency (Zu-Yuan, 1988). Zu-Yuan asserted that gang crimes had become more prevalent in China. In 1983, the Chinese government took strong action against criminal gangs, but had not eliminated them completely. These apparent increases may reflect real changes in behavior, or nothing more than changes in record keeping or definitions of incidents by Chinese authorities.

Some of the Chinese street gangs identify with the triads or with feudal trade associations. Such gangs are organized into strata with rules and well-defined leaders. Leaders of street gangs may jointly belong to triads as well as their gangs. Triads often view the performance of street gang members as a probationary period before full triad membership. Matheron (1988) stated that this period was known as "hanging the blue lantern." Youth may progress up to regular "street gangs," which were more violent and had stronger business ties to the triads. Gang fights, extortion, and other criminal activities were common within these gangs. A note of caution must be exercised regarding triads. Chu (2000: 26) found that in China, ". . . there is a tendency for youths to group themselves into gangs, whose members profess triad affiliation to achieve recognition of their power and to intensify their illegal activities." Chu added, "However, they have no true allegiance to any triad society." This practice is strikingly similar to individuals in the United States who claim gang membership (known as "claimers") or alliances without justification. Finally, modern triads can be viewed as social networks where individual members share resources to organize criminal activities. These networks do not have strict hierarchical structures nor control by highly centralized operations.

In 1991, Zhang et al. (1997) conducted a survey of prison inmates in Tianjin. Of the respondents, about 90 percent indicated they had participated in crimes with spontaneous groups of other individuals. While street gang crime was rare during the 1950s and 1960s, Zhang et al. believe that gang-related crime began to occur in the 1970s and 1980s (Zhang, 2002; Zhang & Messner, 1995; Zhang et al., 1997). The 1970s started drastic social-economic reforms that changed Chinese society at many levels, including the climate for street gangs to arise.

Chinese authorities distinguish among co-offending (crime committed by two or more people), organized crime (groups of people defined by well-organized structure and rules), and criminal gangs (three or more people and by youth in particular). To be considered a criminal gang, a group of people must be involved in illegal activity. Criminal gangs are less organized, and have limited cohesion and role diffusion than Chinese organized crime. Because some of these classifications are overlapping, official discretion regarding what is or is not considered or gang-related occurs.

Zhang et al. (1997) found that gang-related crime was not especially serious but did include burglary, larceny, and other types of felonies. Core members of the Chinese gangs were the most likely to recidivate. Street gangs members were recruited from fellow factory associates and provincial workers. The work unit served as the base from which gangs were formed. Some coworkers worked in the day and then operated as street gangs during nonworking hours. This pattern is reflective of Chinese culture in general, where work associations transfer into private relationships and associations. The intense work interactions spilled over into the recruitment of street gang members. In the Chinese tradition, being loyal to friends is a primary moral standard affecting interpersonal interaction and relationships, especially among youth (Zhang et al., 1997). Thus, street gangs fit nicely with the moral standard of being loyal to others.

According to Zhang et al., (1997), Chinese gang members were typically youth aged between 15 to 25 years and male. Members who were about 16 years old appeared to be the most active in crime. The gangs had very loose organizational structures that were age-graded and territorial, with core and peripheral members. Gang organizational structures varied across regions. Some gangs had clearly defined leaders and divisions of labor for criminal activities. Gangs' names were usually linked to hometowns, but some gangs lacked names.

Chinese Community Responses to Street Gangs

Official Chinese response to street gangs is philosophically based in strong deterrence, including swift, certain, and severe punishment. This approach parallels general Chinese criminal justice practices. The Chinese view gang crime as more serious because it is a collective rather than individual threat to the social order. Chinese officials generally respond to gang-related crime with more severe sanctions than non-gang crime. However, Chinese law, as of 1997, had not developed special penal codes for gangs or gang-related crime. The general Chinese approach is simply to crack down on gang-related crime.

STREET GANGS IN HONG KONG

Youth street gangs exist and thrive in Hong Kong. Authorities have known about the presence in Hong Kong of very large organized crime syndicates or triads for decades. Triads are not considered to be street gangs but in a variety of capacities, are formed from and associate with Hong Kong's street gangs. For decades, the triads characterized themselves as nationalistic organizations, picking up on issues of national interest but as Grennan et al. (2000) note, triads in the 1970s drastically changed and became more criminal than nationalistic oriented.

Some of Hong Kong's triads actively recruited youth to join or perform criminal activities (Lo, 1992). There may be as many as 50 triads operating in Hong Kong with an estimated 150,000 members (Posner, 1991). Such estimated numbers are suspicious, as street gangs sometimes claim triad alliances that are unsubstantiated. A Royal Hong Kong Police Annual Report noted:

> In the slum areas of the city and densely populated new residential areas, there is a tendency for youths to group themselves into gangs, whose members profess triad affiliation to achieve recognition of their power and to intensify their illegal activities. However, they have no true allegiance to any triad society. (Cited by Chu 2000:26)

This claiming affiliation is common and similar to patterns observed in the United States by youth gangs identifying themselves as Crips, Bloods, Disciples, Mafia, or other larger "powerful" groups.

Hong Kong's triads are traditional, have vertical organizational structures, and have age-graded strata. The degree of organizational structure of triads is debatable. Westerners often view triads as well organized secret societies with godfather figures at the top. Asian authorities see them as loosely organized gangs operating under the same name. Yiu Kong Chu (2000) reported that Hong Kong triads were neither centrally structured nor unorganized entities, but loose cartels comprised of numerous societies that adopted similar organizational structures and rituals that bound their members together. The three largest triads in Hong Kong are the Sun Yee On, 14K, and Yee On. Organizational roles and statuses differed and a typical organization from top to bottom might be: *Shan Chu* (Mountain Master), *Fu Shan Chu* (Deputy Mountain Master), *Heung Chu* (Incense Maker for ceremonies), *Sin Fung* (Vanguard–recruitment), *Hung Kwan* (Red Pole –fighter), *Pak-Tsz Sin* (White Paper Fan–general administration), *Cho hai* (Straw Sandal–liaison), and 49 *Chai* (ordinary members).

Triads provided "real" protection services from attacks from street gangs, suppressed competitors, recovered stolen property, and also engaged in criminal activities such as extortion, loan sharking, drug sales, prostitution, and debt collection. Street-level drug distribution was largely controlled by the triads and they were known to "license" (protect) dealers for fees (Chu, 2000: 37). They also "licensed" (rented) ideal spots to street hawkers for selling goods. Triads also offered protection services for festivals and frequently openly participated in parades and ceremonies. Their participation served to establish their presence and power in the community. Finally, triads typically used violence to enhance the status of the group but also to establish individual members' reputations. Violence was typically a means to an end for triads.

So much of a triad's operations was perceived by outsiders and members alike as wrapped up in intrigue, brutality, mystery, and fear. The triad worked hard to keep this mysterious powerful image in the community. Hong Kong's triads were characterized by elaborate initiation rituals. Triad members were "chosen" as opposed to simply joining. While triads were composed of male members of all ages, it is clear that youth were chosen to join in lower entry-level roles. Members of the triads selected members based on whether they were loyal and capable of criminal acts. Youth were sometimes rented by adults in the triads. Specifically, stronger youth were selected to serve as couriers for drugs and gambling. Strength was measured by the youth's ability to endure pain. Youth were also involved in drug sales. Members have been exclusively of Chinese ethnicity, but recently Chu (2000) reported that triads have started recruiting Indian and Pakistani youth.

The triads had secret rituals, passwords, and codes of conduct. New members were taught the history of the triad and its rituals. Rituals were designed to weed out youth that could not endure pain or be disloyal to the triad. At some point, initiation rituals always included taking loyalty oaths. Some rituals sacrificed chickens and mixed blood to symbolize strong blood ties within the triad. New members sometimes paid initiation fees to join. The concept of "Face" (honor) was important to the Chinese community and triad members were no different. To be humiliated in the community was not taken well by triad members and violent reprisals were taken by triad members who felt they had lost "face" in their communities.

Lo (1993:54) elaborated on the relationship between triads and street gangs, "In Hong Kong, delinquent gangs were associated with Chinese triad societies, and thus their norms are mainly transmitted from triad rules and codes." This conclusion was paralleled by Lee et al. (1996), who observed that there was a strong association with street gangs and triad societies and their corresponding subcultural norms and values. Lo (1993) listed some of the common triad codes for behavior that surface in the street gangs of Hong Kong: (1) Don't join other gangs; (2) No squealing; (3) Don't report anything to the police; (4) Obey triad leaders; (5) Help gang members in fighting; (6) Give financial help to gang members in times of trouble; (7) Don't be scared in committing crimes; (8) Don't cheat gang members; and (9) Don't speak ill of gang members behind their backs or spread disadvantageous information about them. Similar rules for street gangs were reported by Lee et al. (1996).

The highly organized (or loosely as you will) triads of Hong Kong represented to many authorities a serious worldwide problem when Hong Kong Island returned to China in 1997. It was reported that the triads had already established outposts in Australia, the Philippines, Canada, and the United States. There was limited evidence in the United States that triads from Hong Kong made serious inroads into the heroin trade in New York (Posner 1991). Few, however, would testify that Hong Kong triads have had the impact that was once feared by authorities.

Lo (1984; 1992; 1993) and Lee et al. (1996) studied the street gangs of Hong Kong. Lo (1984) found delinquent gangs in Hong Kong were not very cohesive. The street gangs only made references to their triad associations during disputes with rival gangs; otherwise they operated with relative autonomy. In 1992, Lo reports that Hong Kong's street gangs were age-graded (ages 11-14, 14-17, and 17-21 years), with the majority of gang members aged between 13 and 18 years. This age range was similar to what Lee et al. (1996) found. Older members aged out upon courtship, marriage, or employment (Lo, 1992).

Regarding gang structures, Lee et al.'s (1996) study of 36 street gangs found that they had core and fringe members. Lo (1992) noted that dyads consisting of *Da Lo* (big brothers or protectors) and *Lan Tsai* (younger brother or follower) were fundamental roles within the gangs' structures. Gang members paid big brothers *lo mo* (red pocket money). The paying of *lo mo* is a traditional Chinese cultural practice. The big brothers made the decisions regarding criminal activities of the gangs. Big Brothers and the core members were senior members of the gang. The gangs also had informal leaders. These street gangs recruited new members from playgrounds. Gang members were male and lived in low-income housing. Much of the gangs' time was spent hanging around street corners. Chu cited a Royal Hong Kong Police Annual Review summary of triad membership:

> The triad member today is in the main a petty gangster who trades on the fear inspired by the sinister mysticism of the ancient name. There is no centralized control of triad groups and only a very loose-knit relationship between gangs operating under the name of the same society. (Chu 2000:22)

In addition to traditional law enforcement, Hong Kong authorities responded to the street gangs by employing detached social workers and operating athletic clubs (Lo, 1992). Authorities hoped the detached social workers would influence youth to become pro-social while at the athletic clubs.

TAIWANESE STREET GANGS

Western and Asian images of gangs and gangsters influence Taiwan's criminal street gangs. Taiwanese street gangs appear to combine Western and Asian influences into their image and operations. Kuo (1973) identified three types of Taiwanese gangs, the *Liumang, tai-pau* (boy gang), and *tai-mei* (girl gang). The term *tai-pau* refers to those youth who join together to assault victims and do criminal mischief. In the late 1940s and 50s, *tai-pau* street gangs operated in Taiwan.

According to one interview and record study, the *tai-pau* and *tai-mei* were drawn from the upper and middle classes of Taiwanese society (Kuo, 1973). In the later stages of a gang's development, youths from other classes might be permitted to join. Street gangs in Taiwan were age-graded, with older members assuming leadership roles. The structure of the street gang was similar to the family and was hierarchical in form. Kuo placed the size of these gangs at five to nine members and seldom over 20. Gangs exceeding 20 members were referred to as pang or crowd and underground organizations were known as *heui* (club).

Street gangs were predominantly male, but there were some female members in mixed gender gangs and some all female *tai-mei*. According to Kuo, the gangs named themselves, had codes of behavior, and rules for controlling members. The gangs stressed gang loyalty and toughness. Gang names carried connotations, such as heroism, fraternity, terrorism, and ferociousness (Kuo, 1973).

Taiwan's gang subcultures were often characterized by distinctive styles of clothing, language, and group norms. American blue jeans, colorful shirts, and folding knives were common among *tai-pau* youth. The *tai-pau* were known for their assaults on people, fights with rival gangs, fights with the police, and other deviant acts. Assaults were used as a means for establishing and reinforcing gang solidarity. The *tai-pau* gangs targeted non- *tai-pau* students and police for some of their attacks. Sexual offenses by gangs and gang members and drunkenness were rare, but some theft and extortion occurred. Theft was discouraged but at times, such as in the case of auto theft when it served the purposes of the gang, it was acceptable. Like other gangs, however, a major pastime for the *tai-pau* was simply hanging out.

Thomas Shaw (1991) conducted a study of Taiwan's *Liumang* (hooligans). These groups identified with local communities and were called *kak-thau*, which meant gang or street corner. The connection between street corner and gang is made immediately, suggesting true street gangs exist in Taiwan. Traditional Taiwanese culture stresses obedience, conformity, and kinship, and only deviants have access to autonomy and personal freedom from authority. In contrast, gangster morality emphasizes community, personal freedom, autonomy, equality, and responsibility. Youth view joining the Luimang (gangs) as providing them with a sense of freedom from oppressive parental authority. The locus of commitment to a gang was the individual and freedom from authority. Gang members were males in their early 20s or younger. Youth growing up together established friendships and relationships that facilitated gang membership. Locals did not have to fight their way into the gang because they knew each other, but outsiders had to be jumped in by the gang to prove loyalty.

Taiwanese *Luimang* street gangs were named after turf and modeled themselves after images found in the media and literature. Much emphasis was given to the references to chivalry found in these references to gangs and gang culture. Gang membership was not so rigorous to provide stiff role definitions and obligations within the gang. The gangs were loosely organized to not inhibit individual freedom, which was at the core of gang member values. The street gangs had leaders called *Lao Da*, which meant boss. Gangs typically had 10 to 20 core members, from which the *Lao Da* was drawn. The gangs had violent struggles within the gangs. Generally, the only way for a gang member to move up the organization was to kill the leader or leaders. Member commitments to the gangs were not enforced ritually or codified in any formal initiation ceremony. Finally, there were clear differences between ethnic street corner gangs, comprised of local youth born in Taiwan, and the mainlander gangs, which were usually older individuals with deeper roots in mainland China.

Taiwanese gangs generally acted to exploit hostilities that were not initiated by the gang but were already present in the community. For example, they became involved in the collection of debts owed to legitimate community businesses using strong-arm tactics. The gangs saw their role as debt collectors as one of implementing fairness to the members of the community. They also were involved in hotly contested political and business issues. They provided at a price, divine mediation through the occult arts or *fali* for those clients adhering to Taoist charms and spells. They were also known to collect protection fees from businesses.

According to Shaw (1991), Taiwanese gangs worked in the community on building images that they were heroes rather than hooligans. The gangs, while pressing the limits of the moral order, reaffirmed the order with their conservative values and actions. These street gangs actually thrived on the perception that they were a natural element of the community. The gangs ensured that outsiders would not threaten local stability and cultural homogeneity. Local residents, many of whom were in *Luimang* street gangs as youth, often perceived the gangs as not threatening to the neighborhood (Shaw, 1991). They helped solidify the neighborhood. In a way, Thomas Shaw (1991: 80) noted, "Gangs thus serve to externalize residents' feelings of attachment and belonging to their urban neighborhoods in spite of the fact that the neighborhood is in no way culturally or structurally discrete, possessing its own regional culture, as was in the case in the past in towns and villages in China."

KOREAN STREET GANGS

Almost 30 years ago, Kang and Kang (1978) studied members of a Korean shoeshine gang. Shoeshine gangs were organized into territories which were used for criminal and business purposes. The legitimate business of shining shoes was the reason for their name and was part of the gang's activities. Membership was exclusively male, and was drawn from urban, minority groups, lower-class Koreans with limited access to social and economic opportunities. The prejudice experienced by these youths appears to have strengthened the bonds among gang members.

Shoeshine gangs were highly organized, with a well-defined hierarchy and strong leadership. Status was determined by one's location in the hierarchy. At the top were the *wang cho*, followed by the *daejang* or generals, then the *hyung him* or elder brothers and oaji or fathers. Youths worked their way up the organizational ladder, which operated similarly to a crime syndicate. Relationships among the gang members were often paternal, and higher-ranking members served as role models for lower ranking members.

Neighborhood territories were well defined, and violent disputes occurred between rival gangs over control of turf. Violence sometimes resulted from such territorial disputes, or the expansion of one gang into another gang's territory. Control over territory was important to the gang because control guaranteed a source of income. In a sense, the territories were considered franchises, and were organized mainly along business lines. In addition to shining shoes, the gang engaged in criminal and delinquent activity in the same territory where they shined shoes. The general impression conveyed by all of this is reminiscent of the pattern of organized adult criminal gangs or youth drug gangs in the United States.

Other researchers have referred to Korean street gangs. For example, in their review of gangs across the world, Grennan et al. (2000) recognized the existence of street gangs in Korea. Grennan et al. did not elaborate much beyond street gang involvement in extortion and black market goods. Some Koreans, they noted, viewed street gang members as "street urchins."

JAPANESE STREET GANGS

Youth gangs and subcultures have been and are present in Japan. Historical evidence from Hiroshima, after the atomic bombs were dropped there, indicates that abandoned and orphaned youths banded together and formed street gangs for survival (Jungk, 1959). These groups of youths resorted to both legal means, such as gathering and selling firewood, and illegal means, such as theft, in order to obtain food. Following the war and corresponding expansion of the black market, a number of new gangs, consisting mostly of delinquents known as *chimpira,* began to appear in Japan (Grennan et al., 2000). The gangs were involved in property crimes and had initiation rituals. These gangs closely resembled postwar European gangs, and were formed in response to the same type of stresses that affected postwar European youths who had been orphaned or abandoned.

Later, Western images of gangs from the 1950s were influential on later Japanese gangs and subcultures, such as the *Yakuza, Bosozoku* (wild tribes), and *Taiyozoku* (children of the sun) (Fyvel, 1961; Loftus, 1977). *Yakuza* or *Boryokudan* (violent ones) gangs date back to the 18th century in Japan. Originally individual gamblers, extortionists, and street peddlers, the *Boryokudan* organized into family-like organizations over time. Over the years, these family-like organizations turned increasingly to criminal activities. The *Yakuza* are similar to Chinese triad societies as they represent organized crime syndicates in Japan and throughout the world. According to Loftus (1977), members of Japanese street gangs came from two-parent families and from middle-class backgrounds. They were predominantly male, and usually consisted of members under 20 years old. Most gangs had about 100 members, with some as large as a thousand.

Joachim Kersten (1993:278) recently classified Japanese gangs into three categories: (1) youth gangs, (2) *Bosozoku*, and (3) *Yakuza*. Kersten concluded that youth gangs were similar to street corner groups in Western countries. The youth gang members were predominantly male and aged between 14 and 20 years. Kersten found a significant feature of Japanese youth gangs was style. As a group, they were markedly different than their non-gang Japanese counterparts. Their style was an attempt to convey an image of toughness, masculine prowess, rebellion against conformist careers, and anti-education. Their emphasis was on the clothing and not focused on political concerns. Their clothing appeared to be right-wing military with an occasional flash of bright colors, such as pink or yellow. Members wore flu-masks during drives to protect identities and prevent illness.

In general, Japanese street gangs have leaders and relatively loose organizational structures. Some street gangs collected dues, but initiation rites were rare to nonexistent. Gangs used logos and symbols to convey membership, and hair and clothing styles were used to identify gang membership and rebellion from mainstream society. As described by Loftus, the essential motivation of these gangs was social rebellion as opposed to violent or economic motives. Although the street gangs were involved in violence confrontations with the police and other gangs, criminal activity was relatively rare. Since the 1970s, however, juvenile delinquency, possibly associated with increased drug use, has increased in Japan (Hotyst, 1982), and street gangs may account for some of this increase.

Japanese *Bosozoku* Gangs

As noted, one form of Japanese street gang is the *Bosozoku*. Kersten (1993) found that *Bosozoku* are slightly older (aged between 17-20 years) than Japanese street gangs and mostly male. Males younger than 18 years typically drove motorcycles and after 18 years cars. Age 20 was consistently the age that *Bosozoku* gangs and driving were viewed as "kid's stuff," which led *Bosozoku* members to leave the gangs. *Bosozoku* participated in nightly high speed, risky, and highly public cruises. *Bosozoku* gangs were highly organized and had informal gang rules, such as fighting with rival gangs when challenged. Some evidence indicates that *Bosozoku* gangs might be responsible for as much as 80 percent of serious juvenile crimes in Japan (Kattoulas, 2001).

Ikuya Sato (1991) undertook a detailed study of Japanese motorcycle (*Bosozoku*) gangs in western Japan. Sato interviewed and was a participant observer of a gang of about 70 members. These street gangs, according to Sato, operated within the general context of play. That is, they viewed evil as fun and used vehicles as their focal points. Much of the gangs' time was spent hanging out at predetermined locations. Occasionally, the gangs went on "boso" drives, which were basically high-speed and high-risk driving excursions across the city. Boso drives were preplanned, highly organized, high-speed forays through city streets. Intersections were blocked by participants as the group of motorcycles and cars so that gang members could drive through at high speeds.

As far as criminal activity is concerned, with a few exceptions, the *Bosozoku* gangs in the past would not be considered serious criminal street gangs. Sato (1991) reported some serious crimes, such as rape and assaults, occurred, but for the most part, these gangs avoided serious crimes. The gangs did have fights with rival youth. However, most of their time was spent hanging out in specified locations. Some drug use was also reported. The main risk they posed for themselves and other Japanese citizens was their truancy from school and high-risk driving. The lack of serious offending by the *Bosozoku* may have changed since Sato's research. Since 1996, Kattoulas (2001) reported *Bosozoku* serious crime has more than doubled.

The reason for the increase since the mid-1990s, according to Kattoulas (2001), is the *Yakuza* have recruited and partnered with *Bosozoku* gangs into criminal activities. Kattoulas indicated that at first the *Bosozoku* were welcomed by the financially strapped *Yakuza*. Over the years, however, the *Yakuza* have preyed on *Bosozoku* gangs by extortion, "road taxes" and other means. The net result has been increased pressure on the *Bosozoku* gangs to commit crimes to pay off the *Yakuza*. In return, the *Yakuza* provide some degree of protection to the *Bosozuku*. Some *Bosozoku* members regret their associations with the *Yakuza* because of the seriousness of offending and manipulation.

Some *Bosozoku* gangs attempted to capture cultural Japanese themes in the names they selected for their groups. Words that capture power, such as those referring to fierce animals, were popular. Thus, they adopted names such as the tigers, sharks, spiders, and cobras. Youth typically joined *Bosozoku* gangs during the junior high school years. The gangs ranged from the teens to the early 20s. As members age, they eventually left the gangs.

Members of *Bosozoku* gangs were both males and females, typically coming from working-class backgrounds. Some members held down low paying sales or store clerk jobs. Many had dropped out of school when faced with the lack of opportunity for higher paying jobs or white-collar careers. They wore their hair in permanent waves and mostly black or white clothing. Western styles of dress were influential for these youth. Embroidered names, such as Black Emperors, Dragons, and Hell Tribe were on some of their jackets. Gangs designed their own gang insignia and flags that they waved during their wild drives through the city. *Bosozoku* gangs have reportedly turned over their banners to the police to indicate the breakup of their groups (Kersten, 1993). Typically, *Bosozoku* gangs have about 25 members, but larger gangs are known to exist (Kattoulas, 2001).

Japanese Community Reaction to the *Bosozoku*

Japanese community response to street gangs has been overreaction. Japanese society, by Western standards, is one of high conformity to traditional social norms. Any group, such as a street gang, that deviates from the social norms is negatively reacted to by the larger community. Minor offenses and nonconformist appearing groups such as gangs are looked upon with great alarm in Japanese society. This rejection by the larger society seems to inspire some youth, including those in street gangs, to push the limits, limits that in Western societies often would go unnoticed.

Since the late 1990s, *Bosozoku* gangs have become increasingly disruptive to Japanese society. For example, they have rioted during street festivals. Their involvement in more serious crimes has lead to increased public concern over safety. *Bosozoku* are no longer teenagers and youth simply taking personal risks and rebelling. They are now becoming full-fledged criminal gangs.

The larger Japanese community has characterized the *Bosozoku* members as victims who suffer from inferiority complexes and chronic frustration from not being able to cope with the demands of modern Japanese society. Japanese society views them as social failures and misdirected. The Japanese media reaction to the *Bosozoku* is clearly a moral panic. The mass media love to write about and glorify the *Bosozoku* as a menace to society. The media often sensationalize the exploits of the gangs. The media depict them as morally confused youth. They in turn play on this attention and often pose for media photos. Writing in the early 1990s, Kersten (1993) concluded that *Bosozoku* and street gangs were not receiving as much attention as they had in the past. Almost a decade later, Kattoulas (2001) contends that they were receiving much more public attention. This is the result of increased involvement of *Bosozoku* in crime. One response has been the development of stiffer penalties for prosecution. Japanese lawmakers have recently lowered the age from 16 to 14 years at which youth could be criminally prosecuted. In addition, there have been calls for *Bosozoku* gangs to be treated as criminal associations similar to the *yakuza* and prosecuted as criminal organizations. Other efforts by the police, such as halting *bosozoku* runs have been implemented.

Japan's *Yakuza* Gangs

In contrast to the *Bosozoku* are the *Yakuza*. Much has been written about Japan's *Yakuza* gangs. *Yakuza* are more criminally oriented and are comprised of adult males. Younger members play apprentice roles within the *Yakuza* structure. *Yakuza* generally have more organizational structure than *Bosozoku* gangs. The *yakuza* form networks of gangs and tend to operate more like business organizations than street gangs. *Yakuza* gangs are involved in legitimate businesses, such as nightclubs, security, insurance and real estate. But on the illegal side, they are involved in narcotics, corruption, prostitution, extortion, bribery, and violence.

The *Yakuza* were known to have business relationships with street gangs and specifically *Bosozoku* (Kattoulas, 2001). *Yakuza* are known to recruit members from the *Bosozoku* and other street gangs. For example, Van Wolferen (1989) reported that 30 to 40 percent of newcomers to the *Yamaguchi-gumi* were former *Bosozoku*. It is also true, according to Kersten (1993), that they hired street gangs to carry out some of their "dirty work." However, Kersten (1993) cautions us that any systematic structure between organized crime and the *Bosozoku* is doubtful. While some *Bosozoku* youth members were prone to joining organized crime groups such as the *Yakuza*, many do not upon finding employment and adulthood. Kersten also suggests that the discrimination and marginalization of youth were key factors shaping the nature of *Bosozoku* and *Yakuza* relationships.

For the most part, the *Yakuza* represent Japanese organized crime. On the whole, they should be considered more similar to organized crime than street gangs but not in the same sense as the Mafia (Vagg, 1997). The big three *Yakuza* crime syndicates are the *Yamaguchi-gumi, Inagawa-kai,* and *Sumiyoshi-kai* (Shigeru, 1998). One of the largest groups is the *Yamaguchi-gumi.* This criminal organization reportedly has about 103 "bosses" and 500 semiautonomous gangs. It is involved in international narcotics, money lending, selling stimulants, exploitation of workers, smuggling, pornography, and illegal gambling. The *Yakuza* are also known to have strong ties to Japanese business and politics. *Yakuza* organizations clearly have "front offices" comprised of public and elected officials who regularly attend their social functions (Vagg, 1997). These large worldwide crime syndicates cannot be considered street gangs in any sense.

Japanese authorities have passed laws directed toward curbing the illegal activities of the *Yakuza*, however, membership in gangs is not a criminal offense in Japan. There may be some general social resistance to eliminating the *Yakuza*. According to Van Wolfren (1989), the *yakuza* also play positive roles in the community. At one level they provide a cultural outlet for youth who would otherwise be involved in street crime. At another level, they police their communities for petty crimes through criminal street gangs to help preserve the social order so people will not shy away from local businesses.

STREET GANGS IN OTHER ASIAN COUNTRIES

One journalistic account provides descriptive and interview information about youth gangs in the Philippines. Luis Francia (1991), relying on observation and interviews, describes Philippine barrio youth gangs. According to Francia, these street gangs are comprised of teenagers and young adults aged to their early 20s. The gangs are fighting gangs that organized around the protection of territory. The lack of official response to local neighborhood disputes by local police and corrupt officials gave rise to youth gangs that filled the need for local social control. Francia found different types of street gangs were present, including *istambays* that were composed of unemployed "toughs," district gangs that covered several neighborhoods, *barkadas* that were harmless "social" gangs, specialized criminal gangs, and gangs based on region.

Francia focused on a Philippine fighting gang that drew its membership from youth seeking protection from other youth. Many of the gang's youth were high school and college students from the area. The gang had unique hand signals and fought with other gangs under agreed upon sets of rules. The gang was criminal, but crime was not the central purpose or focus of the gang. The gang had an elaborate initiation ritual that involved blindfolds, various degrees of questioning, and striking with sticks or paddles. Gang members used drugs, such as glue and crack, but drug use was not encouraged. The gang had a formal leader but not an elaborate organizational structure. The gang leader had a person called an *aladay* who could best be described as a "gofer" and "groupie." The *aladay*, in return for service to the gang and leader, was protected by the gang. Gang members sometimes worked for adults who belonged to adult criminal gangs. Gang members either aged out or were recruited into adult criminal gangs operating in the barrio.

Additional journalistic accounts of Philippine street gangs are present, some of which are very violent. The Philippine media reported on a street gang linked to several homicides in Manila (*Philippine Daily Inquirer*, 2002). Aning (2001) also reported on a 14-year-old gang leader of the Markang Bungo gang who was arrested for two gang-related homicides.

Similar to the *Bosozoku* are the motorcycle gangs of Bangkok (Fairclough, 1993). Young males, ranging from teenage to early 20s who have dropped out of school and lack steady jobs, race through the streets of Bangkok similar to the *Bosozoku* in Japan. Although they identified themselves as gangs, they were not involved in street crimes. Apart from risking their own lives and gambling, these groups do not appear to be true street gangs per se even though they are generally disruptive and dangerous in their communities. Their lack of involvement in criminal offending distinguishes them from street gangs.

The media have also reported on street gangs operating in the city of Jakarta, Indonesia. One reported gang, the "Red Axe," was named after their use of red axes during the commission of crimes. Members of the gang are known to rob bus passengers and motorists stopped at traffic intersections using red axes (*The Jakarta Post*, 2001). Gang members used the axes to breakout vehicle windows and rob victims of cell phones and money. The Jakarta police have standing orders to shoot gang members attempting to escape. The authorities encouraged motorists to equip their cars with flashing signals to alert police of street gang robberies in progress (*The Straits Times*, 1999).

Teo and Phaun (1997) provide a journalistic description of teenage (*paikia*) street gangs in Singapore. These gangs are comprised of teenage boys aged between 13 and 19 years who adopt Chinese secret society names for their street gangs. Their gangs have slogans and speak in coded argot similar to gangs of the 1970s. Teo and Phaun note that the police label these gangs as "pseudo-street gangs" and members as "bluff gangsters" because the gangs consist of wannabe members instead of true traditional gangs and gang members. Some of the members are students while others are school dropouts. Gang members select their members through interviews. When asked why they joined these gangs, members indicated that they joined out of boredom, curiosity, a need to belong, or for identity. Some also joined for protection from local bully gangs.

These gangs ranged from five to 15 members, which is smaller than traditional Chinese street gangs. Gang members may not know each other before joining the gang because they sometimes come from different districts in Singapore. Gang members spend much of their time in shopping centers, arcades, and dance clubs. The gang members dress according to specific styles of clothing, much of it being upscale designer clothes such as Versace and Valentino. The choice of clothing implies that many members are from affluent Malaysian backgrounds. The most common clothing colors are black and white. Whether these gangs are involved in enough criminal activity to label them as street gangs is debatable. These groups do label themselves as gangs and they do break the law, but authorities do not see them as true street gangs.

Police reports on street gangs in Singapore suggest that some street gangs are becoming more loosely organized and violent. Assistant

Police Superintendent Goh Lam Liong stated, "The gangs of today are organized loosely and do not observe any code of ethics and their main activity is to while away their time. But they fight over the most trivial matters, such as staring or bumping accidentally into them" (Kin, 1999:62). According to journalist Chong Chee Kin (1999), Malaysian street gang members are different from gang members of the past. They dress flashier and have hairstyles that identify them as gang members. They are less involved in territorial disputes and criminal activities such as gambling and extortion. They are younger than previous street gang members who were typically aged between 20 and 30 years. Now members are aged between 13 to 19 years. In the past, gangs recruited on the basis of ethnicity (solely Malay), but today, they recruit from Malays, Indians, Eurasians, and other ethnic groups. Today these ethnically diverse gang members pay fees to gang leaders. Membership in the gangs is fluid with youth frequently moving in and out of the gangs out of boredom. Kin believes today's gangs are more violent than in the past.

Government officials claim that Cambodian youths who lived in the United States and participated in street gangs are returning to Cambodia and operating as American-style gangs (McDowell, 1995). Following the elections in 1993, Cambodian youth have been returning to the country and developing street gangs in the capital city of Phnom Penh. The gangs commit robberies, rapes, murders, and other serious crimes. The gangs also hire outsiders to carry out street crimes. Khmer Rouge violence and atrocities were common experiences for some of the gang youth, hence they are accustomed to street violence. Members of the street gangs wear baggy jeans, t-shirts, and American baseball caps. To reflect their Cambodian heritage, some have tattoos of spiritual scripture and wear Buddha pendants for protection.

Finally, journalists have noted the presence of a street gang named Black Metal in Northern Malaysia (Bernama, 2001). This gang is thought to spread occult practices among Malaysian youth. The gang reportedly recruits new members from schools. The gang has an anti-God philosophy and practices satanic rituals. Whether Black Metal and similar groups in Malaysia are true street gangs is unclear given the paucity of information.

CLOSING OBSERVATIONS ABOUT RUSSIAN AND ASIAN STREET GANGS

Street gangs have been and are present in some regions of Asia. In Russia, there is evidence suggesting that street gangs or law violating youth groups were present in Russia at least by the of the 20th century. These groups were certainly present in the period immediately following the end of World War II, as abandoned youth turned to the streets for survival. As the repressive Soviet regimes of Stalin and other dictators grew in power, chances are great that any group resembling a street gang was repressed. With the increase in freedom that occurred during the fall of the Soviet Union, the environment became more open to Western influences and culture. A part of this Western culture was the concept of the street gang. Anything Western was embraced by many as an alternative to the economic decline and stagnation associated with the old Soviet Union. Economic and social reforms coupled with a declining economy created an ideal environment for the development of deviant subcultures, law-violating youth groups, organized crime, and street gangs.

Russian street gangs share many characteristics with their Western counterparts. Most are loosely organized, age-graded, lack clearly defined structures, involved in a variety of crimes, highly cohesive, social in nature, protective of territory, distinctive in style of dress, and are linked to specific subcultural values. It should be noted that some Russian street gangs depart from having loose organizational structures and have clearly defined roles and hierarchical statuses for members. Russian street gangs place comparatively little emphasis on ethnicity but considerably more attention to traditional soviet versus Western influences. Omel'chenko (1996) notes the absence of ethnic origin as a basis in the formation of Russian gangs. Rather, some Russian street gangs focus on attacking Westernized subcultures or gangs of youth. This focus on the negative effects of Westernization of youth is somewhat unique to Russian street gangs.

Russian street gangs are more provincial in origin and orientation and at times take on larger social-economic issues. It is clear the current condition of the Russian economy and its struggles influence the nature of street gangs. One way this influence surfaces is the emphasis of Russian gangs on some gangs reacting to Western influences and culture. These street gangs are aggressive with those who adopt

Western ideas and style. Gangs with this focus specifically look for victims who have adopted non-traditional values and culture. A second way Russian reform and economic change affects street gangs is the steady evolution of gangs into business enterprises. Russian jobs are scarce and the economy is poor. Street gangs provide an opportunity for some youth to earn incomes who otherwise would not.

Various references to different types of Russian street gangs exist in the literature. For example, there are neo-fascist, left-wing, female, skinhead, biker, punk, criminal, and hooligan, among others. While some Russian gangs have a keen sense of territory and neighborhood, street gang membership is formed from work groups, for those with jobs. This pattern is also present in China. The workplace for some Russian gangs serves as the basis for association and in some cases gang formation.

It is clear that Russian gangs have some unique characteristics, but they in fact have adopted many ideas from the West. Part of this derived from an on-going interest and fascination of things from the West. While western cultural influences are evident, Russian street gangs are distinctly Russian in many respects. As the Russian economy continues to struggle for reform, it is likely that street gangs and more criminally oriented groups will continue to flourish. Attempts by Russian authorities to curb street gang and organized crime growth have been ineffective to date. Until authorities have adequate services and a viable infrastructure in place, the prospects look dim and gangs will grow. Street gangs will offer a viable alternative to Russian youth unless other pro-social options become available, such as work or school.

Based on the above descriptions of street gangs, it is fair to conclude that gangs, some of them associated with distinct subcultures, have existed in the Soviet Union and persist in contemporary Russia. The influence of the West on Russian street gangs is evident, yet they are distinctly Russian in character. What the future holds for street gangs in the Russia is a matter for speculation. One possibility is that preoccupation with the restructuring of Russian society will draw attention away from street gangs and youth subcultures, as the social movements in the United States in the 1960s appear to have done. There is a real risk that education, social and recreational programs, and funding for Russia's youth will diminish in difficult economic times, further worsening the situation for youth. Another possibility is that the rapid social change being experienced by Russia will give rise to increased street gang activity. It is evident that enormous changes occurred between 1960 and 1990, mostly in the direction of more extensive and more clearly identifiable street gang activity (Gallagher, 1992). The economic strife present in Russia will likely continue to create fertile ground for the development of street gangs. It remains to be seen whether the trend in increased street gang activity will continue, or will be reversed by the continued restructuring of the old Soviet Union.

India also has a long history of groups that could be considered gangs. The importance of the caste or class system in India should be acknowledged. Gangs were formed on the basis of one's caste. The focus of India's street gangs has always been on property (street) crime or political influence. Based on a very limited number of studies, the pattern in India seems to be that some law-violating youth groups develop into true street gangs over time. Somewhat unique to these gangs is the intergang mobility among gang members. Gang members are relatively free to move from one gang to another when they choose. Often their decisions regarding membership are based on the criminal success of the gang. This pattern is atypical to street gangs in the United States where, in most instances, gang membership fluctuates, but loyalty to a gang remains fairly consistent whether the gang member is active or not. In India, loyalty is extended to the gang leaders but not necessarily to the gang as a group.

Regarding street gangs in eastern Asia, the ancestral image of triad subculture made a lasting impression on street gangs. It shaped, at least philosophically, street gangs in China, Hong Kong, Taiwan, Japan, and other Asian countries. In many eastern Asian countries, aspects of traditional tong or triad philosophy to some degree flavor the nature of street gangs in some regions.

Asian gangs, especially those in Japan, seem to gravitate toward socially upsetting and rebelling against the larger traditional Japanese society. Japanese society is highly conformist and structured compared to the West. Style and rebellion seem to be more important in generating gang cohesiveness than criminal activity for many street level gangs. However, in recent years, the relative focus on risk-taking and social rebellion witnessed in *Bosozoku* gangs is being replaced with more serious criminal activities. *Bosozoku* links to the *yakuza* have resulted in more serious offending by these groups.

In other Asian countries, such as Cambodia, Thailand, Indonesia, Malaysia, and other countries there is evidence of street gangs, some of which appear to have adopted American, Chinese triad, or Japanese *Bosozoku* street gang cultures. For those countries touched by civil war and the accompanying violence, street gang violence may be viewed as a natural thing.

Chapter 6

STREET GANGS IN AFRICA, THE MIDDLE EAST, AUSTRALIA, AND THE PACIFIC ISLANDS

S treet gangs are present in other parts of the world, but information about them is limited. The biggest gap in our information concerns street gangs in Africa and the Middle East. We know little about street gangs in the African continent with the exception of South Africa where prison and street gangs have been written about for years. There have been other exceptions, such as Short and Strodtbeck (1974), who mentioned the Tso Tsio (Tsotsis) of South Africa, and Weinberg (1964), who reported on juvenile group delinquency in Ghana.

Africa is a continent going through major socioeconomic and political changes. The tremendous impacts of African drought, famine, poverty, civil war, and the spread of disease such as HIV, have negatively touched many and left numerous youth on their own to raise themselves. In addition, Africa has a high population growth rate of about 3.6 percent per year, resulting in its population doubling from 174 million in 1985 to about 361 million by 2000 (Urban Management Programme, 2000). An estimated two-thirds of the African population are youth. For the year 2000, one estimate placed the number of street children in Africa at about 32 million (Urban Management Programme, 2000).

Many of these changes have and will continue to have dramatic effects on Africa's youth and street gangs. The turmoil in many African countries has created ripe conditions for the development of street gangs and law-violating youth groups. The streets are the only option available to some youth. It is this potential for youth street crime and the relative absence of sound street gang research that makes Africa one of the most intriguing of areas to study gangs and law-violating groups.

The impact of Africa's many civil and ethnic wars on the formation of criminal street gangs and quasi-military groups deserves special attention. African rebels and warlords often recruit or force youth and children to serve in their military forces. Children and youth are expected to fight in wars and civil disturbances as full combatants. Children and youth are particularly attractive to adults as armed soldiers because they are easy to recruit, work at low cost, and are very trainable. They are particularly capable of atrocities against others, as they often lack parental direction and complete moral upbringings. These youth commit mass murders, mutilations, arson, theft, rape, and a variety of other serious offenses against their victims. Children and youth are being used as rebel soldiers in a variety of African countries. The problem is so significant that the United Nations held a special session in 2002 on the exploitation of children in war.

The recently completed civil war in Sierra Leone is a good example of the exploitation of children and youth. According to journalist Tom Masland (2002), Sierra Leone's children and youth were forced to commit major crimes against civilian populations. The children and youth who were involved in civil atrocities have all of the characteristics one would associate with for future criminal and street gang behavior. Masland (2002) reported that ex-rebel youth had easy access to firearms, had been trained, used drugs (marijuana), lacked parental authority, and had extremely violent histories. These factors, combined with an implied lack of sense of community, absence of legitimate economic opportunities, poor schooling, and other factors are often associated with street crime and gangs. The prospects for street gang and criminal group formation in Sierra Leone and other similar African countries are great unless significant measures are taken to curb their expansion. Given the current economic and political situations in many African countries, effective gang abatement strategies seem remote.

We have more information about street gangs in other areas of the Southern Hemisphere, such as Australia, New Zealand, and the Pacific Islands of Papua New Guinea, and Guam. Scholars have studied and documented street gangs in these countries, which may be reflective of the presence of gang scholars or an indication of increased street gang prevalence in these countries.

SOUTH AFRICAN STREET GANGS

We know more about street gangs in South Africa than any other African country. This knowledge is partially due to the fact that South Africa has had for decades and continues to have a sizable street gang presence, especially in its metropolitan areas. Street gangs have garnered much attention from South African government agencies, institutes, and universities. The South African media have also paid considerable attention to street gangs and violence (*New Pittsburgh Courier*, 1999). Many recent studies of gangs have been conducted in postapartheid South Africa that help fill a large gap in our understanding of street gangs (Burnett, 1999; Dissel, 1997; Glaser, 1992; Healey, 2000; Houston & Prinsloo, 1998; Mooney, 1998; Pinnock, 1985, 1995; Pinnock & Douglas-Hamilton, 1997, 1998; Scheper-Hughes, 1995).

Researchers have found a wide variety of South African street gangs and self-defense units that act similar to gangs. Cora Burnett (1999) found numerous references to South African gangs that differed in degree of organizational structure, and stratification. She typed the gangs as defense, conflict, reform, criminal, prison, or family Mafia gangs. In addition to street gangs, South Africa also has several self-defense units (SDUs). Some communities formed SDUs to deal with threats to community safety and carry out political resistance. South African SDUs can be likened to vigilante groups because they often take the law into their own hands and attack gangs and gang members. Some SDUs have established community security and death squads. According to Shärf (1997), though they sometimes operated similar to street gangs, they were different. Shärf reported they were less self-serving, had a different accountability to the community, and were decreasing in prevalence compared to street gangs.

History of Street Gangs in South Africa

Street gangs and criminal groups are not a recent phenomenon in South Africa (Kynoch, 1999, 2000). A considerable body of research on street gangs describes the many forms of gangs in South African history. For example, references to notorious criminal gangs known as "freebooters" and highwaymen, such as Scotty Smith, are found in the history of South Africa. We know that street gangs have existed in South Africa since at least the turn of the 20th century (Kynoch, 1999). In the early 20th century, gangs called the Amalaita operated in Durban. Gary Kynoch found a Zulu-based gang called the Ninevites terrorized black city inhabitants in the early 20th century. Clive Glaser (1988, 1992, 1994, 1998a, 1998b, 2000) traced the history of street gangs in the townships to the mid-1930s and through the 1970s. Glaser reported that during World War II, street gangs were present in many of the townships. Members of these street gangs admired fighting skill, success with women, and criminal daring. Gang members mostly were respected for their fighting ability. Glaser (2000) reported the male South African street gangs of the late 1930s and 1950s were known as *tsotsi* or *bo-tsotsi.*

According to Glaser (2000), the tsotsi or bo-tsotsi, were expressions of young urban masculinity. A bo-tsotsi gang member was typically a young black male who dressed, spoke, and acted in a clearly tsotsi manner. Members of bo-tsotsi street gangs were mostly working class, urbanized, and from the same geographical locations. Bo-tsotsi gangs permitted females to become members, but they were allowed to assume only secondary roles to the males. The emphasis on masculinity of these gangs limited the degree and nature of female participation (Glaser, 1998a). Females spent some time with the gangs but were often excluded from the gangs' main activities. Females in the gangs were referred to as "molls" and were used as spies, sex toys, showpieces, and assistants in crime. Gangs provided their molls with protection from sexual assaults from outsiders. They were viewed as property of the gang and were expected to be loyal to their gang boyfriends. Glaser (1992) noted that there were some instances of female auxiliary gangs during the same time span.

Bo-tsotsi gangs were highly territorial and fought to protect turf from rivals. These characteristics continue to be true for contemporary street gangs (Burnett, 1999; Dissel, 1997; Pinnock & Douglas-Hamilton, 1997, 1998). Bo-tsotsi males imitated the "American" style of gangs and indulged in some form of criminal activity, such as pickpocketing, murder, robbery, violence, kidnapping, rape, and other crimes. They rejected middle-class values, such as hard work, but aspired to accumulate wealth. They viewed work as undignified and criminal activities as an acceptable means to wealth. High school education was not generally available to many, further contributing to the rise in these and later other street gangs (Glaser, 2000).

Other historical references to South African gangs exist. Gary Kynoch (2000) traced the history of Russian (*Mara Shea* or *Ama-Rashea*) gangs in the gold mining compounds of South Africa. During the 1930s and 1940s, the gangs were called Russians because of the perception by black South Africans of Russians being strong and fierce people. These gangs were involved in a variety of criminal activities.

During the 1960s, youth street gangs, such as the Black Swines, and in the 1970s, the Hazels, operated in South Africa (Glaser, 1994). Weinberg (1964) found that these South African street gangs fought and battled over turf, but such violence was infrequent compared to similar violence in the United States. Weinberg also reported that cohesive relationships existed in organized youth gangs whose members were required to abide by the gang's rules, and whose predatory orientations and methods were taught to gang members.

During the 1970s, street gang culture aligned with the political resistance and reform movements in the South African schools. Following the political changes of the mid-1970s, street gangs again separated from reform movements and reoriented themselves from political objectives back to crime. However, some gangs did not fully break from their political connections. For instance, some gangs actually cooperated with South African authorities and the police to quell political resistance during the 1980s. The gangs attacked leaders of the political reform movements and school children.

Cultural and Apartheid Factors and South African Street Gangs

Consistent in all of the works on South Africa is the important role apartheid played in the formation and nature of street gangs (Healey, 2000). The scars of apartheid are evidenced today in the extreme poverty, hatred, and ethnic disruption that all promote the formation of street gangs. The white Afrikaner policy of confining people to specific areas outside of the cities under apartheid held back the economic development of underprivileged and further marginalized black youth. The imposed Afrikaner culture essentially destroyed tradition-al black African family structures (Dissel, 1997). For example, the break up of tribal groups and neighborhoods by forced segregation into camps and ghettos broke down the sense of belonging and community of some tribal groups. Don Pinnock wrote of the forced removals of people:

> One of the greatest complaints about Group Area removals was that individual people were moved to the Cape Flats and not whole neighborhoods. The stresses resulting from these changes brought with them psychological difficulties and skewed "coping" behavior. Martial relations were upset; and the divorce, desertion rate rose. Parent-child relations also became problematic. (Pinnock, 1995:30)

Gang members also believed that it was demeaning to do "white man's work," and viewed street gangs as an acceptable alternative (Glaser, 1992). Hawthorne (2000) provided another perspective. Hawthorne found that during apartheid, the government relocated the "colored" in the Cape Flats outside of Capetown. This resulted in a disruption of family life and contributed to the rise of gangsterism because youth formed gangs to protect themselves from other youth. Along these lines, Don Pinnock (1995) insisted that youth street gangs in the Cape Flats were a response to the absence of community cohesion. The forced relocation of people led to declines in neighborhood social control and order. Youth drifted into crime and street gangs in light of this decline of the social order. Before the forced Group Areas Act (relocations), street gangs existed but were less violent and provided some level of social control to their communities (Pinnock & Douglas-Hamilton, 1997). Furthermore, the forced relocation resulted in some youth losing their neighborhood connections with elders who, in their cultural tradition, served as role models. Lacking pro-social role models, some youth turned to gangs for leadership and role models. Street gangs offered these youth the organizational structure they sought. In contrast to Pinnock and Douglas-Hamilton's view, Clive Glaser (2000) contended that the decline in neighborhood cohesion didn't promote gangs but rather gangs were more likely to develop where neighborhood cohesion was high (Glaser, 1998a). Gangs reflected neighborhood loyalty and pride. Glaser believed that what matters more than neighborhood cohesion were youth peer pressure and strong neighborhood ties (identification) in driving youth to joining street gangs.

In the opinion of some, as political freedom grew, street gangs reorganized with greater violence, increasing ruthlessness, and a stronger orientation towards business and economic gain (Hawthorne, 2000). In Johannesburg/Soweto, Glaser (2000) suggested that gang subculture was energized in the context of social deprivation and hampered social mobility. For urban males and out-of-school youth, the gangs provided a sense of security and dignity otherwise unavailable. Gangs provided members with a sense of belonging and opportunities for power, acceptance, purpose, and wealth (Dissel, 1998). Of course, for most members, gang participation did not lead to accumulated wealth (Healey, 2000).

Although circumstances have been changing in recent years in postapartheid South Africa, the country remains one of extreme deprivation for many black South Africans. The sections of communities restricted to black Africans are overcrowded, have poor housing, and are slums. Public amenities are minimal, family incomes low, and unemployment high. The racial and ethnic hatred spawned by apartheid, while on the mend, is nevertheless present in some sectors and will continue to be for years to come. These factors continue to fuel the formation of street gangs.

Cora Burnett (1999) focused the role of poverty in shaping the formation of street gangs and gang violence in South Africa. Burnett concluded that gangs became significant reference groups for impoverished youth that allowed them to obtain material things, such as cars and status symbols, otherwise unattainable through legitimate means. Burnett's study of Davidsonville found that gangs intimidated people, committed burglaries, and sold marijuana (dagga) along with other drugs for money. Burnett concluded that street gangs in Davidsonville were a manifestation of the area's extreme poverty.

Researchers have consistently emphasized the importance of ritual, symbolism, and rites of passage relative to South African street gangs. Street gangs were consistently interpreted as meeting needs of South African tribal youth for passage to adulthood. Pinnock and Douglas-Hamilton underscored the importance of initiation rituals to street gangs in the suburbs of Cape Town when they wrote:

> . . . young gang members have to 'break a bottle neck' be the person to light a broken bottle-neck filled with a mixture of dagga and mandrax. Among older

members, the inner circle of the gang may be gained by hunting and killing an enemy gangster. (Pinnock & Douglas-Hamilton, 1998:311)

When tribal initiation rites used to mark the transition of males to adulthood were eliminated, the street gangs filled the void by developing their own initiation rites. In a similar vein, Don Pinnock (1995:33) wrote, "Poverty, unemployment and urbanward migration swelled the ranks of the young. For many, joining gangs became a way to make friends, a sekiree of income and a means of survival in the wasteland." He added, "With the backing of the web in state coercion, the only defense the youths had was to build something coherent out of the one thing they had left–each other."

Don Pinnock and Dudu Douglas-Hamilton (1997) summarized what they believed to be the causes of gangsterism in South Africa. First, they linked the rise of street gangs to apartheid and the supplementation of existing cultural practices with those of the street gangs. In brief, gangs filled the cultural void created by the forced migration and met the needs of youth for role models, leadership, organization, and group values.

A second reason, Pinnock and Douglas-Hamilton suggested, was the social causes of gang promotion, such as blocked opportunities, the mass media, need for protection, and peer pressure. Third, they suggested that gender relations encouraged males to control and dominate women and play a role. The gangs provided an avenue for males to express their masculinity. According to Kynoch (1999), aggressive masculinity was an important feature of South African street gangs. Masculine identity was expressed through violent behavior, often directed toward females. Finally, Pinnock and Douglas-Hamilton contended that personal causes, such as the desire by some youth to get back at an unjust society, were important. Youth, they suggested, rebelled against a society that abused and treated them poorly. This was a pattern similar to what occurs among marginalized youth and gang youth in the United States and other countries.

Cultural Factors Affecting Street Gangs in South Africa

A long history of American cultural and gang influences flavor South African street gangs (Glaser, 1992; Houston & Prinsloo, 1998). Glaser (1992:49) noted, "As far as clothes were concerned, the most admired men were those who would imitate American gangster style, as portrayed in American movies, most effectively." The American zoot suit style was popular among South African street gangs in the 1940s. Today, American style baggy pants, sporting clothes made by Nike, leather jackets, baseball caps, and other clothing suggestive of gang membership are popular among South African youth. American media has been a powerful force shaping South African gang styles. Healey (2000) observed that young people viewed gangsterism with an "idealized lens." South African street gang members have idealistic and romantic notions about street gangs and their corresponding lifestyles.

Similar to American street gangs, South African gangs developed their own argot, which helped distinguish members from nonmembers and reinforced their sense of gang membership. Gang members used tattoos to symbolize their gang affiliation. Secret symbols were incorporated into some tattoos representing gang membership. Hand signals, known only to gang members were also used for communication. Gangs also marked territory with graffiti and occasionally used flags to symbolize membership.

Examples of South African Street Gangs

Research has found that contemporary South African street gangs have been involved in the same crimes as their bo-tsotsi predecessors. Contemporary South African street gangs are involved in car thefts, car-jackings, murders, burglaries, robberies, and other crimes (Dissel, 1997). Street gangs also fought rival gangs over control of territory. Glaser (2000:8) concluded, "Youth gang wars in Johannesburg were fought essentially over territory." Increasingly, these street gangs used guns when committing crimes and fighting over territory. Among gang members, drug sales and use were common (Burnett, 1999). South Africa is known to have a burgeoning drug trade with the increasing importation of crack cocaine. However, the drug of choice among gang members may be Mandrax, once a popularly prescribed barbiturate. Drug dealers crush the Mandrax and combine it with marijuana for smoking. Similar to most street gangs throughout the world, gang members spent considerable time just hanging out (Pinnock & Douglas-Hamilton, 1998). However, some researchers observed that some street gangs were beyond simply hanging out. They note that South African street gangs were sometimes linked to sophisticated crime networks (Kynoch, 1999).

Street gang members viewed individual performance in gang battles as important for status with the gang. Those judged the most fearless and brave built reputations and had higher status within the street gangs. Pinnock and Douglas-Hamilton (1998) reported that as an initiation for some street gangs, new members were asked to murder a gang target and hence proved their loyalty and desire to belong to the gang.

Ledochowski (1991) provided another description of youth gangs in the townships of South Africa. Noting the collapse of community support and control structures and the cultural traditions that supported them, he contends that township youth bound together in gangs to form identities and to earn livings. The gangs, referred to as *skollie* (ruffian) gangs, were organized along military lines with hierarchical structures. Youth were often pressured into joining the gangs for protection. Gang members had tattoos that signified membership in the gang. Public reaction to gang tattoos limited members' ability to gain employment in legitimate jobs, even when they decided to leave the gang. The gangs were involved in illegal drug and liquor sales. A primary purpose for the gangs was predatory (property) crime that provided members with an income. Ledochowski believed American media images of gangs and gang styles and the years of oppression living under an apartheid system largely influenced the gang members. Insofar as we have evidence on these gangs, there appears to be some marked similarities between them and American street gangs.

Cora Burnett (1999) spent three and one half years studying adolescent street gangs in Davidsonville. Burnett's study of gang violence in Davidsonville reported on impoverished male adolescents who joined street gangs for social and economic reasons. The central role violence played in shaping the street gang's structure and activities flavors Burnett's analysis of gangs. She found that the street gangs formed temporarily and typically during holidays. Most gang members were school-aged boys. The gangs actively recruited boys who were known to fight well. Besides fighting well, the recruits had to live within the gang's territory. Street gang membership began during adolescence and expanded to include postadolescent members, maybe for the same reasons as in the United States, where economic depravation and opportunities for some are blocked (Burnett, 1999). Gang members were relatively free to leave the gang when they wanted.

Burnett (1999) found street gang sizes ranged from 15 to 30 members. The gangs had norms and were territorial. They marked their territories with gang graffiti or symbols. They selected gang names that underscored themes of power, violence, and territory. The gangs' abilities to control and protect their territories were affected by their access to weapons. The more access to weapons, the more powerful the gang became. Violent territorial disputes with rival gangs were common. Street gang affiliation offered members security but also increased the risk of rival gang retaliation. Violence was seen as a means to get back at rival gangs. The gangs used violence as a means to establish and maintain authority in the community (Burnett, 1999). Violence was also used to defend territory and obtain material things. Street gang crime was mostly for economic gain. Street gang crimes included thefts, robberies, intergang conflicts, assaults, homicides, and mutilations. Street gangs used mutilations to communicate their power to others in the community. Burnett observed that street gangs had formal leaders who played central roles in the operations, but much of the activities and were conducted by small subgroups that may not be sanctioned by the larger gang.

Pinnock and Douglas-Hamilton (1997) viewed South African society as a highly militant and violent. In their opinion, South Africa afforded a way of living that encouraged the use of force and brutality to resolve issues rather than negotiation. They characterized street gangs in the western cape of South Africa to be a way of life for some youth. They concluded that gang members lived day-to-day. Members of street gangs often displayed an attitude of fearlessness and they did not show any emotions. Gang members viewed the display of emotions as representing vulnerability.

Street gang members obtained most of their income from selling drugs and alcohol, burglary, and theft. Extortion of small shops for protection was also a means of making money. The gangs terrorized shop owners and attempted to control territories for the criminal business purposes of extortion and drug sales. The gangs had unwritten codes of behavior, styles of clothing, and tattoos for members. The codes of the gangs permitted drug use among gang members, which was common. When a youth joined a gang, he or she received a "chappie" or tattoo identifying him as a member of the gang. Women could join but lacked power and played limited supportive roles.

Pinnock and Douglas-Hamilton (1997) suggested there were seven basic types of South African street gangs. First were corner kids who were street-oriented youth aged 10 or younger who were involved in petty offending. Second were defense gangs that formed for the protection of turf and committed property crimes to support themselves. The third was community protection units that were groups of residents who responded to criminal gangs. Usually older, they used violence to ensure community safety from gang offenses. The fourth were reform gangs that were not formed in the streets but in the schools and reformatories. Youth that join reform gangs, as opposed to street gangs, joined for protection and friendship. Youth also joined these gangs because after they completed reform school, their families and communities often rejected them. Reform gangs offered some of these youth the only viable option for support and on-going relationships. According to Pinnock and Douglas-Hamilton (1997), there were also prison gangs, Mafiosi, and syndicates. These three types were not street gangs, but they influenced the character of street gangs. For example, a prison gang named the Mongrels had close working relationships with street gangs on the outside.

Pinnock and Douglas-Hamilton noted that street gangs referred to their elders as "generals." One became a general through his proven abilities. A second level of leadership in the street gangs included the drug lords and *Shebeen* owners. These second-in-command members occasionally met to discuss gang strategy. Teachers were the third level in street gangs. They instructed new members on gang rules. The next level was the "killers," who had the gang's permission to kill and make street-level decisions regarding homicides. Finally, there were the rank and file members of the gang.

Ed O'Loughlin (1995) provided a short journalistic glimpse of Cape Town's street gangs. The gangs were comprised of Cape Town males who viewed themselves as alienated and marginalized from mainstream South African society. Unemployment was very high in the areas where they lived. The areas had few schools, businesses, parks, and other pro-social opportunities. The biggest gang called itself the Young Americans and other street gangs had names like Sexy Boys, Mongrels, Ugly Cats, Music Makers, Nice Kids, Naughty Boys, and Genuine TV Kids. The gangs frequently modeled themselves after American street gangs. The gangs provided protection to residents for doing favors for the gang, such as storing weapons and drugs. Youth were often forced to join gangs for protection. O'Loughlin found that the gangs fought bloody battles over turf to control protection rackets, prostitution, and drug sales. The community response to these street gangs was mixed. The community was mostly against the gangs but equally unfavorable regarding the police. Years of police apathy, brutality, and corruption colored their perceptions of law enforcement.

Wilfred Schärf (1997) provided another view of South African street gangs. He observed that they viewed themselves as the product of unfair political and economic systems. They rationalized that crime victims deserved to be preyed on because they were the "haves" of society. The gangs did not victimize the poor even though it was known in the community that some gangs members victimized the impoverished. Scarf reported that gang members had low levels of educational attainment and were typically aged between 13 and 25 years.

Houston and Prinsloo's (1998) comparison study of street and prison gangs reported that "mouthpieces" or ringleaders were common among street gangs. Members saw gang leaders as evil, sly, and daring. Amanda Dissel (1997) found that adults often served as leaders of these street gangs. Occasionally, the parents of gang youth also were members. Street gangs initiated new members according to rituals, possibly filling a cultural rite of passage to adulthood (Dissel, 1997). Don Pinnock and Dudu Douglas-Hamilton (1997) suggested that some South African youth longed for rituals and gang initiations met this need. Some street gangs required new members to murder specific targets to prove their worthiness to join a gang.

South African Community Responses to Street Gangs

South African media play a major role in defining and perhaps even strengthening street gangs. The media has been flooded with images of gang violence, such as the practice of setting bodies on fire with "necklaces" of gasoline-filled tires hung around the victims' necks. These images leave lasting impressions on the general public and buttress the perception that gangs were powerful and extremely violent. These images also send a message that gangs were powerful influences in their respective areas (Healey, 2000). These media images also led youth to seek the power offered by gangs.

Community responses to street gangs ranged from tolerance and support to violent suppression. Gary Kynoch (1999) noted that historically many communities supported local street gangs. Community tolerance stemmed from the protective and economic roles gangs played. Gang youth viewed themselves as defenders of the community, and the communities sometimes agreed (Dissel, 1997). Community lack of confidence in official law enforcement fueled the desire to have local gangs for protection from outside groups and gangs. Street gangs generally protected their turf at all cost (Houston & Prinsloo, 1998). Often victims of gang violence were youth from other gangs or neighborhoods who attempted crimes in the street gang's neighborhood.

Because the local police were reluctant or ineffective in controlling street gangs, numerous community groups formed defense associations to confront the gangs. In some communities, Moslem and other religious groups formed versions of street gangs or militias to gain back control of their neighborhoods from violent drug dealing gangs. These militia groups were known to murder street gang members. One group, known as People Against Gangsterism and Drugs (PAGAD), has conducted an urban war against drug lords, crime syndicates, and street gangs (Hawthorne, 2000; Pinnock & Douglas-Hamilton, 1997). PAGAD has also had conflicts with the police. The PAGAD groups have undoubtedly contributed to the amount of violence in South Africa (Kynoch, 1999). Some of these defense groups participated in the very same crimes they were formed to prevent. The self-defense groups began to take on the characteristics of criminally oriented street gangs and it is now difficult to distinguish between the two.

Other less organized community responses to gangs, such as calling the police, were seen as temporary solutions to the problem. South African authorities have implemented a program labeled MADAM, which stands for the Multi-Agency Delivery Action Mechanism. MADAM provided support to communities with gang problems. In addition, pressure from PAGDAD and similar groups led to the formation of an organization known as CORE (Community Outreach Forum), which was comprised of gang leaders who have declared they want to get out of gangs (Schärf, 1997). In addition, South Africa has been a leader in the restorative justice movement. The National Unity and Reconciliation Act provided a restorative justice approach to crime and gangs, such as family conferencing (Schärf, 1997).

South African law enforcement agencies developed special gang units specifically designed to address street gang violence. Law enforcement agencies also have established SWAT teams to respond to gangs. Some of the law enforcement efforts have been hampered because the police living in the same neighborhoods were sometimes reluctant to confront the gangs because of fear of retaliation. Even with local resistance and the lack of cooperation, numerous gang members have been incarcerated. For example, in 1994, 16,000 South African youth under the age of 20 were incarcerated mostly as a result of gang activities (Kanji, 1996). In addition to locking up offendes, there have been legislative attempts to curb and suppress gang activities through statutes similar to the RICO (Racketeering Influenced Corrupt Organizations) laws in the United States (Agence France Presse, 1998).

This is not to suggest that alternatives to gang suppression haven't been tried. The South African police have had some success in establishing truces among rival gangs (Pinnock & Douglas-Hamilton, 1997). South Africans also have established "boys' club" programs that serve as alternatives to street gangs. However, these efforts have proven to be ineffective in curbing street gang involvement (Glaser, 1992). Others, such as Pinnock and Douglas-Hamilton (1997) and Dissel (1997) promote a restorative justice model to respond to gang and individual crime in South Africa. South Africa's National Institute for Crime Prevention and Rehabilitation of Offenders (NICPRO) has been working on establishing restorative justice programs focused on reintegrating offenders back into their communities rather than returning to their gangs.

NIGERIAN STREET GANGS

Nigerian organized criminal activities are well recognized by international criminologists. Nigerian organized criminal groups have established themselves as major players in worldwide distribution of cocaine, heroin, and marijuana. Since the 1970s, Nigerian gangs have been involved in organized crime activities (Grennan et al., 2000). Nigerian criminal groups' ages range from 24 to 35 years but have been as young as 14 years old. Most gang members are male. Nigerian gangs have been involved in a variety of fraudulent activities, such as credit card, bank, student tuition, insurance, and welfare frauds. Nigerian criminal groups are noted for their ability to cooperate with each other and avoid rival-group violence. For example, different criminal groups share information regarding law enforcement efforts and help protect each other's interests. The degree of organization of these Nigerian groups suggests that they are not street gangs per se, but organized crime groups with loose structures. Members of these groups are free to branch off into criminal activities without the blessing of the "barons" or leadership of the organization. Little is known about Nigerian street gangs, which have very little contact with organized crime organizations except to occasionally sell drugs (Grennan et al., 2000).

Some information is available on the groups of Nigerian males who raid entire neighborhoods in the evenings. According to journalist Pitman (2001), armed groups or gangs sent notices to sections of Nigerian communities warning them that they planned to rob them in the future and that they should be prepared. These groups, which may be street gangs, wanted victims to be home when the robberies occurred and be prepared with their money. The gangs beat or shot to death those victims unable or unwilling to pay. Victims prepared envelopes with money to avoid such assaults. Small groups were known to tear down walls to get at victims locked in their homes. Law enforcement in the capital Lagos has been ineffective in halting these assaults and robberies. Meanwhile, these groups continued to ransack neighborhoods with little to no resistance. In the evenings when it was dark, it was particularly dangerous as gangs of armed men patrolled the streets looking for victims. These groups even attacked police stations. Little else has been reported about these groups; which if they were street gangs, were organized around serious criminal activities.

Agence France Presse (2000) reported on street gangs, known as "Area Boys" to locals, in the capital city of Lagos. According to this media account, groups of Area Boys recently warned shop owners of an impending mass gang assault by Yoruba youth on the area. Many shops and businesses closed in anticipation of the assault by the youth. Gangs of Area Boys targeted Hausa owned shops and businesses during the raid. Many Hausa businesses were looted before the Lagos police arrived. The Hausa, the other major ethnic group in Nigeria, also had street gangs that fought rival Yoruba street gangs and assaulted Yoruba residents and businesses (Agence France Presse, 2002).

Cultural and ethnic tribal differences formed the basis for these criminal groups and gangs in Nigeria.

KENYAN STREET GANGS

Kenya, similar to other African countries, has been experiencing ethnic violence between competing groups. Coastal ethnic groups have formed well-organized gangs that attack business and communities of inland ethnic groups (McKinley, 1997). These gangs were divided along ethnic and political lines and were more likely politically motivated criminal groups than true street gangs. In countries similar to Kenya, it is difficult to separate street gangs from civil war or law-violating groups.

In Kenya and other African countries reports of large gangs attacking sections of cities or whole communities are common. For example, an African News Services Report (2002a) told of a large gang of 200 attacking a section of Nairobi and leaving 20 dead. Victims had their throats slit and bodies mutilated. During the attack, it was evident that it was highly planned, well organized, and occurred at a time that residents were returning home from work. Following the attack, the press reported the "gang" members dissolved back into the community. It is difficult to determine if this event was gang related, as indicated in the press, or a mob acting in a criminal manner. Violence on this scale suggests ethnic and political violence on an organized and grand scale more than street gang phenomena.

Aylward Shorter and Edwin Onyancha (1999) conducted a case study of street children in Nairobi (Xinhua). They discovered that some of Nairobi's street children resorted to street gangs for survival. Shorter and Onyancha (1999) described one street gang that had a well-defined leader and about 20 male members. The average age of members was estimated to be 14 years. The gang was involved in pickpocketing, which members called *kusanya* (Swahili "to collect") and drug use. Drugs were readily available to gang members with glue sniffing being inexpensive and very popular. The gang also used marijuana (*bhang*) as a drug.

This street gang and others offered members security against the violent and hostile streets of Nairobi. The gangs provided backup support for members and helped obtain food and other basic necessities. The gangs gave youth a sense of identity and belonging, the latter being absent for many youth with the dissolution of their families. Shorter and Onyancha believed that Nairobi's gangs were surrogate families for children. In the gang, members were taught to share gains with other gang members to help them all survive. Gang members generally took care of each other's needs. Shorter and Onyancha noted that it was exceptional for a child not to belong to a gang.

Shorter and Onyancha (1999) reported that gang members participated at different levels in the gangs. Members who participated in gangs on a limited (part-time) basis were less involved in criminal activities than those who functioned as full-time members. Major differences existed between children who lived at home and those who lived on the streets. Home dwellers were typically part-time gang members and those who lived on the streets were full-time gang members. The more the youth were involved with gangs, the more they were criminally inclined.

Street gangs drew members from their neighborhoods. Youth from other areas moving into new neighborhoods had a more difficult time joining local gangs. Youth joining the gangs were required to go through rituals that included teasing, meeting the leader, and tests of endurance to determine their worthiness of membership and appropriate rank in the gang's hierarchy. Gang members provoked new members into fights, asked them to run errands for members, etc., all directed at testing the character of the new member. Females were allowed to join the gangs but were generally sexually abused by the gang when they joined. Female gang members often associated with one male and were fiercely protected by that male from others.

Nairobi's street gangs had well-defined levels of hierarchy. The levels included the high command (gang leaders), junior officers, and lower ranks. Gang leaders controlled the finances of the gang, which mostly was used to buy food. One's rank in the gang was determined by how much pain the member could take. Gang members took pride in scars and injuries resulting from conflicts with mobs or rival gangs.

Nairobi's street gangs were highly territorial and the gangs defended their respective territories. Gang leaders sometimes negotiated agreements with rival gang leaders to control the level of violence. The gangs had codes of honor that supported certain values, such as sharing of food, shelter, and wealth with other gang members. Some gangs even set-up funds for medical expenses for gang members and their families, should there be a need for medical care.

Shorter and Onyancha (1999) observed that the street gangs of Nairobi presented some of the most humane values in Kenya, as gang members worked cooperatively to help each other and share what little they had as surrogate families for desperate youth. In Nairobi, street children built crude shelters called *chuom* that served as bases for operations. The *chuom* were makeshift shelters where the youth lived, sought protection, and otherwise survived. During the day, those sharing a chuom turned to the streets to make a living. *Chuom* members scavenged, washed dishes, begged, and worked in a variety of odd jobs during the day. They might also be involved in illegal activities, such as drug sales (*bhang*). All of the members' earnings were shared with others in the *chuom*. Female members also might rely on prostitution to make money. Within the *chuoms*, males played the role of husbands and the females wives. Gang members played specific roles and some served as leaders. Regarding youth in Kenya, the Urban Management Programme concluded:

> Street children as any social entity have a distinct culture with a structure that defines roles and responsibilities of each member. Street children depend less on their families or other people who they consider strangers and cannot share their experiences. Instead, they rely more on the meaningful ties they have established within their groups or gangs. (Urban Management Programme, 2000:3)

The street gangs provided children with the families they lacked and served important functions for youth. They took care of youth who would otherwise be defenseless and alone. Youth lacking emotional and physical support from their biological families turned to the *chuom* to meet these needs.

Gangs operating out of *chuom* had designated territories that they defended against rivals. Given some of the economic needs of gangs, it was financially important for them to control their territories. For instance, gangs protected the areas they depended on for scavenging from rival gangs (Urban Management Programme, 2000). Certain strategic areas, such as in the business center of Nairobi, were important for gangs to control for illegal purposes. Those gangs involved in theft, pickpocketing, prostitution, and other crimes fought to control areas of the city where success was assured. Competition among gangs for territory increased their cohesiveness.

The Kenyan community response to the street gangs has been insignificant to date. Kenyan efforts to work with street gangs have been limited. Shorter and Onyancha (1999) reported that some agencies helped gangs be surrogate families, obtain health care, and provided training. The government has made additional efforts to help the gangs develop recycling centers to make money and provide educational training.

The Urban Management Programme of UNICEF, operating in Nairobi, made several recommendations on how authorities should handle street children and gangs. It recommended that these youth be redirected into pro-social activities through programs such as Big Brothers and Big Sisters. It also recommended members of street gangs and *chuoms* be involved in identifying and solving problems. If given the opportunity to conform with society, the Urban Management Programme optimistically held that these youth would easily conform to socially approved patterns of behavior. Finally, Kenyan police recently cracked down on street gangs in Nairobi. According to one press account, public muggings and robberies of pedestrians and motorists had become so prevalent that the police had arrested masses of people involved in such gangs (World Sources, 2002).

STREET GANGS IN OTHER AFRICAN COUNTRIES

Journalists have reported the presence of "street gangs" in other African nations, such as Liberia (Fecci, 1997; Hill, 1996) and the Middle East. Liberia, torn by a bloody civil war, has evolved into a free-for-all for bands of well-armed youth. These groups may represent law-violating youth or possibly street gangs. The groups were not politically motivated and functioned for the sole purpose of committing crimes. The groups violently controlled their respective territories. Media accounts of cannibalism, dissection, mutilation, and other atrocities committed on Liberians by well-armed groups of youth are abundant. Hill (1996) provided antidotal evidence of preteen and teenage groups killing people for their possessions and the thrill of having them beg for mercy. These armed groups, often operated under the general direction of warlords, terrorized and extorted local populations. They generally lacked local support, as they victimized citizens within their territories.

Over 30 years ago, J.S. La Fontaine (1970) concluded that in Kinshasa, Zaire, youth gangs were present and were very territorial. Regarding the gangs, La Fontaine (1970:204) noted, "The concept of territory includes the sole right to recruit members within it, sexual access to young girls living within it, and the right to use the area to satisfy requirements for money, food and drugs." He then added, "A large part of the gang's time is spent in fighting other gangs for exclusive control of a territory or in endeavoring to encroach on the territories of other gangs, particularly by kidnapping or seducing the girls "belonging" to other gangs."

Other reports of African street gangs are present. Street gangs have been reported in Kampala Uganda (African News Service, 2002b). The African News Service reported that Kampala's street gangs were better organized, armed, and trained in marital arts than in the past. These gangs used cell phones to communicate gang-related information. Robbery appeared to be the crime of choice for these gangs. The gangs were spread throughout Kampala and its suburbs. The gangs consisted of former street kids, some of whom held down regular jobs during the day and joined their gangs at night. The names of some of the gangs included the Hit Bombers and VJ. The gangs targeted women and smaller or medium-sized men because they viewed them as easier targets. The gangs hung around fitness gyms during the day. They used the fitness gyms for body building and to develop fighting skills. Victims of the gangs were often unwilling to cooperate with authorities out of fear of gang reprisal.

In Ethiopia, a country where violence and civil strife are common, some of its crime has been linked to street gangs. According to Veale and Adefrisew (1993), violence was present mostly among children who lived in street gangs. Specifically, when members of a gang were insulted or attacked, the gang responded by counterattacking the other gang or individual. Although Ethiopian street gangs were present and violent, Veale and Adefrisew (1992) did not view them as a serious problem.

STREET GANGS IN THE MIDDLE EAST

The presence of street gangs in the Middle East is difficult to ascertain given the political turmoil characteristic of the region. Differentiating street gangs from law violating youth groups, organized crime, politically motivated groups, or organizations is difficult. The political unrest characteristic of the region blurs distinctions between street gangs and informal political action groups. In addition, very little research has been conducted in these countries regarding street gangs. Given the relative rarity of street gangs and a perception that gangs don't exist within many of these countries, it should come as no surprise we know little about what actually might be occurring.

Palestinian Street Gangs

Scholars have identified Palestinian street gangs on the West Bank. Grennan et al. (2000) characterized these gangs as being similar to American street gangs. Members ranged from age 12 to 30 years, with the older members serving as gang leaders. The gangs were armed and posed a threat to Israeli and Palestinian residents. However, unlike American street gangs, the Palestinian gangs had strong political agendas aligned with the Palestinian desire for independence from Israel. Criminal activities of these gangs included robberies, political kidnappings, extortion, homicides, and drug dealing.

One media report provided a glimpse of how some of the gangs operated. Deutsche Presse Agentur (1995) described clashes between Palestinian police and a street gang known as the Fatah Hawks. The Fatah Hawks were established by the Palestinian Liberation Organization (PLO) to combat drug traffickers in the area. However, some of the Fatah Hawks turned to criminal activities, such as extortion and homicide.

Israeli Street Gangs

Given the on-going political turmoil in Israel, it is difficult to unravel what is occurring regarding street gangs. Much of the observed group street crime behavior is clearly not representative of street gangs. Yet, there is some evidence that small street gangs exist in

Israel. Certainly, these gangs are not as prevalent as they are in other countries.

Moshe Sherer (1990) studied 43 Jewish and 57 Arabic members of street gangs, and compared them to teenage junior and high school students living in Israel. Regardless of ethnicity, street gang members were more involved in criminal activities than junior and high school students. Sherer noted that typical street corner gangs, whether Jewish or Arabic, were not prone toward violence. Members were often between the ages of 12 and 18 years old, had dropped out of school, and were unemployed.

Arabic gang members were the most involved in crime. Popular crimes for the gang youth were motor vehicle theft, assault, drug abuse, vandalism, and disorderly conduct. Sherer, consistent with gang research throughout the world, found that gang members offended at higher rates than their nongang junior and high school counterparts. Nongang school children were, however, more likely to be involved in political protests. Sherer proposed that police discrimination against Arabic youth, community reporting practices, and the tension between Arabic and Jewish peoples accounted for some but not all of the higher crime rates for Arabic gang youth. He offered other explanations, such as normlessness, the lack of opportunity, and Israeli police enforcement practices.

Eugene Tarakovsky and Julia Mirsky (2001) provided a description of what they labeled bullying gangs in Israel. These gangs were comprised of adolescents who had recently immigrated to Israel from the former Soviet Union. They found the bullying gangs operated in some of the special high schools established to handle immigrant youth. The bully gangs picked on and assaulted other immigrant youth. They attributed the formation of bullying gangs to the immaturity of the immigrant adolescents, their migration to a foreign host culture, and models of violent behavior imported from their home culture. According to Tarakowsky and Mirsky (2001), the migration of these youth resulted in the loss of habitat, family, friends, and familiar environments. The adjustment from Soviet to Israeli culture was a difficult one for these youth. In addition, the absence of parental figures in the lives of the youth contributed to insecurity, anxiety, and formation of bullying gangs.

The bully gangs were mostly comprised of males, but a few females were allowed to participate. Male gang members viewed these females as only associates and the property of the gang. Gang members used alcohol and drugs for amusement. The gangs terrorized, extorted, stole from, and assaulted weaker immigrant youth in the special schools. The gangs had hierarchical structures and well-defined sets of gang rules.

Moshe Hazani (1989) described another form of Israeli youth group that in many other countries would be considered a street gang. In Israel, some youth were involved with *charakas*. In Hebrew slang, a *charaka* was when youth stole and drove automobiles recklessly through the streets for excitement. The *charaka* in many respects is similar to the *bosozoku* of Japan, where Japanese youth drive in groups at high speeds through their communities. A key difference is that in Israel, the cars were stolen, whereas in Japan, they were not.

Similar to *bosozoku*, the *charaka* were highly structured groups and events. Young males crammed into cars and took turns driving. Part of the objective of a *charaka* was to taunt the police and not be apprehended. The groups had norms and a code of honor, such as member loyalty to the group, not cooperating with the police, "manly honor," and other norms similar to street gangs. Members also adhered to the larger social values of hard work, family, and taking responsibility of one's life. Members were adolescent males, mostly under age 20, from the same neighborhoods, had working-class backgrounds, had jobs, and had dropped out of school.

The groups, similar to some street gangs, had a core group headed by a leader and usually about five associates. Under the associates were younger members who were typically boys under age 15. The groups were involved with motor vehicle theft, hashish smoking, theft, vandalism, but little street violence. Community reaction to *charaka*s was dependent on the generation of the respondent. Older Israelis disapproved of the practice, middle-aged were passive observers, and the young were supportive.

Whether the groups involved with *charaka*s were true street gangs cannot be determined from Hazani's (1989) study. The groups do seem to be youth street gangs because of their involvement in crime, persistence over time, rudimentary organizational structures, and other characteristics. The one aspect of these groups was that communities did not identify them as street gangs. Perhaps this final piece of the gang puzzle is the next evolutionary step of these groups.

OTHER STREET GANGS IN AFRICA AND THE MIDDLE EAST

Grennan et al. (2000) reported on the presence of a youth street gang operating in the United Arab Emirates. The gang's membership ranged from 15 to 18 years of age. This specific gang was known to have committed a homicide. Little else was reported on the activities of this specific gang. Other gangs have reportedly been involved in drug sales to Europe, suggesting links between these street gangs and organized crime. The extent of street gangs is unknown but is likely very low in other Middle Eastern countries. Interestingly, in Iraq, there have been reports of street gangs that were involved in auto thefts and burglaries (Cockburn, 1995).

STREET GANGS IN THE PACIFIC AND SOUTHERN HEMISPHERE

Street gangs are known to Australia and other islands of the South Pacific. A considerable body of research has focused on street gangs in Australia, New Zealand, and Papua, New Guinea. However, there is still much that needs to be studied in these and other Southern Hemisphere countries. In many Polynesian and Pacific Island cultures, family, kinship, community cohesion, folk wisdom, and religious ritual have shaped the contexts in which gangs have formed in many of these island societies. Hence, the study of street gangs in these regions takes on a special character.

AUSTRALIAN STREET GANGS

Bodgies and *Widgies* are terms used to identify some youth street gangs in Australia (Bessant & Watts, 1992; Fyvel, 1961; Short & Strodtbeck, 1974). Bodgies and Widgies borrowed their styles mostly from American film, clothing, and popular music. Although street gangs exist in Australia, they do not appear to be as prevalent as in other industrialized countries of the world. According to some researchers, highly structured youth gangs were not common in Australia (Daniels, 1977). Daniels (1977) noted that much of the juvenile delinquency in Australia was not gang-based, but was group delinquency. Klein (1995a) cited data provided by Kenneth Polk of the University of Melbourne who also suggested that the problem in Australia was one of loosely structured groups with little or no organization or permanence of membership. These groups used public transportation, congregated in and moved through public spaces, and sought low-cost or no-cost entertainment. They were typically lower- or working-class males, who sometimes engaged in fist and knife fights. Others viewed the gangs as a prominent feature of Australian society, especially during the 1950s (Bessant & Watts, 1992).

Researchers have reported on Australian street gangs of the late 1940s and 1950s. Bessant and Watts (1992) studied street and school gangs from 1946 to 1956. They described gangs that were violent when faced with challenges to their territory or honor. Bessant and Watts noted that these gangs were very territorial and viewed their role as protecting turf. Gangs were named after territories or locales. The gangs were involved mostly in assaults and vandalism. Gang members were drawn from youth aged 12 to 18 years and were organized along ethnic lines. The gangs had distinctive styles of dress that included jeans, tartan shirts, t-shirts, zoot suits, and "Tony Curtis" hairstyles. Gang members ascribed to the values of toughness, honor, and masculinity. Italian and Greek immigrants were viewed as challenges to the gangs and were targets of gang violence.

Similar to other studies, Bessant and Watts concluded that the community responded to media attention paid to these gangs with a moral panic. According to Bessant (1994), Australian media overreacted to an unwarranted fear of gangs in the early 1990s. Compared to their real threat to Australian society, Australians overreacted to the problem. This overreaction took many forms, such as strict curfews for youth and a perception that many youth were unemployed and hence involved in crime.

Besides public concerns regarding aboriginal youth and gangs, Australians have also focused on immigrant and refugee youth and gangs. For example, in Brisbane, police reported that street gangs based on ethnic backgrounds such as Pacific Islander, Vietnamese, white Australian, and aboriginal homeless youth have formed (Haberfield, 2000). Vietnamese street gangs and organized crime organizations have recently been a source of concern for Australian officials.

In Australia, ethnic Vietnamese gangs were involved in crimes such as gambling, drug sales, extortion, robbery, home invasions, and assorted other crimes. The more organized groups were actively involved in the importation and distribution of heroin. The gangs tended to victimize people and businesses within the immigrant Vietnamese community. The gangs were loosely organized and operated at a local rather than national level for the most part. They were highly mobile and reportedly very violent. Violence was used as a means to an end (usually profit) rather than an end in itself.

In Sydney, Vietnamese gang members sported gang tattoos and were very active in heroin sales. The notorious and most widely known Vietnamese gang was the 5T gang. The 5T gang was founded in the mid 1990s. The 108 gang was another Vietnamese gang that operated in Sydney. Comprised of mostly teenagers and young adults, the gang had about 200 members. Similar to other Vietnamese gangs in Australia, the 5T gang preferred to victimize members of the Vietnamese community.

The Parliamentary Joint Committee on the National Crime Authority (1995) noted that it was unclear if these groups represented organized crime or local juvenile delinquency problems. Currently they are considered to be local juvenile delinquency problems that had the potential to become national organized crime organizations. Clearly the Joint Committee believed their criminal activities were increasing, including their involvement in the distribution of heroin in Australia.

Another immigrant population receiving attention has been immigrants from Hong Kong, fleeing from Chinese rule in 1997. Australian officials have been concerned that the triads of Hong Kong have migrated to Queensland. Although there has been tremendous immigration of people from several Asian countries, including Hong Kong, there is little evidence that Hong Kong's triads have moved to Australia (Goldworthy, 1998). This is not to say that there is no triad involvement in Australian crime, especially the heroin trade, but not to the extent anticipated by authorities.

Poynting et al. (1999) interviewed a small sample of Arabic-speaking immigrant youth aged 16 to 19 years. They concluded that much of the Australian media's concern about immigrant youth was unwarranted. They suggested that public outrage over ethnic gangs represented a moral panic rather than actual gang behavior or activity.

They observed that the stereotyping of ethnic gangs by the media further escalated racism in Australia.

Bessant (1994) contended Australia was not following the same patterns as the United States in developing a juvenile offender underclass. The Australian experience, Bessant contends, was quite different. Different because Australians had a long-history of associating criminality with aboriginal populations, it followed that many Anglo heritage Australians viewed aboriginal peoples as prone to join street gangs. Thus, street gangs were strongly associated with aboriginal and recent immigrant youth rather than youth with Anglo or European backgrounds.

David Moore (1994) studied skinheads in Australia. He found the Australian skinheads were typically unemployed, aged between 17 to 21 years with some being as young as 14 years. He reported that they came from Irish or English backgrounds. Drinking was a big part of their activities. They did not organize themselves into traditional gang structures. Moore concluded that the skinheads did not operate as gangs per se but represented quasi-groups or action sets. Moore focused on the modes of violence among the skinheads and found recurring themes. First, skinhead violence represented an opportunity for skinheads to demonstrate their loyalty to the skinhead movement as a whole and to close drinking friends. Violence also represented a prospect to establish or reaffirm reputations as skinheads and style. Skinhead violence reaffirmed the collective solidarity of the group (Moore, 1994).

STREET GANGS IN NEW ZEALAND AND OTHER PACIFIC ISLANDS

Street gangs were known to New Zealand and other islands of the South Pacific. A considerable body of research has focused on street gangs in New Zealand and Papua, New Guinea. Historically, crime and delinquency in New Zealand has been popularly perceived as a Maori and Polynesian problem. Maori and Polynesian groups have not fit and integrated well with European settler cultures. They are disproportionately represented in New Zealand's criminal justice system. Among many European heritage settlers, there is a social equation between being Maori or Polynesian and being criminal or violent. New Zealand's crime statistics do not support this perception.

Neil Cameron (1983), over 20 years ago, noted that Maori gangs had been defined as a crime problem, which began in the mid-1960s with the bikie (motorcycle) gangs. By the early 1980s, the gangs expanded. Cameron viewed Maori gangs as cohesive groups that challenged traditional and European cultural values and customs. Although occasionally involved in serious offenses, they had always been marginally involved with crime. Nevertheless, the media milked Maori gang crime for all its worth, further feeding negative stereotypes about Maori males as being prone to violence and crime.

New Zealand definitely has street gangs. Pahmi Winter (1998) provided a description of some of them. Winter discovered that skinhead, bikie, white power, ethnic (such as the Mongrel Mob), and Asian triad gangs operated in New Zealand. The primary purpose of these gangs was to provide members with a sense of belonging. However, some gangs focused on criminal and antisocial activities. For example, one gang's slogan was "rape, pillage, and plunder" (Winter 1998:259). Criminal activities by gang members were individualized and not dictated by other gang members. Members of these gangs were youth who remained in the gangs until their early 20s. Most of the gang members were Maori, but other cultural and ethnic groups also joined these gangs.

Pahmi Winter (1998) linked the rise of gangs in New Zealand to the structural and economic upheavals of New Zealand following World War II. Following the war, families in New Zealand disintegrated, and a moral panic ensued. Migration of populations to New Zealand's cities seeking employment was viewed as contributing to the rise of gangs. The gangs described by Winter were most likely syndicated crime organizations and not true street gangs.

New Zealand's community response to these groups included a heavy emphasis on crime prevention. Authorities implemented a work-trust movement to provide youth with gainful employment. Both of the dominant criminal groups, the Black Power and Mongrel Mob, sought collaboration with the government. For example, both groups suggested that criminal activity could be limited with cooperation and concessions from authorities. In Winter's opinion, these groups developed considerable skill in manipulating New Zealand's authorities. However, the general public viewed gang members as essentially evil.

Another study of participation in New Zealand gangs was conducted by Erin Eggleston (1997). Eggleston focused on the nature of female participation in gangs. Eggleston interviewed 43 male inmates and conducted a participant observation study of street gangs. The gangs studied by Eggleston were predominantly Maori. Eggleston found that females participate in gangs in Auckland. Eggleston's study reported that male members mistreated female gang members. The males gang raped, beat, and called females "bitches," "hos," or "rootbags." This poor treatment of female gang members is consistent with some but not all of the gang research in the United States. Male gang members made the rules for female participation in the gang. One rule was that if a female was a girlfriend of a gang member, she was automatically considered a gang member. Some gangs developed initiation rituals, such as being beaten by walking down a line. Besides the negative approaches to females, males viewed their role as provider to females but never allowed female members to transcend gang space in public. Males saw female gang members as "small timers" and not key players. The role of females in mixed gender gangs was almost a total lack of respect, degradation, and treatment of them as sex objects.

Street Gangs in Papua New Guinea

A surprising number of recent studies have been conducted on gangs in Papua New Guinea and specifically Port Moresby (Anonymous, 1995b; Dinnen, 1995, 1997; 1998; Goddard, 1992, 1995; B. Harris, 1988; Kulick, 1993; Nibbrig & Nibbrig, 1992) and East Sepik Province (Roscoe, 1999a, 1999b). This research focused on what are called raskols and raskol (rascal) gangs.

To understand street gangs in New Guinea, the notion of the rascal or "raskolism" needs to be understood. Sinclair Dinnen (1995) defined the term raskol or rascal as a label for a member of a gang that was involved in criminal activities. He elaborated further that although temporary wealth was the product of rascal criminal activities, it was not what was ultimately important. While the acquisition of wealth was an objective of rascal gangs, social prestige and reputation were viewed as more important. Youth were not propelled into committing property crime for the accumulation of wealth. Rather, gang members viewed the accumulation of wealth as drawing the undesirable attention of police and relatives (Goddard, 1992). Wealth was to be spent immediately to gain status and prestige in the community. Dinnen (1995) noted employment can be a disincentive as relatives and others pressed for money from those having jobs. The notion of "playing at crime" was viewed by gang members as an attractive alternative to legitimate employment (Goddard, 1992). Goddard (1992) concluded that traditional explanations of gangs in the context of inequality, poverty, and social disintegration did not fully apply to gangs in Papua, New Guinea. Explanations of rascal gangs, to Dinnen (1995; 1998), cannot be seen as a consequence of the lack of economic and employment opportunities. Rather, gangs were an easy means to temporary wealth and reputation in the community. Rascal crime was more a matter of opportunity than economic necessity. The acquisition of Western consumer goods motivated some to join gangs and commit crimes (Roscoe, 1999).

Rascal gangs were involved in theft and they referred to the goods they stole as "cargo" (Kulick, 1993; Nibbrig & Nibbrig, 1992). Rascals also were involved in petty offenses, such as minor burglaries, motor vehicle thefts, petty street crimes (B. Harris, 1988), vandalism, pickpocketing, and homicides (Goddard, 1992; 1995). In rural East Sepik, rascal gangs were involved in highway robberies, vandalism, rapes, and murders, but rape and murder continue to be rare in the rural provinces (Roscoe, 1999a). Rascal gangs were sometimes involved with white-collar crimes, such as making and selling fake identity cards for illegal immigrants to the island. Most of the victims of rascal gangs were the poor inhabitants of the island. Poor women were common victims of rapes. Theft from unprotected homes was also frequent and tourists or business owners were also targeted. Some note that gangs were wrongfully credited for criminal actions by authorities (B. Harris, 1988).

Nibbrig and Nibbrig (1992) reported that the rascal gang lifestyle was attractive to youth as it allowed them to "run" with the big boys. The gangs offered excitement and adventure and provided opportunities for male bonding (Nibbrig & Nibbrig, 1992). To youth, the gangs afforded a romanticized lifestyle of fast money and prestige in the community. Rascalism offered power and a sense of adventure to gang members. Finally, Goddard (1992) noted that joining a gang paralleled the start of criminal activity by youth.

Cultural Factors in Papua New Guinea

According to Sinclair Dinnen, the urban street gangs of Papua, New Guinea were largely a product of social traditions and customs. Gang members gained status and support by escalating success in crime and the redistribution of wealth to family members and lesser criminals. In short, a "favors" system or gift economy operated for the street gangs. One's gang and community prestige was evident in having a car, women, and buying beer but also in how much wealth was redistributed to others. Individuals able to give away large amounts of wealth were known as "big men," which was a traditional cultural concept in Papua New Guinea (Goddard, 1995). Being a "big man" obligated the individual to distribute wealth to others but also created a sense of obligation of others receiving the wealth. The redistribution or sharing of wealth represented a Melanesian cultural pattern.

Other cultural factors have been explored as contributing to the unique nature of Papuan gangs. For example, Goddard (1995) believed the social disruption resulting from urbanization and industrialization of the country was an overriding factor in the creation of street crime and gangs. Others stressed the role New Guinea's colonial past played in the creation of rascal gangs. Nibbrig and Nibbrig (1992) viewed the island's colonial past as creating socioeconomic inequalities and blocked opportunities that fostered youth to become rascals and gang members. According to Nibbrig and Nibbrig (1992), rascals were driven by the inequities resulting from colonization. They also suggested that male dominance in Papua New Guinea's cultural tradition played a role in the formation of gangs. Sinclair Dinnen (1998) noted that urban rascal gangs exhibited a rich mix of social and cultural traditions.

Characteristics of Papua New Guinea's Street Gang Members

Most of the gang members were male and aged between nine to 25 years (Kulick, 1993). Females assisted the gangs but were not generally considered to be full gang members. Many gang members had dropped out of school before age 12. Socioeconomic backgrounds of gang members varied (Goddard, 1995). Most of the gang members were Melanesian and unemployed or worked in low paying jobs. Gang organized around ethnic lines with a few gangs being comprised of youth from mixed ethnic backgrounds (Goddard, 1992). Although most were Melanesian youth, increasingly, the rascal gangs were becoming more ethnically mixed. Some noted that the highland culture (village), an ethnic subdivision on the island, contributed to the perception of rascal gangs as being more violent (Nibbrig & Nibbrig, 1992). Rascals who married typically abandoned their gang lifestyles under pressure from kin and obligations to their new families (Roscoe, 1999).

Rascal gangs adopted names and identities for their gangs (Dinnen, 1995). Some sense of gang territory was observed by Nibbrig and Nibbrig (1992). Gang territories were determined by geographical location and not by conflict among the gangs. The gangs did not generally fight over territory. No gang tattoos were mentioned by Goddard (1995). The only gang rule was loyalty to the group (Dinnen, 1998).

Organizational Structure of Street Gangs in Papua New Guinea

The rascal gangs did not have links to organized crime, but there were four main groups of rascal gangs: the Bomai, Koboni, Mafia, and 585. Within these four main groups, rascal gangs formed loosely associated subgroups with very fluid organizational structures (Dinnen, 1998). The degree of organization structure may be changing to looser structures. During the mid-1980s, Nibbrig and Nibbrig (1992) noted there were fewer but better organized rascal gangs.

Regarding organizational structure, rascal gangs generally had core leaders and lieutenants, full but less active members, and supporters (B. Harris, 1988). The leaders were those who could most easily mobilize the gang into action. Leaders, known as "big men," were defined as those members with great cargoes (Kulick, 1993; Nibbrig & Nibbrig, 1992). Cargoes were frequently shared with gang and non-gang members. Buying beer and drugs with one's wealth gave status and power in the community. Rascal gang leaders tended to be older than other members of the gangs, and were in the late 20s to early 30s. The supporters identified with the gang but were never initiated into membership. Some individuals claimed to be the in rascal gangs for prestige and status but were not members. This pattern is common with "claimer" and "wannabe" youth in the United States. Entry into the gangs was not a formal initiation rite (Dinnen, 1998) but a process characterized by escalating involvement by youth into the gang's criminal activities (Goddard, 1992). Exiting the gang was not formal or difficult.

Community Response to Rascal Street Gangs

Authorities viewed rascals and rascal gangs as a threat to the people and the stability of the country. During the 1980s, the community had a sense of helplessness regarding the rascal gangs because it believed nothing could be done about them (Nibbrig & Nibbrig, 1992). This perception was fueled by a lack of confidence regarding government and police. Currently, the perception held by many is that things have become worse than the 1980s.

Authorities have overtly condemned rascals as a menace and have tried gang suppression strategies. Police have conducted gang sweeps and assaulted gang members. In some cases, villages supported rascal gangs and they were seen as altruistic superheroes, surrounded by adventure and socioeconomic power. Numerous folktales about the exploits of rascal gangs were present in New Guinea. For example, community members sometimes made references to the special powers of rascals, such as their use of magic and their alleged ability to become invisible or immune to bullets (Kulick, 1993). Some communities even viewed rascals as cultural heroes or "Robin Hoods" (Kulick, 1993). Some villagers saw the police and rascals as doing the same work and it was difficult to distinguish between the two. Some citizens even refused to cooperate with authorities except in rare cases (Dinnen, 1998). These perceptions were not universal to the island. Roscoe (1999) reported that in the East Sepik region, rural villagers did not view rascals as having special powers.

Sinclair Dinnen (1995) reported that organizational retreats between rascal gang youth and individuals in high political office sometimes occurred. Communities reportedly had difficulties breaking up rascal gangs because the gangs dispersed wealth across the neighborhoods (Goddard, 1992). Neighbors were often allowed to share in the spoils of rascal crimes, hence making them unwilling to cooperate with authorities. However, business owners and victims did not always share this positive view of the gangs. The media also took a negative view of rascal gangs and often overdramatized gang members as being more violent than the facts indicated (Dinnen, 1995).

Most of the criminal activities of rascal gangs were conducted in the urban areas of the island. When law enforcement agencies cracked down on the gangs or gang members, they would retreat back to their remote and welcoming villages until the heat died down. The villagers believed the rascals were fighting a guerilla war against corrupt politicians, greedy business owners, and missionaries (Kulick, 1993). More recent evidence indicates a permanent rascal gang presence in rural areas of New Guinea (Roscoe, 1999).

A somewhat unique occurrence with rascal gangs were the mass surrenders described by Goddard (1995) and Dinnen (1995). Goddard wrote:

> A common occurrence in Papua, New Guinea is the sudden mass "surrender" of large groups of criminals to authorities. Brokers, under church influence, would enter negotiations with gang leaders that would lead to mass gang surrenders. This process usually entailed a public conversion (charismatic or fundamentalist) to Christianity, the handing over of guns and ammunition to the police, public apology for past crimes, and often (despite the criminal's history of offenses including violence and occasional killings) a waiving of any prosecutions. (Goddard 1995: 2)

Sinclair Dinnen (1995) suggested that these gang surrenders might have great potential for the abatement of rascal gangs, if accompanied by employment opportunities for gang members. However, Hazlehurst and Hazlehurst (1999) were doubtful that offering employment would have much impact on the gang situation in Papua, New Guinea. They suggested that surrendering may be a mechanism used by gangs to simply reconfigure their organizations.

Papua New Guinea remains a country where street gangs continued to operate in-spite of law enforcement efforts to curb their activities and promote public safety. Governmental attempts to establish curfews and control gangs have had little success. Until the citizens agree to support the government's efforts and view law enforcement as having a legitimate role in controlling gangs, the gangs will continue to operate.

What can be drawn from the studies of rascal gangs in Papua, New Guinea is the fundamental notions of gangs arising from urbanization, unemployment, modernization, and poverty take backstage to the important role of cultural tradition. Gangs and gang membership were fuelled more by the Melanesian cultural traditions of establishing prestige and social obligation through the sharing of wealth obtained by "playing" the criminal game. Summarizing the cultural context around these gangs, Goddard (1992:20) wrote that these gangs, ". . . represent an integration of pre-capitalist social behavior into a cash-economic environment." These gangs, Goddard observed, can best be understood in terms of their cultural relationships of support and reciprocation among individuals viewed as leaders (big men) and the wide range of individuals involved in criminal activity.

Street Gangs in Guam

Stephen Schmitz and John Christopher (1997) identified street gangs on the island of Guam. They found different types of gangs on Guam, including village, Filipino, and copycat that were styled after the American Crip and Blood gangs. These criminal street gangs were involved in burglary, robbery, auto theft, theft, and assault.

Traditional culture on Guam promoted group membership over individualism, but some values have eroded in contemporary times as the island was confronted with modernization and Western influences. The erosion of traditional culture, when coupled with American models about gangs, resulted in fertile conditions for the development of street gangs in Guam.

According Schmitz and Christopher (1997), traditional moral visions characterized gang members. Moral visions were culturally based assumptions that shaped how individuals experienced life and the views they adopted toward life. Gang members ascribed to a moral vision based on traditional tribal warrior values. These values included bravery, solidarity, physical aggression, and the rejection of social mores. Guam's street gang members rejected Western individualism in favor of group goals. Gangs provided norms, rules, and demanded loyalty from members.

Although Schmitz and Christopher placed the age of Guam's street gang members at between 13 to 17 years, membership began during the elementary school years. Elementary school children indicated they joined "lollipop gangs" that were affiliated with older gangs. This is a pattern similar to the age grading (cliques) observed in American

Hispanic gangs (see Chapter 2). Likewise, gangs were known to recruit new members from the elementary schools. Elementary school children saw gangs as good because they provide protection, entertainment, and excitement for members. Youth saw gangs as providing a sense of honor, bravery, and solidarity missing from traditional society. Gang members were viewed as role models and appealing because they represented an alternative to traditional collectives and modern individualism.

CONCLUSION: STREET GANGS IN AFRICA, MIDDLE EAST, AUSTRALIA, POLYNESIA, AND THE SOUTH PACIFIC

The overwhelming sense one has in reviewing street gangs in many African countries, especially those south of the equator, is one of childhood lost. Civil wars, colonialism, poverty, famine, loss of parents, drought, HIV, failing economies, repressive political regimes, wars, diseases, and other social calamities have reeked havoc on many children and youth. The scars of colonialism and apartheid left their mark on many African countries, especially South Africa.

Robbed of childhood and faced with poor prospects, some African youth have turned to street gangs for survival. Many youth undoubtedly have nothing to lose by turning to gangs and crime. In South Africa, some have observed the tensions of township life, stress on families, and inability of families to protect children have led numbers of children to join "substitute" families, such as prostitute gangs and street gangs (Kanji, 1996). This pattern was repeated in other African countries where street gangs or groups operated as substitute families for homeless and abandoned youth. The novel *Lord of the Flies* comes to mind when thinking about the situation in many African countries, at least those regions along and south of the equator. Africa has numerous youth who lived by their own rules and sometimes these rules were violent and predatory. In general, the future looks dim for many youth and bright for street gangs and paramilitary groups willing to arm youth. For scholars interested in street gangs, the situation in Africa bares watching, as the future may prove negative.

Ethnic and tribal divisions in some African countries helped create street gangs of young adults that selectively victimized opposing ethnic group communities on a grand scale. Reports from Burundi (Lorch, 1995), Zaire (McKinley, 1996), Rwanda (McKinley, 1996) and Kenya (McKinley, 1996) describe a pattern of bands of ethnically similar groups or gangs attacking communities and committing crimes and atrocities. How much of these activities represent street gang activity or political militias has not been systematically sorted out. The degree of organization of some of these groups suggest gangs, but their motives go well beyond simple street crime.

It was noted previously that most of what is known about street gangs in Africa comes from South Africa. Even in South Africa, where sound research has occurred or been undertaken, more needs to be done. The paucity of information about street gangs and criminal groups in other African countries is great and the surface has barely been scratched. Scattered evidence indicates that street gangs were present in some Middle Eastern countries, such as Pakistan and Israel. Until this region of the world stabilizes, it will be difficult to ascertain the existence and prevalence of street gangs. In some Middle Eastern countries, street gangs undoubtedly, or at least law violating youth groups, exist. Again the role of migration of peoples seems an important consideration. This was certainly the case with some of the gangs in Israel, where Russian immigrants had formed bully gangs in response to their new and old countries. In some Middle Eastern (Asian) countries, like Pakistan, gangs and groups operated with a degree of community support and although they are not specifically referred to as gangs, they operate as such. This pattern may be present in other Middle Eastern and Northern African countries but without research, we are left to speculation.

The street gang situation for Australia and other countries in the Southern Hemisphere and Pacific is less desperate. From the studies we have on street gangs in this vast region of the world, it appears that while western gang influences were present, the gangs in these countries have incorporated many aspects of their traditional cultures into the gangs. For example, the sharing of material gains by gang members in New Guinea, while similar to some street gangs in Africa and *choums*, remains unique. African street gangs and choums shared wealth mostly for survival and status. New Guinea's street gangs did it for prestige and status only, as survival was not the issue, but social status, no matter how temporary was a concern.

In Australia, some street gangs followed the skinhead model as a style. However, other forms of street gangs existed. Tricia Fox, a criminologist at Queensland University of Technology, observed that homeless teenagers have turned to street crime to support themselves, and because they were bored (Haberfield, 2000). She added that the youth have a sense of common identity as a group. Some of these youth in all likelihood have or will join street gangs.

Street gangs in Australia mirror gangs in other Anglo-European countries, but this may be changing as large numbers of immigrants move to the country and bring their cultural experiences with them. The immigration of peoples from a variety of Asian countries has raised concerns about the expansion of street gangs and organized crime. There is some evidence that this may be occurring, but the extent is unknown.

In other Southern Hemisphere and Pacific countries, street gangs were present and seem to combine local cultural traditions into the operations of the gang. The street gangs of Papua New Guinea and Guam were unique and reflected their native cultures. They had not bought into the Western notions of success and modernization.

Chapter 7

CLOSING OBSERVATIONS ON STREET GANGS THROUGHOUT THE WORLD

The studies reviewed in this book raise the question of whether American concepts and theories about gangs are useful in understanding gangs, law-violating youth groups, and youth subcultures in other countries. There are substantial differences among gangs in different countries at varying times, but there is also evidence that the American youth subcultures of the 1950s through the present have made a lasting impression on street gangs throughout the world. In turn, the United States and other countries also have been influenced by British gangs, most notably the skinheads. Likewise, Chinese secret societies and organized crime have partially shaped street gangs in several countries. However, in some areas, street gang phenomena appear to spring from independent cultural influences, as exemplified by the relatively nonviolent Argentine and Puerto Rican gangs of the 1960s and 1970s and the street gangs of Papua New Guinea and Guam that incorporate traditional cultural values into their operations.

WORLDWIDE TRENDS AND STREET GANGS

The world's population of homeless and unsupervised youth has been growing at an alarming rate. As noted, there may be as many as 100 million street children in the world (United Nations, 1999). These children and youth need to find ways of surviving and street gangs provide them with a mechanism for doing so. Street gangs are an effective coping strategy for coping with life and many of these youth will be at risk of joining street gangs.

214

World Immigration Patterns and Street Gangs

The movement of national and ethnic populations has been linked to the development of street gangs in host countries. In the United States, immigration to the country by waves of foreigners promoted the rise of street gangs. For example, when ethnic groups such as the Irish, Southern Europeans, Eastern Europeans, Mexicans/Latinos, and Chinese moved to the United States, some members of these groups formed street gangs. The cliché that whatever group was the "last off the boat" is the group likely to form street gangs in response to prejudice and discrimination is reflective of what occurred. For example, in the 19th century, Irish immigrants formed street gangs partially for power and socioeconomic reasons but also in response to the prejudice and discrimination they faced from Anglo Americans. More recently, immigrant Cambodian refugees have reportedly formed street gangs for protection from white, Hispanic, and African-American street gangs in southern California (Willwerth, 1991). The pattern has been repeated when marginalized immigrant groups and their children form street gangs.

This pattern is paralleled in other countries, including Germany, Great Britain, France, Slovakia, Czech Republic, Sweden, Slovenia, and others. The immigration of peoples from ex-Eastern European Bloc countries, Africa, Asia, Central America, the Middle East, and other regions has promoted groups and gangs in the new host countries. This is most evident in some of the neo-fascist and nationalistic movements in these countries, such as the skinheads. This is significant for street gangs as all indications are the migration of peoples will continue in the future.

Likewise, the formation of antiimmigration groups and street gangs almost always gives rise to the formation of defensive groups and gangs among immigrants. This is the case with the Turkish Power Boys in Germany, Sikh and Yardie gangs in London, and North African ethnic street gangs in Scandinavia and Paris. Repeated attacks by racist and hate groups or gangs promotes the rise of reactionary street gangs comprised mostly of youth from the targeted groups. Even within countries, such as Brazil, the migration of ethnic groups within national borders fuels the formation of ethnically-based street gangs. The low-income northern Brazilians migrating to the south face street gangs fuelled by socioeconomic and ethnic prejudice and discrimination (Vincent, 1992).

Related to migration, the passage of deportation laws in many countries has promoted the expansion of street gangs. Criminal adults and youth, when deported back to their native countries, tend to establish street gangs based on what they learned while living in the United States. This pattern was reported in Belize (Miller-Matthei & Smith, 1998), Central American (DeCesare, 1999), Cambodia (McDowell, 1995), South African (Glaser, 1992), Russia (Pilkington, 1994) and other countries. There is little evidence that street gangs purposely migrate to countries to establish themselves. However, some organized crime networks, such as the drug cartels, do establish groups in other countries to expand their criminal activities. What confuses the picture is organized crime groups sometimes employ local street gangs across national boundaries to carry out assignments, and in doing so give the impression that street gangs are crossing national boundaries when in fact they are not.

Urbanization, Industrialization, and Street Gangs

One theme in the literature is that crime and delinquency are most likely to occur in urban settings. For youth, Fischer (1975) proposed that only in urban areas are delinquents present in sufficient numbers to establish a delinquent subculture and hence gangs. It may also be necessary for a critical mass of youths to be present in some proximity to one another in order for a gang to form. Opportunities for joining gangs are therefore greater in urban areas than in the countryside. Others have questioned the *critical mass* theme (Erickson & Jensen, 1977), but there is general agreement that street gangs have historically been primarily an urban slum phenomenon (Miller, 1975).

Street gangs are in fact more prevalent in urban than in rural settings and appear to be more widespread in more developed, industrialized countries than in less developed, nonindustrial countries. Increasingly, there are exceptions to this pattern in some developing countries. In Chapters 5 and 6, rural street gangs were noted in Papua New Guinea, South Africa, Pakistan, and other countries. In addition, some street gangs move back and forth from urban areas to the countryside. For example, street gangs in New Guinea reportedly move from urban areas to rural following crime sprees or law enforcement crackdowns (Roscoe, 1999a; 1999b). In developed countries with large urban settings, a common pattern is the commuting street gangs that use mass transit to travel to areas of the city to commit gang-related crimes. This was found to be the case in Olso, Norway (Lien, 2001), Paris (Henley, 2001; Klein, 1995a; Kroeker & Haut, 1995). In addition, Klein (1996; 2001) observed this pattern in Stockholm, Zurich, Stuttgart, and Frankfurt.

The urbanization hypothesis claims that unskilled rural peasants expand city populations and criminalize urban areas because they want to live like city residents but lack the necessary skills. However, urbanization, in the opinion of some, does not apply to all street gangs. For example, Mahabir (1988) concluded that urbanization did not account for crimes or gangs in Trinidad, Tobago, or Jamaica. Although this may be the case in Trinidad and Tobago, this review suggests that street gangs will continue to be more predominant in urban areas.

Modernization and Street Gangs

It is generally assumed that high rates of urban crime accompany industrial development and modernization (Clinard & Abbot, 1973). The assumption is that crime and delinquency increase with modernization as traditions break down. If this were the case, we would expect to find street gangs more prevalent in industrialized and modernized areas. Street gangs do appear to be more prevalent in the modernized and industrialized countries.

However, there is evidence that this pattern is not present in all countries or cultures. For example, street gangs in Guam reject the values associated with modernity, that is individualism. Street gangs have a shared sense of meaning, honor, safety, and stability (Schmitz & Christopher, 1997). Schmitz and Christopher concluded street gangs in Guam are a vehicle to demonstrate rejection of and importance of independence from Western individualistic mentality. Modernization/ urbanization and the accumulation of wealth in Papua New Guinea are dissimilar to the patterns observed in the United States (Bessant, 1994). But the situations in Guam and Papua New Guinea are the exception rather than the rule. Although modernization does not cause gangs, it most likely seems to ripen the conditions for them to develop and flourish.

Street Gangs and Economic Functions

It is apparent from reviewing the studies and journalist accounts that many street gangs are increasingly developing economic functions, some legitimate and others not. This observation is consistent with Hazlehurst and Hazlehurst (1998), who concluded that gangs throughout the world have adopted economic functions. Examples are numerous, such as the many street gangs involved in drug sales in the United States, Dinnen's (1995; 1997; 1998) notation of Melanesian gangs and "wok," and the informal economy operated by rascal gangs in New Guinea. The *choums* of Africa are clearly social but also economic entities designed to provide financial support for homeless youth. Street gangs throughout the world play an important role in the local and national economies of countries excluded from the world's economic success story. The unfulfilled promise of the good life promotes the expansion of street gangs, as they are assumed to be the only mechanism available to some to survive. There is every reason to suspect that street gangs will continue to play a role in the world's informal economy indirectly on the macro and directly on micro levels. The expansion of the world's illegal drug trade, as well as other crimes such as smuggling, can only promote street gangs.

The Worldwide Street Gang Subculture

Much of what is observed across the world and attributed to gang or gang affiliations is probably imitative behaviors. Many activities considered gang or gang-related are actually law-violating youth groups or simple group delinquency. Imitative behaviors by youth of gang phenomena such as dress and style are common in a world with instant worldwide communications through satellites and advanced telecommunications. The youth of many countries are exposed to the American gangster lifestyle and many find this style worthy of imitation, whether they are involved in criminal behavior or not. Hip Hop, rap, gangsta, and other contemporary music that incorporates gang imagery and values will continue to be embraced by at-risk youth throughout the world, whether they are in gangs or not. For example, youth in the Netherlands have modeled their street gangs after Afro-American gangs (see Chapter 3).

Communities Will Continue to Play Important Roles In Defining Street Gangs as Problems

Communities play an important role in defining street gangs as problems or as valued or nonthreatening features of the environment. There are several examples of community support for street gangs in this review. For example, rascal/raskol gangs of Papua New Guinea have high levels of community support. They buy beer and share their wealth with their respective communities. They also control media images by staging mass surrenders and religious conversions to build community sympathy and forgiveness. For instance, the Peckham Girls of London enjoyed community support (Archer, 1995). Many of the street gangs in South Africa and South America have community support. The street gangs of Rio de Janeiro's *favela's* have community support, or at least tolerance. Finally, some European communities provide tacit support or act indifferently to hate groups and skinhead street gangs opposed to immigrants.

STREET GANG STRUCTURES THROUGHOUT THE WORLD

Street gangs throughout the world do not typically exhibit formal organizational structures but show variation across regions and countries (Spergel, 1990). A similar observation about gang organizational structures has been made about gangs in the United States (Sanders, 1994). Most street gangs throughout the world are loosely organized, have varying leaders, are only sporadically violent, hangout a lot, and are most of the time fairly boring (Klein, 2001). With the exception of some of the Far East, gang structures appear to be loose, non-hierarchical, and leadership is not always well defined. In part, this may reflect the absence of clear distinctions in the research between law-violating youth groups, subcultures, and gangs.

Using Klein's (2001) dimensions of gang structures as a guide for gangs, European gangs tend to be specialty and compressed gangs. In Sweden, Germany, and England, Klein (2001) found varieties of street gangs that did not correspond well with American-style, traditional street gangs with their larger territorial based "agglomeration" of youth. But in other countries and cities such as Berlin, Brussels, and

Russia, Klein found gang structures similar to the traditional American street gang. Some of the authors concluded that there was evidence that Rotterdam and Den Haag had specialty gangs (Klein, 2001; Van Gemert, 2001); Den Haag had law-violating youth groups (Gruter & Versteegh, 2001); Copenhagen had ethnic gangs (Stevns, 2001) or compressed (Klein, 2001); Frankfurt had compressed gangs (Tertilt, 2001); and Oslo had compressed gangs (Klein, 2001).

Applying Klein's 2001 characteristics of gang structures to the studies of this review, it is apparent that all of the various structures find representation around the world, with some more common than others. Using the information provided by the studies and references, it is possible to classify street gangs by study and county. Because the studies did not always fully cover all the aspects of gangs, one can only speculate where they might fall in the scheme. When information was missing, these gangs were noted by an asterisk.

If the information is interpreted correctly, traditional street gangs are not common in the studies of street gangs. Neo-traditional street gangs are, however, common, but are not the most common structure. The most common structures are compressed and specialty gangs.

Traditional gangs are long-lasting, large, with distinct subgroups, wide age range, and are strongly territorial. The following descriptions of street gangs included in this review approximate these characteristics: Argentina (DeFleur, 1967b), Germany (Klein, 2001), Netherlands (Baur, 1964), Russia (Salagaev, 2001), South Africa (Glaser, 2000; Kynoch, 1999; 2000; Weinberg, 1964), and Zaire (La Fontaine, 1970*).

Neo-Traditional have short histories, are medium sized, have distinct subgroups, are strongly territorial, The following examples appear to resemble this gang structure: Australia (Bessant & Watts, 1992; Haberfield, 2000), Cambodia (McDowell, 1995), Canada (Gordon, 1998; Le Blanc & Lanctôt, 1994), China (Lee et al., 1996 Shaw, 1991; Vagg, 1997; Zhang et al., 1997), El Salvador (DeCesare, 1999), England (Mares, 2001), France (Cavan & Cavan, 1968; Kroeker & Haut, 1995; Monsod, 1967), Guatemala (Carrell, 1998), India (Sidhva, 1997; Singh, 1969), Jamaica (Gunst, 1989; 1995; Joseph, 1999), Netherlands (Van Gemert, 2001), New Zealand (Winter, 1998), Palestine (Grennan et al., 2000), Puerto Rico (Ferracuti et al., 1975), Russia (Likhanov, 1991; Omel'chenko, 1996), Slovenia (Dekleva, 2001), South Africa (Glaser, 1992; Houston & Prinsloo, 1998; Ledochowski, 1991; Pinnock & Douglas-Hamilton, 1997), and Trinidad & Tobago (McCree, 1998).

Compressed have short histories, are small, lack subgroups, and have narrow age ranges. Possible examples of this gang structure include: Brazil (Vincent, 1992), Canada (Barron, 1997; Barron & Tindall, 1993; Kennedy & Barron, 1993), China (Lo, 1984; Zhang et al., 1997), Denmark (Stevns, 2001; Klein, 2001), El Salvador (Rohter, 1997; Sanchez, 1995), England (Humphries, 1981; Archer, 1995; Mares, 2001), Ethiopia (Veale & Adefrisew, 1993), France (Esterle-Hedibel, 2001), Germany (Tertilt, 1997), Guam (Schmitz & Christopher, 1997), Guatemala (Mojica, 2001), Israel (Sherer, 1990; Tarakovsky & Mirsky, 2001), Japan (Grennan et al., 2000; Jungk 1959; Kersten, 1993), Kenya (Shorter & Onyancha, 1999), Malaysia (Teo & Phaun, 1997), Mexico (Trussell, 1999; Valenzuela, 1988), Northern Ireland (Montgomery, 1997), Netherlands (Klein, 2001), New Zealand (Winter, 1998), Norway (Klein, 2001), Pakistan (Ali, 1989), Papua New Guinea (Anonymous, 1995a; Dinnen, 1995, 1998; Goddard, 1995; B. Harris, 1988; Kulick, 1993; Nibbrig & Nibbrig, 1992: Roscoe, 1999, 1999a), Philippines (Francia, 1991), South Africa (Burnett, 1999; Pinnock, 1995; Pinnock & Douglas-Hamilton, 1997), Sweden (Klein, 2001), Taiwan (Kuo, 1973), and Trinidad and Tobago (Mahabir, 1988; McCree, 1998).

Collective gangs last from 10 to 15 years, are medium to large, lack subgroups, and have medium to wide age ranges. Studies that may reflect this street gang structure include: Australia (Moore, 1994), Burundi (Lorch, 1995), Israel (Hazani, 1989), Japan (Kattoulas, 2001; Kersten, 1993), Kenya (McKinley, 1996), Nigeria (Agence France Presse, 2002), Norway (Lien, 2001), Russia (Bushnell, 1990; Chalidze, 1977; Fain, 1990; Pilkington, 1994), Rwanda (McKinley, 1996), Sierra Leonne (Masland, 2002), and Zaire (McKinley, 1996).

Specialty gangs have a duration of under 10 years, are small, have no subgroups, have usually narrow age ranges, are territorial, and have a narrow criminal focus. Examples include: Australia (Haberfield, 2000), Belgium (Vercaigne, 1997), Brazil (Dimenstein, 1991; Anonymous, 1989-90), Cambodia (McDowell, 1995), China (Chu's, 2000; Lo, 1993; Matheron, 1988; Vagg, 1997: Zhang et al., 1997), Columbia (Salazar, 1994), England (Ross, 1972), France (Janssen, 1986), Germany (Levin & McDevitt, 1993), Hungary (Grennan et al., 2000), India (Clinard & Abbott, 1973; Grennan et al., 2000; Srivastava, 1955; Shukla, 1981-82), Japan (Grennan et al., 2000; Kattoulas, 2001; Kersten, 1993), Kenya (Shorter & Onyancha 1999),

Korea (Kang & Kang, 1978), Netherlands (Klein, 2001; Van Gemert, 2001), New Zealand (Winter, 1998), Nigeria (Agence France Presse, 2000; Grennan et al., 2000; Pitman, 2001), Papua New Guinea (Anonymous, 1995a; Dinnen, 1995, 1998; Goddard, 1995; B. Harris, 1988; Kulick, 1993; Nibbrig & Nibbrig, 1992; Roscoe, 1999; 1999a), Russia (Likhanov, 1991; Pilkington, 1994; Salagaev, 2001; Shabad, 1988; Wilson-Smith, 1989), Sierra Leone (Masland, 2002), South Africa (Burnett, 1999; Dissel, 1997: Pinnock & Douglas-Hamilton, 1997), Sweden (Björgo, 1993), Taiwan (Kuo, 1973), Trinidad & Tobago (McCree, 1998), and Uganda (African News Service, 2002a).

MULTIPLE MARGINALITY AND THE WORLD'S STREET GANGS

The concept of multiple marginality first advanced by Vigil (1988) and Vigil and Yun (2001) and their colleagues gains support from this review of street gangs around the world. Cultural, economic, ethnic, racial, language, and other forms of prejudice and discrimination fuel much of what is observed in the formation and continuation of street gangs. The world is most certainly marginalizing large populations of youth that when faced with overwhelming odds for success or survival may turn to street gangs for remedies. This is occurring in several countries in Africa, South America, and for that matter, most of the remainder of the world.

Vigil and Yun (2002:174) wrote, ". . . the seeds of the solutions to gangs are found in the root causes. Even though larger-than-life historical and structural forces have undermined social control institutions, such as families, schooling, and law enforcement, there is an opportunity to salvage many of the children who have been marginalized and left to the streets." We should promote the idea that something can and should be done about the world's marginalized populations and street gangs.

REFERENCES

Abadinsky, H. (1990). *Organized crime.* Chicago: Nelson Hall.

African News Services. (2002a). Mysterious gang kills 20 in Nairobi. *Africa News,* March 4, 2002.

African News Services. (2002a). Uganda: Robbers raid Kampala. *Africa News,* April 24, 2002.

Agence France Presse. (1998). International News. *Agence France Presse,* May 7, 11:48.

Agence France Presse. (2000). Street gangs create panic in Lagos loot stalls (International News). *Agence France Presse,* October 18, 2000.

Agence France Presse. (2002). Troops patrol Nigerian city after bloody ethnic unrest. *Agence France Presse,* February 6, 2002.

Alain, M. (1995). The rise and fall of motorcycle gangs in Quebec. *Federal Probation,* June, 59:54-57.

Alexandrescu, G. (1996). Street children in Bucharest. *Childhood,* 3:(2) 267-270.

Ali, S. (1989). Milking the rich. *Far Eastern Economic Review,* October 5, 146:41-42.

Aning, J. (2001). Metro 14-year old gang "boss" arrested. *Philippine Inquirer,* September, 11:21.

Anonymous. (1989-90). International news: Brazil: Gang wars mean overtime. *Law and Order,* 38:(8) 6.

Anonymous. (1994). A new U.S. import in El Salvador. *Criminal Justice in the Americas,* 7:(4) 21-22.

Anonymous. (1995a). Gangs and cops vie for Rio. *World Press Review,* 18:(1) 18.

Anonymous. (1995b). Rascals rule. *The Economist,* October 15, 336:26.

Anonymous. (1998). The Americas: Welcome to paradise, Jamaica-style. *Economist,* October 3, 349:40.

Anonymous. (1999). Europe: Nasty, ubiquitous and unloved. *Economist,* March 20, 350: (8111) 56-57.

Anti-Defamation League. (1995). *The skinhead international: A worldwide survey of neo-nazi skinheads.* New York: Anti-Defamation League.

Archer, D. (1995). Riot GRRRL and raisin girl: Femininity within the female gang the power of the popular. *The British Criminology Conferences: Selected Proceedings,* Vol. 1.

Asbury, H. (1927). *The gangs of New York.* Garden City, NY: Garden City Publishing Company.

Ash, S. (2002). Youth gangs becoming more active. *The Guelph Mercury,* May 11: A7.

Attwood, L. (1996). Young people, sex and sexual identity. In H. Pilkington (Ed.), *Generation and identity in contemporary Russia.* London: Routledge.

Augustine, Saint. (1949). *Confessions.* New York: Modern Library.

Baker, R. (1988). Homeboys: Players in a deadly drama. *Los Angeles Times,* June 26.

Banks, G. (2000). The tattooed generation: Salvadoran children bring home American gang culture. *Dissent,* 47: (1) 22-29.

Banks, K. (1985). A wave of gang violence. *Maclean's,* April 8, 98:50-51.

Barron, S.W. (1997). Canadian male street skinheads: Street gang or street terrorists? *The Canadian Review of Sociology and Anthropology,* 34:(2) 125-153.

Barron, S.W., & Tindall, D. (1993). Network structure and delinquent attitudes with a juvenile gang. *Social Networks,* 15:(3) 255-273.

Baur, E.J. (1964). The trend of juvenile offences in the Netherlands and the United States. *Journal of Criminal Law, Criminology, and Police Science,* 55:359-369.

Beirne, P. & Nelken, D. (Eds.). (1997). *Issues in comparative criminology.* Aldershot, England: Dartmouth.

Belfast Telegraph. (2001). Troubled area is becoming wild west. *Belfast Telegraph,* No. 3, 2001.

Bellamy, J. (1973). *Crime and public order in England in the later Middle Ages.* London: Routledge and Kegan Paul.

Bergman, B. (1995). Wild in the streets. *Maclean's,* August 14, 108:18-19.

Bernama (Malaysian National News Agency). 2001. "Black Metal" street gang trying to recruit students. *Malaysia General News,* July 16.

Berry, N. (1988). Radical Sikh. *New Society,* March, 11:16-18.

Bessant, J., & Watts, R. (1992). Being bad is good: Explorations of the bodgie gang culture in Southeast Australia, 1948-1956. *The Gang Journal,* 1:31-55.

Bessant, J. (1994). The American juvenile underclass and the cultural colonization of young Australians under conditions of modernity. *Journal of Gang Research,* 2:15-33.

Binder, A., Geis, G., & Bruce, D. (1988). *Juvenile delinquency: Historical, cultural, and legal perspectives.* New York: Macmillan.

Binder, D. (1990). Violence by skinheads startling East Germans. *New York Times International,* August 21: A-2.

Bindman, S. (1991). Street gangs pose major problem, RCMP report says; Young Offenders Act hampers police efforts. *Southampton News,* September 3:A3.

Bing, L. (1992). *Do or die.* New York: Harper Perennial.

Bjerregaard, B., & Smith, C. (1993). Gender differences in gang participation, delinquency and substance abuse. In M.W. Klein et al. (Eds.). *The modern gang reader.* Los Angeles: Roxbury.

Bjorgo, T. (1993). Violence against immigrants and refugees in Scandinavia. In T. Bjorgo and R. Witte (eds.), *Racist violence in Europe.* New York: St. Martin's Press.

Bjorgo T. (1997). *Racist and right wing violence in Scandinavia.* Stockholm: Tano Aschehoug.

Bjorgo, T., & Witte, R. (Eds.). (1993). *Racist violence in Europe.* New York: St. Martin's Press.

Block, C.R., & Block, R. (1993). *Street gang crime in Chicago.* Washington, D.C.: National Institute of Justice.

Bobrowski, L.J. (1988). *Collecting, organizing, and reporting street gang crime.* Chicago: Special Functions Group, Chicago Police Department, Mimeo.

Bollag, B. (1999). Foreign students in Slovakia fear they will be victims of racist violence. *Chronicle of Higher Education,* 46: (10) A79.

Bookin-Weiner, H., & Horowitz, R. (1983). The end of the youth gang: Fad or fact? *Criminology,* 21:585-602.

Borger, J. (1999). Army ordered to wage war on Kingston's gangs. *The Manchester Guardian,* July 14:13.

Bowker, L., & Klein, M.W. (1983). The etiology of female juvenile delinquency and gang membership: A test of psychological and social structural explanations. *Adolescence,* 18:739-751.

Brady, J. P. (1983). People's Republic of China. In E.H. Johnson (Ed.), *International handbook of contemporary developments in criminology.* Westport, CT: Greenwood Press.

Braithewaite, J. (1989). *Crime, shame and reintegration.* Cambridge: Cambridge University Press.

Brake, M. (1974). The skinheads: An English working class subculture. *Youth and Society,* 6:179-20.

Brake, M. (1985). *Comparative youth culture.* London: Routledge and Kegan Paul.

Brown, A. (1994). Rio street gangs join dance of death funk music scene becomes outpouring of fury for slum kids. *The Toronto Star,* September 18:E6.

Brown, W.K. (1977). Black female gangs in Philadelphia. *International Journal of Offender Therapy and Comparative Criminology,* 21:221-228.

Brown, W.K. (1978). Graffiti, identity, and the delinquent gang. *International Journal of Offender Therapy and Comparative Criminology,* 22:39-45.

Bruman, C. (1983). Boat people in a new land. *Maclean's,* October, 96: 19.

Brunner, R. (1974). Focal points of juvenile crime: Typology and conditions. In Congress Report. *Juvenile Crime and Resocialization.* Stuttgart, West Germany: Springer-Verlag.

Buford, B. (1990). *Among the thugs.* New York: Vintage Books.

Bullington, B. (1977). *Heroin use in the barrio.* Lexington, MA: D.C. Heath.

Burke, R., & Sunley, R. (1998). Post-modernism and youth subcultures in Britain in the 1990s. In K. Hazlehurst & C. Hazlehurst (eds.)., *Gangs and youth subcultures: International explorations.* New Brunswick, NJ: Transaction.

Burkeman, O. (2000). Gang wars fuel race fears in Bradford: The murder of a young black man amid a spate of shootings heightens tension between Asian and Afro-Caribbean communities. *The Guardian,* August, 19:1.7.

Burnett, C. (1999). Gang violence as survival strategy in the context of poverty in Davidsonville. *Society in Transition,* 30:(1) 1-12.

Burt, C. (1925). *The young delinquent.* New York: Appleton.

Bushnell, J. (1990). Introduction: The history and study of Soviet youth subculture. *Soviet Sociology,* 29:3-10.

Bynum, J.E., & Thompson, W.E. (1988). *Juvenile delinquency: A sociological approach.* Boston: Allyn and Bacon.

Came, B., Lewis, P., Hart, J., Wolff, D., O'Farrell, E., Ogston, L., Allen, G., Gregor, A., & Black, L. (1989a). A growing menace: Violent skinheads are raising urban fears. *Maclean's,* January 23, 102:43-44.

Came, B., Gilles, L., Howse, J., Kaihla, P., Wickens, B., & Burke, D. (1989b). Gang terror. *Maclean's*, May 22, 102:36-39.

Cameron, N. (1983). New Zealand. In E. H. Johnson (Ed.), *International handbook of contemporary developments in criminology*. Westport, CT: Greenwood Press.

Campbell, A. (1984a). *The girls in the gang: A report from New York City*. Oxford, England: Basil Blackwell.

Campbell, A. (1984b). Girl's talk: The social representation of aggression by female gang members. *Criminal Justice and Behavior*, 11:139-156.

Campbell, A. (1991). *The girls in the gang*. Cambridge, MA: Basil Blackwell.

Campbell, A., & Muncer, S. (1989). Them and us: A comparison of the cultural context of American gangs and British subcultures. *Deviant Behavior*, 10:271-288.

Campbell, A., Munce, S., & Galea, J. (1982). American gangs and British subcultures: A comparison. *International Journal of Offender Therapy and Comparative Criminology*, 26:76-89.

Campbell, J. (1991). We are the bully boys. In R. Rosen & P. McSharry (Eds.), *Street gangs: Gaining turf, losing ground*. New York: The Rosen Publishing Group.

Campos, R., Raffaelli, M., Ude, W., Greco, M., Ruff, A., Rolf, J., Antunes, C.M. (1994). Social networks and daily activities of street youth in Belo-Horizonte Brazil. *Child Development*, 65:(2) 319-330.

Canadian Press. (1995). Winnipeg gangs move from joy rides to muggings, killings. *The Canadian Press*, August 1:A4.

Capp, B. (1977). English youth groups and the Pinder of Wakefield. *Past and Present*, 76:127-133.

Carey, S. (1985). I just hate 'em that's all. *New Society*, July, 26:123-125.

Carrell, S. (1998). When street cleaning is killing kids. *Scotland on Sunday*, April 19:18.

Caryl, C. (1998). Rapping in red square. *U.S. News and World Report*, 124:(19) 38-42.

Cavan, R.S. & Cavan, J.T. (1968). *Delinquency and crime: Cross-cultural perspectives*. Philadelphia: Lippincott.

Chalidze, V. (1977). Criminal Russia: *A study of crime in the Soviet Union*. New York: Random House.

Chambliss, W.J. (1973). The saints and the roughnecks. *Society*, 11:341-355.

Chapman, D. (1998). Girl gang leaders led "reign of terror." *The Toronto Sun*, April 24:1.

Chavira, R. (1980). West coast story. *Nuestro*, May 4:21.

Chein, I., Gerald, D.L., Lee, R.S., & Rosenfeld, E. (1964). *The road to H: Narcotics, delinquency, and social policy*. New York: Basic Books.

Chin, K. (1986). *Chinese triad societies, tongs, organized crime, and street gangs in Asia and the United States*. Ph.D. Dissertation, University of Pennsylvania.

Chin, K. (1990a). *Chinese subculture and criminality: Non-traditional crime groups in America*. New York: Greenwood Press.

Chin, K. (1990b). Chinese gangs and extortion. In C.R. Huff (Ed.), *Gangs in America*. Newbury Park, CA: Sage.

Chu, Y.K. (1994). The triad threat to Europe. *Policing*, 10:(3) 206-215.

Chu, Y.K. (2000). *The triads as business*. London: Routledge.

Clarke, J. (1976). The skinheads and magical recovery of working class communities. In S. Hall, J. Clarke, T. Jefferson, & B. Roberts (Eds.). *Resistance through rituals.* London: Hutchinson.

Clinard, M.B. (1960). A cross cultural replication of urbanism to criminal behavior. *American Sociological Review,* 25:253-257.

Clinard, M.B., & Abbott, D. (1973). *Crime in Developing Countries: A Comparative Perspective.* New York: Wiley.

Cockburn, J.S. (1977). *Crime in England* 1550-1800. Princeton, NJ: Princeton University Press.

Cockburn, P. (1995). Iraq sinks under tidal wave of crime. *The Independent,* October12: 17.

Cohen, S. (1973). Mods and rockers: The inventory of manufactured news. In S. Cohen & J. Young (Eds.). *The manufacture of news.* Beverly Hills, CA: Sage.

Cohen, S. (1980). *Folk devils and moral panics: The creation of the mods and rockers.* Oxford: Martin Robertson.

Coleman, J.S. (1970). *The circle.* Ludlow, MA: Pro Litho.

Collins, H.C. (1979). *Street gangs.* New York: New York City Police Department.

Conklin, J.E. (1989). *Criminology.* New York: Macmillan.

Connell, R. and R. Lopez. (1996). Homeboys' reign of terror. *The Observer,* November 24: 9.

Connor, W.D. (1972). *Deviance in Soviet society: Crime, delinquency, and alcoholism.* New York: Columbia University Press.

Cooper, B.M. (1987). Motor city breakdown. *Village Voice,* December 1:23-25.

Coplon, J. (1988). Skinhead nation. *Rolling Stone,* 540:54-95.

Covey, H.C., Menard, S., & Franzese, B. 1997. *Juvenile gangs.* Springfield, IL: Charles C Thomas.

Cummings, L.L. (1994). Fighting by the rules: Women street fighting in Chihuahua, Mexico. *Sex Roles,* 30:189-198.

Cureton, S.R. (2002). Introducing Hoover: I'll ride for you, gangsta. In C.R. Huff (Ed.), *Gangs in America III.* Newbury Park, CA: Sage.

Curry, G.D. (1998). Female gang involvement. *Journal of Research in Crime and Delinquency,* 35:(1) 100-118.

Curry, G.D., & Spergel, I. (1988). Gang homicide, delinquency, and community. *Criminology,* 26:381-405.

Daniels, P. (1977). How relevant are delinquency theories? In P. Wilson (Ed.), *Delinquency in Australia: A critical appraisal.* St. Lucia, Australia: University of Queensland Press.

Danker, U. (1988). Bandits and the state: Robbers and the authorities in the Holy Roman Empire in the late seventeenth and eighteenth centuries. In R. Evans (Ed.), *The German underworld: Deviants and outcasts in German history.* London: Routledge and Kegan Paul.

Davies, A. (1998). Street gangs, crime and policing in Glasgow during the 1930s: The case of the Beehive Boys. *Social History,* 23: (3) 251-267.

Davies, A. (1999). These viragoes are no less cruel than the lads. *The British Journal of Criminology,* 39:72-89.

Davis, J.R. (1978). *Terrorists–Youth, biker, and prison violence.* San Diego, CA: Grossmont Press.

Davis, N. (1971). The reasons of misrule: Youth groups and charivaris in sixteenth century France. *Past and Present,* 50:41-75.

Dawley, D. (1992). *A nation of lords: The autobiography of the vice lords.* Prospect Heights, IL: Waveland Press.

Decker, S., & Kempf-Leonard, K. (1991). Constructing gangs: The social definition of youth activities. *Criminal Justice Policy Review,* 5: 271-291.

Decker, S., & Van Winkle, B. (1994). "Slinging dope": The role of gangs and gang members in drug sales. *Justice Quarterly,* 11:583-604.

DeCesare, D. (1998). The children of war: Street gangs in El Salvador. *NACLA Report on the Americas,* July 32:21-29.

DeCesare, D. (1999). Deporting America's gang culture. *Mother Jones,* 24:(4) 44-51.

DeFleur, L.B. (1967a). Ecological variables in the cross-cultural study of delinquency. *Social Forces,* 45:536-570.

DeFleur, L.B. (1967b). Delinquent gangs in cross-cultural perspective: The case of Cordoba. *Journal of Research in Crime and Delinquency,* 4:132-141.

Dekleva, B. (2001). Gang-like groups in Slovenia. In M. W. Klein et al. (Eds.), *The eurogang paradox: Street gangs and youth groups in the U.S. and Europe.* Dordrecht: Kluwer Academic Pubs.

Deutsche Presse-Agentur. (1995). Palestinian police battle violent gangs. *Deutsche Presse-Agentur-International News,* December 17.

Deutsche Presse-Agentur. (1997). Girl gangs robbed schoolgirls in Spain. *Deutsche Presse-Agentur-International News,* February 4.

Deziel, S. (2001). Gang warfare in paradise. *Maclean's,* 13:(30) 13.

Dimenstein, G. (1991). *Brazil war on children.* London: Latin America Bureau.

Dinnen, S. (1995). Praise the Lord and pass the ammunition–criminal group surrender in Papua New Guinea. *Oceania,* 66:103-118.

Dinnen, S. (1997). Law, order, and state in Papua New Guinea. Discussion Paper 97/1 State, Society and Governance in Melanesia Project: Australian National University.

Dinnen, S. (1998). Urban raskolism and criminal groups in Papua New Guinea. In K. Hazlehurst & C. Hazlehurst (Eds.), *Gangs and youth subcultures: International explorations.* New Brunswick, NJ: Transaction.

Dissel, A. (1997). Youth, street gangs and violence in South Africa. *Proceedings of the International Symposium held in Abidjan, Ivory Coast,* May 1997.

Dissel, A. (1998). Youth street gangs and violence in South Africa. Cape Town, South Africa: Braamfontein Centre for the Study of Violence and Reconciliation.

Dolan, E.G., & Finney, S. (1984). *Youth gangs.* New York: Simon and Schuster.

Downes, D. (1966). The gang myth. *Listener,* April 14, 75:534-537.

Downes, D. (1996). *The delinquent solution.* New York: The Free Press.

Drori, I., & Gayle, D.J. (1990). Youth employment strategies in a Jamaican sugar-belt area. *Human Organization,* 49:(4) 364-372.

Drowns, R.W., & Hess, K.M. (1990). *Juvenile justice.* St. Paul, MN: West.

Durkheim, E. (1933) (originally published in 1893). *The division of labor in society.* New York: Free Press.

Dyer, G. (1999). Street gangs gauge race relations. *The Jakarta Post*, March 4.

Eggleston, E.J. (1997). Boys' talk: Exploring gender discussions with New Zealand male youth gang members. *Caribbean Journal of Criminology and Social Psychology*, 2:100-114.

Egley, A., Jr. (2000). *Highlights of the 1999 national youth gang survey (Fact sheet #2000-20)*. Washington, DC: U.S. Department of Justice, OJJDP.

Elliott, D.S., & Ageton, S.S. (1980). Reconciling race and class differences in self-reported and official estimates of delinquency. *American Sociological Review*, 40:95-110.

Elliott, D.S., & Huizinga, D. (1983). Social class and delinquent behavior in a national youth panel: 1976-1980. *Criminology*, 21:149-177.

Elliott, D.S., Huizinga, D. & Ageton, S.S. (1985). *Explaining delinquency and drug use*. Beverly Hills, CA: Sage.

Elton, C. (2001). From San Salvador's streets to a study program. *The Christian Science Monitor*. April 19:7.

Empey, L. (1967). Delinquency theory and recent research. *Journal of Research in Crime and Delinquency*, 4:28-42.

English, T.J. (1995). *Born to kill: America's most notorious Vietnamese gang, and the changing face of organized crime*. New York: William Morrow.

Erickson, M.L., & Jensen, G.F. (1977). Delinquency is still group behavior! Toward revitalizing the group premise in the sociology of deviance. *Journal of Criminal Law and Criminology*, 68:262-273.

Erlanger, H.S. (1979). Estrangement, machismo, and gang violence. *Social Science Quarterly*, 60:235-248.

Erlich, R. (2001). Jamaican gangs give peace a chance. *The Christian Science Monitor*. April 9:8.

Esbensen, F-A., Deschenes, E.P., & Winfree, L.T. Jr. (1999). Differences between gang girls and gang boys: Results from a multi-site survey. *Youth and Society*, 31: (1) 27-53.

Esbensen, F-A., & Huizinga, D. (1993). Gangs, drugs, and delinquency in a survey of urban youth. *Criminology*, 31:565-589.

Esbensen, F-A., Huizinga, D., & Weiher, A.W. (1993). Gang and non-gang youth: Differences in explanatory factors. *Journal of Contemporary Criminal Justice*, 9:(2) 94-116.

Esbensen, F-A., Peterson, D., Freng, A., & Taylor, T.J. (2002). Initiation of drug use, drug sales, and violent offending among a sample of gang and non-gang youth. In C.R. Huff (Ed.), *Gangs in America III*. Newbury Park, CA: Sage.

Esbensen, F-A., & Winfree, L.T., Jr. (1998). Race and gender differences between gang and non-gang youth: Results from a multi-site survey. *Justice Quarterly*, 15:(4) 505-526.

Esterle-Hedibel, M. (2001). Youth gangs in France: A socio-ethnographic approach. In M.W. Klein et al. (Eds.), *The eurogang paradox: Street gangs and youth groups in the U.S. and Europe*. Dordrecht: Kluwer Academic Pubs.

Etter, G. W. (1999). Skinheads: Manifestations of the warrior culture of the new urban tribes. *Journal of Gang Research*, 6:(3) 9-21.

Fagan, J. (1989). The social organization of drug use and drug dealing among urban gangs. *Criminology,* 24:439-471.

Fagan, J. (1990). Social processes of delinquency and drug use among urban gangs. In C.R. Huff (Ed.), *Gangs in America.* Newbury Park, CA: Sage.

Fain, A.P. (1990). Specific features of informal youth associations in large cities. *Soviet Sociology,* 29:19-42.

Fairclough, G. (1993). Traveller's tales–Bangkok's night-riders: Tryst with destiny. *Far Eastern Economic Review,* 156:(38) 36-37.

Far Eastern Economic Review. (1989). Chinese crime pays. *Far Eastern Economic Review,* January 12, 143:30.

Fasilo, R., & Leckie, S. (1993). *Canadian media coverage of gangs: A content analysis.* Ottawa, Canada: Solicitor General of Canada.

Fecci, J. (1997). Africa's gang-bangers. *Soldier of Fortune,* 22:(11) 44-47, 69-70.

Feldman, H.W., Mandel, J., & Fields, A. (1985). In the neighborhood: A strategy for delivering early intervention services to young drug users in their natural environments. In A. Friedman & G. Beschner (Eds.), *Treatment services for adolescent substance users.* Rockville, MD: National Institute of Drug Abuse.

Ferracuti, F., Dinitz, S. & de Brenes, A. (1975). *Delinquents and nondelinquents in the Puerto Rican slum culture.* Columbus, OH: Ohio State University Press.

Fexia, C. (1995). Urban tribes and the Chavos gang: Juvenile cultures in Catalonia and Mexico. *Nueva Anthropoligia,* 14: (47) 71-93.

Fischer, C. (1975). Toward a subcultural theory of urbanism. *American Journal of Sociology,* 80:1319-1330.

Fleisher, M.S. (1998). *Dead end kids: Gang girls and the boys they know.* Madison, WI: University of Wisconsin Press.

Fleisher, M.S. (2002). Doing field research on diverse gangs: Interpreting youth gangs as social networks. In C.R. Huff (Ed.), *Gangs in America III.* Newbury Park, CA: Sage.

Fong, R.S., Vogel, R.E., & Buentello, S. (1996). Prison gang dynamics: A research update. In J.M. Miller & J.P. Rush (Eds.), *Gangs: A criminal justice approach.* Cincinnati, OH: Anderson.

Francia, L. (1991). The dusty realm of Bagong barrio. In R. Rosen & P. McSharry (Eds.), *Street Gangs: Gaining Turf, Losing Ground.* New York: The Rosen Publishing Group.

Friedman, C.J., Mann, F., & Adelman, H. (1976). Juvenile street gangs: The victimization of youth. *Adolescence,* 11:527-533.

Fritz, M. (1992). Eye for an eye: Turkish community simmers after killings. *The Associated Press,* November 25.

Fyvel, T.R. (1961). *The insecure offenders.* Harmondsworth, England: Penguin.

Gallagher, J.P. (1992). As law enforcement crumbles, Russian crime, gangs proliferate. *Chicago Tribune.* September 2: Section 1:6.

Gambetta, D. (1993). *The Sicilian Mafia: The business of private protection.* Cambridge, MA: Harvard University Press.

Garvin, G. (2000). Salvadoran cops go into the mean streets to fight lawlessness. *The San Diego Union-Tribune.* May 6:2S-3.

Gay, B.W. & Marquart, J.W. (1993). Jamaican posses: A new form of organized crime. *Journal of Crime and Justice*, 16:(2) 139-170.

Gillis, J. (1974). *Youth and History*. London: Academic Press.

Giordano, P.C. (1978). Girls, guys, and gangs: The changing context of female delinquency. *Journal of Criminal Law and Criminology*, 69:126-132.

Giordano, P.C., Cernkovich, S.A., & Pugh, M.D. (1986). Friendships and delinquency. *American Journal of Sociology*, 91:1170-1202.

Glaser, C. (1988). Students, Tsotsis and the Congress Youth League Organization on the Rand in the 1940s and 1950s. *Perspectives in Education*, 10:(2) 1-15.

Glaser, C. (1992). The mark of Zorro: Sexuality and gender relations in the Tsotsi subculture on the Witwaterstrand. *African Studies*, 51:47-67.

Glaser, C. (1994). *Youth culture and politics in Soweto*, 1958-1976. Ph.D. Dissertation, Cambridge University.

Glaser, C. (1998a). Swines, Hazels and the Dirty Dozen: Masculinity, territoriality and the youth gangs of Soweto, 1960-1976. *Journal of Southern African Studies*. 24:(4) 719-736.

Glaser, C. (1998b). We must infiltrate the Tsotsis': School politics and youth gangs in Soweto, 1968-1976. *Journal of Southern African Studies*, 24:(2) 301-323.

Glaser, C. (2000). *Bo-Tsotsi–The youth gangs of Soweto*, 1935-1976. Portmouth, NH: Henneman.

Glionna, J.M. (1993). Pals in the posse: Teen culture has seized the word as a hip name for groups; Not all harmless. *The Los Angeles Times*, February 26:B-3.

Goddard, M. (1992). Bigman, thief: The social organization of gangs in Port Moresby. *Canberra Anthropology*, 15:20-34.

Goddard, M. (1995). The rascal road: crime, prestige, and development in Papua New Guinea. *The Contemporary Pacific Review*, 7: 55-80.

Goldworthy, T. (1998). Triad activity in Australia. *Lawnet Journal.* January 7.

Goldstein, A.P., & Glick, B., Carthan, W., & Blancero, D.A. (1994). *The prosocial gang: Implementing aggression replacement training*. Thousand Oaks, CA: Sage.

Gordon, R.M. (1998) Street gangs and criminal business organizations: A Canadian perspective. In K. Hazlehurst & C. Hazlehurst (Eds.), *Gangs and youth subcultures: International explorations*. New Brunswick, NJ: Transaction.

Gordon, R.M. (2000). Criminal business organizations, street gangs and 'wanna be' groups: A Vancouver perspective. *Canadian Journal of Criminology*, 42:(1) 39-60.

Gordon, S. (2002a). Bossing mom's big boy: Gregory Wooley made it to the top. *Montreal Gazette*, April 1:A6.

Gordon, S. (2002b). Street gangs push boundaries: "Home turf" no longer applies as groups seek to expand throughout city, cops say. *Montreal Gazette*, April 8:A1.

Grennan, S., Britz, M.T., Rush, J., & Barker, T. (2000). *Gangs: An international approach.* Upper Saddle River, NJ: Prentice Hall.

Gruter, P., & Versteegh, P. (2001). Toward a problem-oriented approach to youth groups in The Hague. In M.W. Klein et al. (Eds.). *The eurogang paradox: Street gangs and youth groups in the U.S. and Europe*. Dordrecht: Kluwer Academic Pubs.

Gunst, L. (1989). Johnny-too-bad and the sufferers. *Nation*, 249 (16):549, 567-569.

Gunst, L. (1995). *Born Fi' Dead: A journey through the Jamaican posse underworld.* New York: Henry Holt.

Haberfield, I. (2000). Gangstas in paradise—fear of street warfare. *Sunday Mail*, February 13:4.

Hagedorn, J.M. (2002). Gangs and the informal economy. In C.R. Huff (Ed.), *Gangs in America III*. Newbury Park, CA: Sage.

Hagedorn, J.M., with Macon, P. (1988). *People and folks.* Chicago: Lake View Press.

Hamm, M.S. (1993). *American skinheads.* Westbrook, CT: Greenwood.

Hanawalt, B. (1979). *Crime and conflict in English communities*, 1300-1348. Cambridge, MA: Harvard University Press.

Hanson, K. (1964). *Rebels in the streets: The story of New York's girl gangs.* Englewood Cliffs, NJ: Prentice-Hall.

Hardman, D.G. (1967). Historical perspectives on gang research. *Journal of Research in Crime and Delinquency*, 4:5-27.

Hardman, D.G. (1969). Small town gangs. *Journal of Criminal Law, Criminology, and Police Science*, 60:173-181.

Harris, B. (1988). The rise of rascalism: Action and reaction in the evolution of rascal gangs (Discussion Paper No. 24). Port Moresby, Papua New Guinea: Institute of Applied Social and Economic Research.

Harris, M.G. (1988). *Cholas: Latino girls and gangs.* New York: AMS Press.

Harris, M.G. (1994). Cholas: Mexican-American girls, and gangs. *Sex Roles*, 30: 289-301.

Hawthorne, P. (2000). Cops and bombers: South Africa's Cape Town struggles to cope with crime among would-be self protection groups. *Time Europe*, February 7:155.

Hazani, M. (1989). The *charaka* complex: Maturation out of delinquency in an Israeli slum. *Journal of Contemporary Ethnography*. 18:(3) 243-270.

Hazlehurst, K., & Hazlehurst, C. (Eds.). (1998). *Gangs and youth subcultures: International explorations.* New Brunswick, NJ: Transaction.

Healey, S. (2000). *Finding social control in the Western Cape: The role of gangs in a current context.* Cape Town South Africa: Institute of Criminology, University of Cape Town.

Hebdige, D. (1976). The meaning of Mod. In S. Hall & T. Jefferson (Eds.), *Resistance through rituals: Youth subcultures in post-war Britain.* New York: Holmes and Meier.

Hebdige, D. (1979). Subculture, *The meaning of style.* London: Methune.

Hedges, C. (1999). In Kosovo, gangs dim the luster of a 'Greater Albania.' *New York Times*, August 8:10.

Heller, C. (1966). *Mexican American youth: Forgotten youth at the crossroads.* New York: Random House.

Henley, J. (2000). Monkeys: The new weapon of Paris gangs. *The Manchester Guardian*, September 27:1.16.

Henley, J. (2001). Youths pick chic Paris mall for gang rumble. *The Manchester Guardian*, January 29:1.13.

Hill, M. (1996). Liberia: A nation fighting itself. *Baltimore Sun*, April 14:1A+.

Hood, R., & Sparks, R. (1970). *Key issues in criminology.* New York: McGraw-Hill.

Hopkins, N. (2000). Drugs turfwar is linked to Telford hangings. *The Guardian*, April 28: 1.1.

Horowitz, R. (1982). Adult delinquent gangs in a Chicano community: Masked intimacy and marginality. *Urban Life*, 11:3-26.

Horowitz, R. (1986). Remaining an outsider: Membership as a threat to research rapport. *Urban Life*, 14:409-430.

Horowitz, R. (1990). Sociological perspectives on gangs. In C.R. Huff (Ed.), *Gangs in America*. Newbury Park, CA: Sage.

Horowitz, R., & Schwartz, G. (1974). Honor, normative ambiguity, and gang violence. *American Sociological Review*. 39:238-251.

Horvath, J. (1997). Skinheads in eastern and central Europe. *Telepolis*, 19:(6) 1-4.

Hotyst, B. (1982). *Comparative criminology*. Lexington, MA: Lexington Books.

Houston, J., & Prinsloo, J. (1998). Prison gangs in South Africa: A comparative analysis. *Journal of Gang Research*, 5:41-52.

Howell, J.C., Moore, J.P., & Egley, A. Jr. (2002). The changing boundaries of youth gangs. In C.R. Huff (ed.). *Gangs in America III*. Newbury Park, CA: Sage.

Huff, C.R. (1989). Youth gangs and public policy. *Crime and Delinquency*, 35:524-537.

Huff, C.R. (Ed.). (2002). *Gangs in America III*. Newbury Park, CA: Sage.

Hufford, D. (2001). Personal correspondence with author.

Huizinga, D., & Schumann, K. F. (2001). Gang membership in Bremen and Denver: Comparative longitudinal data. In M.W. Klein et al. (Eds.), *The eurogang paradox: Street gangs and youth groups in the U.S. and Europe*. Dordrecht: Kluwer Academic Pubs.

Humphries, S. (1981). *Hooligans or rebels? An oral history of working class childhood and youth, 1889-1939*. Oxford: Basil Blackwell.

Inciardi, J.A., & Surratt, H.L. (1998). Children in the streets of Brazil: Drug use, crime, violence, and HIV risks. *Substance Use and Misuse*, 33:(7) 1461-1480.

Jackson, P.G. (1989). Theories and findings about youth gangs. *Criminal Justice Abstracts*, 21:(2) 313-329.

Jakarta Post. (2001). Police shoot dead two "Red Axe" members. *The Jakarta Post*, January 29.

Janeksela, G.M. (1992). The significance of comparative analysis of juvenile delinquency and juvenile justice. *International Journal of Comparative and Applied Criminal Justice*, 16:(2) 137-150.

Janeksela, G. M., Farington, D. P., Hatch, A. et al. (1992). Special issue: Comparative juvenile delinquency. *International Journal of Comparative and Applied Criminal Justice*, 16:(2) 137-261.

Jankowski, M.S. (1991). *Islands in the street: Gangs and American urban society*. Berkeley: University of California Press.

Janssen, B. (1986). Pickpockets in Paris: Gypsy children. *Maclean's*, December 8, 99:70-71.

Jansyn, L., Jr. (1966). Solidarity and delinquency in a street corner group. *American Sociological Review*. 31:600-614.

Jefferson, T. (1976). Cultural responses of the Teds. In S. Hall & T. Jefferson (Eds.), *Resistance through rituals: Youth subcultures in post-war Britain*. New York: Holmes and Meier.

Jefferies, S. (2000). France horrified by rise of the teenage killers: Turf wars and macho culture increase in violent crime by juveniles. *The Manchester Guardian*, December 13: 1.15.

Jefferies, S. (2001). Gunshop opens near scene of shooting: Protesters fear for children of estate plagued by gangs. *The Manchester Guardian*, January 15:1.13.

Joe, D., & Robinson, N. (1980. Chinatown's immigrant gangs: The new young warrior class. *Criminology*, 18:337-345.

Joe, K.A. (1994). The new criminal conspiracy? Asian gangs and organized crime in San Francisco. *Journal of Research in Crime and Delinquency*, 31:390-415.

Johnson, C., Webster, B. & Connors, E. (1995). *Prosecuting gangs: A national assessment.* Washington, D.C. National Institute of Justice.

Johnson, D. (1997). Police turning to deportation: Law used to fight ethnic-gang crime. *The Gazette*, December 6:A3.

Johnstone, J.W.C. (1981). Youth gangs and black suburbs. *Pacific Sociological Review*, 24:355-375.

Johnstone, J.W.C. (1983). Recruitment to a youth gang. *Youth and Society*, 14: 281-300.

Jones, L. (2000). LA's deportees send crime rate soaring in El Salvador. *The Guardian Weekly*, March 2.

Joseph, J. (1999). Jamaican posses and transnational crimes. *Journal of Gang Research*, 6: 41-47.

Jungk, R. (1959). *Children of the ashes.* New York: Harcourt, Brace, and World.

Kaiser, G. (1983). Federal Republic of Germany. In E.H. Johnson (Ed.), *International Handbook of Contemporary Developments in Criminology: Europe, Africa, the Middle East, and Asia.* Westport, CT: Greenwood Press.

Kang, G.E., & Kang, T.S. (1978). The Korean urban shoeshine gang: A minority community. *Urban Anthropology*, 7:171-183.

Kanji, W. (1996). *Review of urbanization issues affecting children and women in the eastern and southern African region.* Nairobi, Kenya: UNICEF Eastern and Southern Region.

Kattoulas, V. (2001). Young, fast and deadly. *Far Eastern Economic Review*, 164:(4) 64-67.

Keiser, R. (1958). *The Vice Lords: Warriors of the streets.* New York: Holt, Rinehart and Winston.

Kennedy, L., & Baron, S. W. (1993). Routine activities and a subculture of violence: A study of violence on the street. *Journal of Research in Crime and Delinquency*, 30:(1) 88-112.

Kersten, J. (1993). Street youths, *bosozoku*, and *yakuza*: Subculture formation and social reactions in Japan. *Crime and Delinquency*, 39:(3) 277-295.

Kersten, J. (1998). German youth subcultures: History, typology and gender-orientations. In K. Hazlehurst & C. Hazlehurst (Eds.), *Gangs and youth subcultures: International explorations.* New Brunswick, NJ: Transaction.

Kersten, J. 2001. Groups of violent young males in Germany. In M.W. Klein et al., *The eurogang paradox: Street gangs and youth groups in the U.S. and Europe.* Dordrecht: Kluwer Academic Pubs.

Kin, C. C. (1999). Modern gangs prone to violence. *The Straits Times*, January 29:62.

Kinnear, K.L. (1996). *Gangs: A reference handbook.* Santa Barbara, CA: ABC-CLIO.

Kinsella, W. (1994). *Web of hate: Inside Canada's far right network.* Toronto: Harper and Collins.

Klein, M.W. (1968). Impressions of juvenile gang members. *Adolescence,* 3:53-78.

Klein, M.W. (1971). *Street gangs and street workers.* Englewood Cliffs, NJ: Prentice Hall.

Klein, M.W. (1995a). *The American street gang.* New York: Oxford University Press.

Klein, M.W. (1995b). Street gang cycles. In J.Q. Wilson & J. Petersilia (Eds.), *Crime.* San Francisco: Institute for Contemporary Studies.

Klein, M.W. (1996). Gangs in the United States and Europe. *European Journal on Criminal Policy and Research,* 4:(2) 63-80.

Klein, M.W. (2001). Gangs in the United States and Europe. In J. Miller, C.L. Maxson, & M.W. Klein (Eds.), *The Modern Gang Reader.* Los Angeles: Roxbury.

Klein, M.W. (2002). Street gangs: A cross-national perspective. In C.R. Huff (Ed.), *Gangs in America III.* Newbury Park, CA: Sage.

Klein, M.W., & Crawford, L.Y. (1967). Groups, gangs, and cohesiveness. *Journal of Research in Crime and Delinquency,* 4:63-75.

Klein, M.W., & Maxson, C.L. (1985). "Rock" sales in south Los Angeles. *Sociology and Social Research,* 69:561-565.

Klein, M.W. & Maxson, C.L. (1989). Street gang violence. In N.A. Weiner & M.E. Wolfgang (Eds.). *Violent Crimes, Violent Criminals.* Newbury Park, CA: Sage.

Klein, M.W., Maxson, C.L., & Cunningham, L. C. (1991). "Crack," street gangs, and violence. *Criminology,* 29:623-650.

Klein, M.W., Maxson, C.L., & Miller, J. (eds.). (1995). *The modern gang reader.* Los Angeles: Roxbury.

Klein, M.W., Kerner, H., Maxson, C.L., & Weitekamp, E.G.M. (Eds.). (2001). *The eurogang paradox: Street gangs and youth groups in the U.S. and Europe.* Dordrecht, Germany: Kluwer Academic Pubs.

Kleiner, R.J., Stub, H.R., & Lanahan, J. (1975). A study of black youth groups: Implications for research, action, and the role of the investigator. *Human Organization,* 34:391-394.

Knight, N. (1982). *Skinhead.* London: Omnibus Press.

Knox, G. (1993). *An introduction to gangs.* Berrien Springs, MI: Vande Vere.

Kornhauser, R.R. (1978). *Social sources of delinquency.* Chicago: University of Chicago Press.

Kroeker, M., & Haut, F. (1995). A tale of two cities: The street gangs of Paris and Los Angeles. *The Police Chief,* 62:(5) 32, 34-35, 44-46.

Kulick, D. (1993). Heroes from hell: Representations of "rascals" in a Papua New Guinea village. *Anthropology Today,* 9:9-14.

Kynoch, G. (1999). From the Ninevites to the Hard Livings gang: Township gangsters and urban violence in twentieth-century South Africa. *African Studies,* 58:(1) 55-85.

Kynoch, G. (2000). Marashea on the mines: Economic, social and criminal networks on the South African gold fields, 1947-1999. *Journal of Southern African Studies,* 26:(1) 79-103.

Kuo, Y. (1973). Identity-diffusion and tai-pau gang delinquency in Taiwan. *Adolescence,* 8:165-170.

LASD (1995). L.A. style: A street gang manual of the Los Angeles County Sheriff's Department, In M.W. Klein, C. L. Maxson, & J. Miller (Eds.), *Modern gang reader.* Los Angeles: University of Southern California Press.

La grée. J.C., & Fai, P.L. (1987). Girls in street gangs in the suburbs of Paris. In V. Maquieira, J.C. La grée, P.L. Fai, & M. de Wool (Eds.), *Teenage lifestyles and criminality in Spain, France and Holland.* San Domenico, Spain: European University Institute.

Labov, T. (1982). Social structure and peer terminology in a black adolescent gang. *Language in Society*, 2:391-411.

Lafont, H. (1982). Youth gangs Les bandes de jeunes. *Communications*, 35:147-158.

La Fontaine, J.S. (1970). Two types of youth group in Kinshasa (Leopoldville). In P, Meyer (Ed.), *Socialization: The approach from social anthropology.* London: Tavistock Publications.

LaFranchi, H. (1996). Latest US export: Youth gang culture to Central America. *The Christian Science Monitor*, November 5:1.

Lamm, Z. (1993). Life in a Brazilian slum. *Swiss Review of World Affairs*, December: 13-15.

Lawrence, D. A. (1998). Trading bullets for soccer balls. *Latin America Press*, March 26, 1:1.

Le Blanc, M., & Lanctôt, N. (1994). Adolescent gang members social and psychological characteristics, gang participation: A selection or activation process? Paper presented at the Annual Meeting of the American Society of Criminology, Miami, November 1994.

Ledochowski, C. (1991). The skollie gangs. In R. Rosen & P. McSharry (Eds.), *Street gangs: Gaining turf, losing ground.* New York: The Rosen Publishing Group.

Lee, F.W.L., Loi, T.W. & Wong, D.S.W. (1996). Intervention in the decision-making of youth gangs. *Groupwork*, 9:(3) 292-302.

Leo, J, Casey M., & Woodbury, R. (1998). Parasites on their own people: Gangs are tougher, better armed, and more violent than ever. *Time*, July 8, 126:76.

Lerman, P. (1967). Gangs, networks, and subcultural delinquency. *American Journal of Sociology*, 73:63.72.

Levin, J., & McDevitt, J. (1993). *Hate crimes: The rising tide of bigotry and bloodshed.* New York: Plenum Press.

Lien, I. (2001). The concept of honor, conflict and violent behavior among youths of Oslo. In M.W. Klein et al. (Eds.), *The eurogang paradox: Street gangs and youth groups in the U.S. and Europe.* Dordrecht, Germany: Kluwer Academic Pubs.

Likhanov, D. (1991). Dirt: From Kazan to Tashkent. In R. Rosen & P. McSharry (Eds.), *Street gangs: Gaining turf, losing ground.* New York: The Rosen Publishing Group.

Lo, T.W. (1984). *Gang dynamics.* Hong Kong, China: Caritas Outreach Services.

Lo, T.W. (1992). Groupwork with youth gangs in Hong Kong. *Groupwork*, 5:(1) 58-71.

Lo, T.W. (1993). Neutralization of group control in youth gangs. *Groupwork*, 6:(1) 51-63.

Loeb, R. (1973). Adolescent groups. *Sociology and Social Research*, 58:13-22.

Loftus, R.P. (1977). The idioms of Japan XVII. *Japan Interpreter*, 11:384-394.

Lorch, D. (1995). Burundi's ethnic divide widens, feeding fear of greater violence. *New York Times* (Late New York Edition), April 2:1.

Louwage, F.E. (1951). Delinquency in Europe after World War II. *Journal of Criminal Law, Criminology, and Police Science*, 42:53-56.

Maguire, S. (1999). Trouble on track as street gangs target the DART. *The People*, April 4:6.

Mahabir, C. (1988). Crime in the Caribbean: Robbers, hustlers, and warriors. *International Journal of the Sociology of Law*, 16:315-338.

Main, J. (1991). The truth about triads. *Policing*, 7:(2) 144-163.

Maltz, M. (1985). Toward defining organized crime. In H. Alexander & G. Caiden (Eds.), *The politics and economics of organized crime*. Lexington, MA: Lexington Books.

Marcial, R. (1998). Young, graffiti, voice: Youth urban identities a round the graffiti expressions in Guadalajara (Mexico). *SocAbstracts*, Accession Number 98s37655.

Mares, D. (2001). Gangstas or lager louts? Working class street gangs in Manchester. In M.W. Klein et al. (Eds.), *The eurogang paradox: Street gangs and youth groups in the U.S. and Europe*. Dordrecht, Germany: Kluwer Academic Pubs.

Margulis, M., & Urresti, M. (1998). Buenos Aires and youth: The urban tribes. *Estudios Sociolgicos*, 16:(46) 25-35.

Marks, J. (1992). For Germany's Turks, an ugly worry. *U.S. News and World Report*, December, 113:718.

Matheron, M.S. (1988). China: Chinese triads, the Oriental mafia. *CJ International*, 4:(3) 3, 4, 26-27.

Masland, T. (2002). We beat and killed people. *Newsweek*, May 13:24-29.

Maxson, C.L., & Klein, M.W. (1994). Investigating gang structures. Paper presented at the Annual Meeting American Society of Criminology, Miami, 1994.

Maxson, C., & Whitlock, M. (2002). Joining the gang: Gender differences in risk factors for gang membership. In C.R. Huff (Ed.), *Gangs in America III*. Newbury Park, CA: Sage.

Mayo, P. (1969). *The making of a criminal: A comparative study of two delinquency areas*. London: Weidenfeld and Nicolson.

McCall, A. (1979). *The medieval underworld*. London: Hamish Hamilton.

McCree, R.D. (1998). Violence: A preliminary look at gangs in Trinidad and Tobago. *Caribbean Journal of Criminology and Social Psychology*, 3:155-173.

McDougall, C. (1994). What Lisbon's young gangs up to? *The Associated Press*, January 25.

McDowell, R. (1995). Returning California gang members hit Phnom Penh streets. *International News*, Deutsche Presse-Agentur, September 9.

McKinnley, J. C. Jr. (1996). Stoked by Rwandans, tribal violence spreads in Zaire. *New York Times* (Late New York Edition), June 16:3.

McKinnley, J. C. Jr. (1997). Ethnic strife in Kenya derails talks on reform. *New York Times* (Late New York Edition), August 21:A3.

Merton, R.K. (1957). *Social Theory and Social Structure*. New York: Free Press.

Mieczkowski, T. (1986). Geeking up and throwing down: Heroin street life in Detroit. *Criminology*, 24:645-666.

Miller-Matthei, L.M. & Smith, D.A. (1998). Belizean "Boyz'n the Hood:" Garifuna labor migration and transnational identity. *Comparative Urban and Community Research*, 6:270-290.

Miller, W.B. (1962). The impact of a "total community" delinquency control project. *Social Problems*, 10:168-191.

Miller, W.B. (1973). Race, sex, and gangs: The Molls. *Society*, 11:(1) 32-35.

Miller, W.B. (1974). American youth gangs: Past and present. In A.S. Blumberg (Ed.), *Current Perspectives on Criminal Behavior*. New York: Knopf.

Miller, W.B. (1975). *Violence by Youth Gangs and Youth Groups as a Crime Problem in Major American Cities*. Washington, D.C. US Govt. Printing Office.

Miller, W.B. (1977). Rumble this time. *Psychology Today*, 10 (2):52-88.

Miller, W.B. (1980). Gangs, groups, and serious youth crime. In D. Shichor & D. Kelly (Eds.), *Critical issues in juvenile delinquency*. Lexington, MA: Lexington Books.

Miller, W.B. (1981). American youth gangs: Past and present. In A.S. Blumberg (Ed.), *Current perspectives on criminal behavior*. New York: Knopf.

Miller, W.B. (1982). *Crime by youth gangs and youth groups in the United States*. Washington, D.C.: Department of Justice, OJJDP.

Mirande, A., & López, J. (1992). Chicano urban youth gangs: A critical analysis of a social problem? *Latino Studies Journal*, 3:(3) 15-28.

Mojica, C. (2001). Going the cooperative way. *The UNESCO Courier*, February, 2:1-7.

Monsod, J. (1967). Juvenile gangs in Paris: Toward a structural analysis. *Journal of Research in Crime and Delinquency*, 4:142-165.

Montgomery, M. (1997). The powerlessness of punishment: Angry pride and delinquent identity. *Reclaiming Children and Youth–Journal of Emotional and Behavioral Problems*, 6:(3) 162-166.

Mooney, K. (1998). Ducktail: Flick-knives and pugnacity: Subcultural and hegemonic masculinities in South Africa, 1948-1960. *Journal of Southern African Studies*, 24:(4) 753-774.

Moore, D. (1994). *The lads in action: Social process in an urban youth subculture*. Hants, England: Ashgate.

Moore, J. B. (1993). *Skinheads shaved for battle: A cultural history of american skinheads*. Bowling Green, OH: Bowling Green State University Popular Press.

Moore, J. (1978). *Homeboys*. Philadelphia: Temple University Press.

Moore, J.W. (1991). *Going down to the barrio: Homeboys and homegirls in change*. Philadelphia: Temple University Press.

Moore, J.W. (1993). Gangs, drugs, and violence. In S. Cummings & D.J. Monti (Eds.), *Gangs: The origins and impact of contemporary youth gangs in the United States*. Albany, NY: University of New York Press.

Moore, J.W., & Hagedorn, J.M. (2001). *Female gangs: A focus on research (Juvenile Justice Bulletin, Youth Gang Services, NCJ No. 186159)*. Washington, DC: U.S. Department of Justice, Office of Juvenile Justice and Delinquency Prevention.

Moore, J., Vigil, D. & Garcia, R. (1983). Residence and territoriality in Chicano gangs. *Social Problems*, 31:182-194.

Moorehead, C. (1990). Fighting for life in the streets: If they manage to find food they still face the terror of police death squads. *The Independent (London)*, November 28:22.

Morales, A. (1992). A clinical model for the prevention of gang violence and homicide. In R.C. Cervantes (Ed.), *Substance abuse and gang violence*. Newbury Park, CA: Sage.

Morash, M. (1983). Gangs, groups, and delinquency. *British Journal of Criminology*, 23:309-331.

Morganthau, T. (1982). Vietnamese gangs in California. *Newsweek*, 100:22.

Morris, S. (2002). Damilola verdict: Hard boys drifting into a life of crime; The accused gang members were known to police. *The Guardian*, April 26:4.

Munoz, I. (1996). Juvenile drug trafficking in El Salvador: Is there an American gang connection? Paper presented at the annual meeting of the Western Society of Criminology, Rohnert Park, California.

Murphy, S. (1978). A year with the gangs of East Los Angeles. *Ms*, 7:(1) 56-64.

Mydans, S. (1990). Life in a girls' gang. Colors and bloody. *New York Times*, January, 29:1,12.

Neuman, W.L., & Berger, R.L. (1988). Competing perspectives on cross-national crime: An evaluation of theory and evidence. *The Sociological Quarterly*, 29:(2) 281-313.

Neuman, W. L. & Berger, R.L. (1997). Competing perspectives on cross-national crime: An evaluation of theory and evidence. In P. Beirne & D. Nelken (Eds.), *Issues in Comparative Criminology*. Aldershot, England: Dartmouth.

New Pittsburgh Courier. (1999). This isn't New York or Los Angeles . . . it's South Africa. *New Pittsburgh Courier*, 90:(27) A2.

Nibbrig, N. & Nibbrig, E.H. (1992). Rascals in paradise: Urban gangs in Papua New Guinea. *Pacific Studies*, 15:(3) 115-134.

Nozina, M. (n.d.). Vietnamese organized crime in the Czech Republic. Prague, Czech Republic: Institute of International Relations.

O'Hagan, F.J. (1976). Gang characteristics: An empirical survey. *Journal of Child Psychology and Psychiatry*, 17:305-314.

Omel'chenko, E. (1996). Young women in provincial gang culture: A case study of Ul'ianovsk. In H. Pilkington (Ed.), *Gender, generation, and identity in contemporary Russia*. London: Routledge.

Operation Safe Streets. (1995). L.A. style: A street gang manual of the Los Angeles County Sheriff's Department. In M.W. Klein et al. (Eds.), *The modern gang reader*. Los Angeles: Roxbury.

Padilla, F. (1992). *The gang as an American enterprise*. New Brunswick, NJ: Rutgers University Press.

Padilla, F. (1995). The working gang. In M.W. Klein, C.L. Maxson, & J. Miller. (Eds.), *The Modern Gang Reader*. Los Angeles: Roxbury.

Parker, H. 1974. *View from the boys*. London: Newton Abbot.

Parks, C.P. (1995). Gang behavior in the schools: Reality or myth? *Educational Psychology Review*, 7:(1) 41-68.

Parliamentary Joint Committee on the National Crime Authority. (1995). *Vietnamese Organized Crime in Australia.* Discussion Paper Sydney, Australia: Parliamentary Joint Committee on the National Crime Authority.

Parsons, T. (1977). *The evolution of societies.* Englewood Cliffs, NJ: Prentice-Hall.

Patrick, J. (1973). *A Glasgow gang observed.* London: Eyre Methuen.

Paz, O. (1961. *The labyrinth of solitude: Life and thought in Mexico.* New York: Grove Press.

Pearson, G. (1983). *Hooligan: A history of reportable fears.* New York: Schocken.

Perkins, U.E. (1987). *Explosion of Chicago's black street gangs 1900 to present.* Chicago: Third World Press.

Pfautz, H.W. (1961). Near-group theory and collective behavior: A critical reformulation. *Social Problems,* 9:167-174.

Philippine Daily Inquirer. (2002). Youth's killing prompts drive vs. street gangs. *Philippine Daily Inquirer,* April 28:25.

Pilkington, H. (1994). *Russia's youth and its culture: A nation's constructors and constructed.* London: Routledge.

Pilkington, H. (Ed.). (1996). *Gender, generation, and identity in contemporary Russia.* London: Routledge.

Pilkington, H. (1996a). Youth culture in contemporary Russia: Gender, consumption and identity. In H. Pilkington (Ed.), Gender, Generation, and Identity in Contemporary Russia. London: Routledge.

Pilkington, H. (1996b). Farewell to the Tusovka: Masculinities and feminities on the Moscow youth scene. In H. Pilkington (Ed.), *Gender, generation, and identity in contemporary Russia.* London: Routledge.

Pinnock, D. (1985). Breaking the web: Gangs and family structure in Cape Town. In D. Davis & M. Slabbert (Eds.), *Crime and power in South Africa Cape Town.* Cape Town, South Africa: David Philip.

Pinnock, D. (1995). Suffer the little children. *Democracy in Action,* 8-9.

Pinnock, D., & Douglas-Hamilton, M. (1997). *Gangs, rituals and rites of passage.* Cape Town South Africa: African Sun Press with the Institute of Criminology, University of Cape Town.

Pinnock, D., & Douglas-Hamilton, M. (1998). In K. Hazlehurst & C. Hazlehurst (Eds.), *Gangs and youth subcultures: International explorations.* New Brunswick, NJ: Transaction.

Pitman, T. (2001). Brazen Nigerian robbers tell victims they're coming. *The Denver Post,* July 13:2A, 24A.

Porché-Burke, L., & Fulton, C. (1992). The impact of gang violence. In R.C. Cervantes, (Ed.), *Substance abuse and gang violence.* Newbury Park, CA: Sage.

Portes, A., Castells, M., & Benton, L.A. (Eds.). (1989). *The informal economy: Studies in advanced and less advanced countries.* Baltimore: Johns Hopkins University Press.

Portugal, I.C., & Urteaga, M. (1998). Mexico: The punk movement and feminine identity. *Chasqui,* 62:17-21.

Posner, G. (1991). Triads. In R. Rosen & P. McSharry (Eds.), *Street gangs: Gaining turf, losing ground.* New York: The Rosen Publishing Group.

Poynting, S., Noble, G. & Tabar, P. (1999). Intersections of masculinity and ethnicity: A study of male Lebanese immigrant youth in western Sydney. *Race, Ethnicity and Education*, 2:(1) 59-77.

Pridemore, W. A. (2002). Social problems and patterns of juvenile delinquency in transitional Russia. *Journal of Research in Crime and Delinquency*, 39:(2) 187-213.

Prothrow-Stith, D. (1991). *Deadly consequences*. New York: Harper Perennial.

Rawlinson, P. (1998). Criminal heirs-organized crime and Russia's youth. In K. Hazlehurst and C. Hazlehurst (Eds.), *Gangs and youth subcultures: International explorations*. New Brunswick, NJ: Transaction.

Reed, B. (1989). Nazi retreat. *New Republic*, April 3, 200:10-11.

Reinhold, R. (1988). In the middle of L.A. gang warfare. *New York Times Magazine*, 5: 2-30.

Rice, B. (1977). The new gangs of Chinatown. *Psychology Today*, 10:60-69.

Rice, R. (1963). A reporter at large: The Persian Queens. *New Yorker*, October 19, 39:153.

Ridgeway, J., & Jean-Pierre, J. (1996). Crime story: The US exports its bad boys back to Haiti. *Village Voice*, 4: (43) 31-34.

Robert, K., & Hermelo, R.G. (1992). Argentina: Where youth is a crime. *Report on the Americas*, 26:(3) 12-15.

Rocha, F. (1991). Razor's edge: Killings continue in Brazil. *New Internationalist*, 226: 1.

Rodriguez, L.J. (1993). *Always running: La vida loca: Gang days in L.A.* Willimantic, CT: Curbstone Press.

Rogerson, C.M. (2000). Emerging from apartheid's shadow: South Africa's informal economy. *Journal of International Affairs*, 53:(2) 673-695.

Rohter, L. (1997). In U.S. deportation policy, A Pandora's box. *The New York Times*, August 10, Section 1:1.

Romero, F. (1991). Children of the streets. *UNESCO Courier*, October, 44:16-18.

Roscoe, P. (1999a). The return of the ambush: 'raskolism' in rural Yangoru, East Sepik province. *Oceania*, 3:171-183.

Roscoe, P. (1999b). War and society in Sepik New Guinea. *Journal of the Royal Anthropological Institute*, 2:(4) 645-666.

Ross, S. (1972). A mug's game. *New Society*, 22:(522) 13-14.

Roth, M. (1997). The emerging yardie problem. *Crime and Justice International*, 16:(45) 5-6.

Roy, P. (1996). Discovering India, imaging Thugee. *The Yale Journal of Criticism*, 9: 121-145.

Salagaev, A. (2001). Evolution of delinquent gangs in Russia. In M.W. Klein et al. (Eds.), *The eurogang paradox: Street gangs and youth groups in the U.S. and Europe*. Dordrecht, Germany: Kluwer Academic Pubs.

Salazar, A. (1992). *Born to die in Medellin*. Nottingham, England: Russell Press.

Salazar, A. (1994). Young assassins of the drug trade. *NACLA Report on the Americas*, 27: (6) 24-28.

Sanchez, R. (1995). Marked for death: In El Salvador, "Shadow" waits for tattooed teens. *Newsday*, July 4:A10.

Sanders, W.B. (1970). *Juvenile offenders for a thousand years: Selected readings from Anglo-Saxon times to 1900.* Chapel Hill, NC: University of North Carolina Press.

Sanders, W.B. (1994). *Gangbangs and drive-bys: Grounded culture and juvenile gang violence.* New York: Aldine De Gruyter.

Sarnecki, J. (1982). *Criminality and peer relations: Study of juvenile delinquency in a Swedish commune.* Stockholm: Brottsforebyggande Radet.

Sarnecki, J. (1986). *Delinquent networks.* Stockholm: National Council for Crime Prevention.

Sarnecki, J., & Pettersson, T. (2001). Criminal networks in Stockholm. In M.W. Klein et al. (Eds.), *The eurogang paradox: Street gangs and youth groups in the U.S. and Europe.* Dordrecht, Germany: Kluwer Academic Pubs.

Sato, I. (1991). *Kamikaze biker: Parody and anomy in affluent Japan.* Chicago: University of Chicago Press.

Save the Children. (1992). *Country report, Brazil.* London: Save the Children.

Schärf, N. (1997). Re-integrating militarized youths (Street gangs and self defense units) into mainstream in South Africa: From hunters to game-keepers. Cape Town, South Africa: Institute of Criminology, University of Cape Town.

Scheper-Hughes, N. (1995). Who's the killer? Popular justice and human rights in a South African squatter camp. *Social Justice,* 22:(3) 143-164.

Scheper-Hughes, N., & Hoffman, D. (1994). *Kids out of place. NACLA Report on the Americas,* 27:(6) 16-23.

Schissel, B. (1997). *Blaming children.* Halifax, Nova Scotia: Fernwood.

Schmitz, S., & Christopher, J.C. (1997). Troubles in Smurftown: Youth gangs and moral visions on Guam. *Child Welfare,* 76:411-428.

Schneider, E.C. (1999). *Vampires, dragons and Egyptian kings: Youth gangs in postwar New York.* Princeton, NJ: Princeton University Press.

Scott, P. (1956). Gangs and delinquent groups in London. *British Journal of Delinquency,* 7:4-21, 25-26.

Sears, E. (1989). Skinheads: A new generation of hate-mongers. *USA Today,* May 1, 117:24-26.

Shabad, S. (1988). Regional report: The Soviet Union–The gangs of Kazan. *World Press Review,* 35:(7) 39.

Shakur, S. (1993). *Monster.* New York: Penguin Books.

Shaw, T.A. (1991). Taiwan: Gangsters or good guys? In M. Freilich, D. Raybeck, & J. Savishinsky (Eds.), *Deviance: Anthropological perspectives.* New York: Bergin and Garvey.

Shelden, R.G., Tracy, S.K., & Brown, W.B. (1997). *Youth gangs in American society.* Belmont, CA: Wadsworth.

Sherer, M. (1990). Criminal activity among Jewish and Arabs youth in Israel. *International Journal of Intercultural Relations,* 14:529-548.

Sheth, H. (1961). *Juvenile delinquency in an Indian setting.* Bombay: Popular Book Depot.

Shigeru, B. (1998). *Yakuza* on the defensive. *Japan Quarterly,* 45:(1) 79-86.

Short, J.F., Jr. (1968). *Gang delinquency and delinquent subcultures.* New York: Harper and Row.

Short, J.F., Jr. (Ed.). (1976a). *Delinquency, crime, and society.* Chicago: University of Chicago Press.

Short, J.F., Jr., (1976b). Gangs, politics, and the social order. In J.F. Short, Jr. (Ed.), *Delinquency, crime, and society.* Chicago: University of Chicago Press.

Short, J.F., Jr., & Strodtbeck, F.L. (1974). *Group process and gang delinquency.* Chicago: University of Chicago Press.

Shorter, A., & Onyancha, E. (1999). *Street children in Africa.* Nairobi, Kenya: Paulines Publications Africa.

Shorter, E. (1977). *The making of the modern family.* New York: Basic Books.

Sidhva, S. (1997). Mafia metropolis. *Far Eastern Economic Review,* November 13, 160: 21, 24, & 28.

Siegel, L.J. (1989). *Criminology.* St. Paul, MN: West.

Singh, I.J. (1969). Subculture in Varanasi City. *Journal of Social Research* (India), 12: (2) 86-91.

Skolnick, J.H, Correl, T., Navarro, E., & Rabb, R. (1990). The social structure of street drug dealing. *American Journal of Police,* 9:1-41.

Shukla, K.S. (1981-82). Adolescent criminal gangs: Structure and functions. *The International Journal of Critical Sociology,* 5:35-49.

Spencer, J.C. (1964). *Stress and release in an urban estate.* London: Tavistock.

Spergel, I. (1964). *Slumtown, racketville, haulburg.* Chicago: University of Chicago Press.

Spergel, I. (1984). Violent gangs in Chicago: In search of social policy. *Social Service Review,* 58:199-226.

Spergel, I. (1986). The violent gang problem in Chicago: A local community approach. *Social Service Review,* 60:94-131.

Spergel, I.A. (1990). Youth gangs: Continuity and change. In N. Morris (Ed.), *Crime and delinquency: An annual review of research, Volume 12.* Chicago: University of Chicago Press.

Spergel, I.A. (1995). *The youth gang problem: A community approach.* New York: Oxford University Press.

Sposito, M.P. (1994). Juvenile sociability and the street: New conflicts and collective action in the city. *Tempo Social: Revista de Sociologia da USP,* 5:(1-2) 161-178.

Srivastava, S.S. (1955). Sociology of juvenile ganging. *Journal of Correctional Work,* 2: 72-81.

Stafford, M. (1984). Gang delinquency. In R.E. Meier (Ed.), *Major forms of crime.* Beverly Hills, CA: Sage.

Stevns, A. (2001). Street gangs and crime prevention in Copenhagen. In M.W. Klein et al. (Eds.), *The eurogang paradox: Street gangs and youth groups in the U.S. and Europe.* Dordrecht, Germany: Kluwer Academic Pubs.

Stites, R. (1992). *Russian popular culture, entertainment and society since 1900.* Cambridge: Cambridge University Press.

Stover, D. (1986). A new breed of youth gang is on the prowl and a bigger threat than ever. *American School Board Journal,* 173:19-21.

Straits Times. (1999). Use rotators as an alert, suggest Jakarta police. *The Straits Times,* January 15:1.

Tacon, P. (1982). Carlinhos: The hard gloss of city polish. *UNICEF News*, 3 (1):4-6.

Takagi, P., & Platt, A. (1978). Behind the gilded ghetto: An analysis of race, class, and crime in Chinatown. *Crime and Social Justice*, 9:2-25.

Tartakovsky, E., & Mirsky, J. (2001). Bullying gangs among immigrant adolescent from the former Soviet Union in Israel. *Journal Interpersonal Violence*, 16:(3) 247-265.

Taylor, I., & Wall, D. (1976). Beyond the skinheads: Comments on the emergence and significance of the slam rock cult. In G. Mungham & G. Pearson (Eds.), *Working Class Youth Culture*. London: Routledge and Kegan Paul.

Teo, G., & Phaun, W. (1997). The "bluff gangsters." *The Strait Times (Singapore)*, July 22:33.Tertilt, H. (1997). Turkish power boys: Toward an interpretation of a violent subculture. *Zeitschrift fur Sozialisationsforschung und Erziehungssoziologie*, 17:(1) 19-29.

Tertilt, H. (2001). Patterns of ethnic violence in a Frankfurt street gang. In M.W. Klein et al. (eds.). *The eurogang paradox: Street gangs and youth groups in the U.S. and Europe*. Dordrecht, Germany: Kluwer Academic Pubs.

Thompson, R. (1984). Adolescent culture in colonial Massachusetts. *Journal of Family History*, 9:863-891.

Thrasher, F. (1927). *The gang*. Chicago: University of Chicago Press.

Tobias, J.J. (1967). *Crime and industrial society in the 19th century*. New York: Schocken Books.

Trussell, R.P. (1999). The children's streets: An ethnographic study of street children in Ciudad Juárez, Mexico. *International Social Work*, 42:189-199.

United Nations. (1999). *Global Profiles on the Situation of Youth: 2000-2025*. New York: United Nations Division of Social Policy and Development.

Urban Management Programme. (2000). *Street children and gangs in African cities*. Narobi, Kenya: Urban Management Programme, United Nations, Centre for Human Settlements.

Vagg, J. (1997). Context and linkage: Reflections on comparative research and internationalism in criminology. In P. Beirne & D. Nelken (Eds.), *Issues in comparative criminology*. Aldershot, England: Dartmouth.

Valenzuela, J.M. (1988). Jalabrava e'sel. Tijuana, Baja California, Mexico: El Colegio de la Frontera Norte.

Van Gemert, F. (2001). Crips in orange: Gangs and groups in the Netherlands. In M.W. Klein et al. (Eds.), *The eurogang paradox: Street gangs and youth groups in the U.S. and Europe*. Dordrecht, Germany: Kluwer Academic Pubs.

Van Wolferen, K. (1989). *The enigma of Japanese power: People and politics in a stateless nation*. New York: Alfred A. Knopf.

Vasagar, J., & Hopkins, N. (2000). Yardie war moves to the streets: Police condemn 'unprecedented' escalation in violence as gunman shoots eight outside South London night club. *The Guardian*, August 1:1.3.

Vasagar, J., Ward, D., Etim, A., & Keating, M. (2001). 'No go for whites' in race hotspots: Community leaders in Oldham dispute police claims over attacks by Asian gangs. *The Manchester Guardian*, April 20: 7.

Vaz, E.W. (1962). Juvenile gang delinquency in Paris. *Social Problems*, 10:23-31.

Vaz, E.W. (Ed.), (1967). *Middle-class juvenile delinquency*. New York: Harper and Row.

Veale, A. & Adefrisew, A. (1992). *Study on street children in four selected towns of ethiopia.* Cork, Ireland: Ethiopia Ministry of Labour and Social Affairs UNICEF, Ethiopia, University College.

Veash, N. (2000a). Systematic gang killings reported on rise in Brazil. *Boston Globe,* February 10: A13.

Veash, N. (2000b). Children of privileged form Brazil crime gangs 'silver-spoon' bandits target the wealthy. *Boston Globe,* February:A2.

Vercaigne, C. (1997). Views from the field: Gangs in sight. *Journal of Gang Research,* 5: (1) 55-61.

Vercaigne, C. (2001). The group aspect of youth crime and youth gangs in Brussels: What we do know and especially what we don't know. In M.W. Klein et al. (Eds.) *The eurogang paradox: Street gangs and youth groups in the U.S. and Europe.* Dordrecht, Germany: Kluwer Academic Pubs.

Vercaigne, C. & Goris, P. (1996). The social exclusion of juveniles and street crime in the city: Research into juvenile criminology and social geography. *Caribbean Journal of Criminology and Social Psychology,* 1:164-188.

Vigil, J.D. (1988). *Barrio gangs.* Austin, TX: University of Texas Press.

Vigil, J.D. (1990). Cholos and gangs: Culture change and street youth in Los Angeles. In C.R. Huff (Ed.), *Gangs in America.* Newbury Park, CA: Sage.

Vigil, J.D., & Yun, S.C. (2002). A cross-cultural framework for understanding gangs: Mulitiple marginality and Los Angeles. In C.R. Huff (Ed.), *Gangs in America III.* Newbury Park, CA: Sage.

Vincent, I. (1992). Neo-nazis, skinheads on the attack in Brazil. *The Globe and Mail,* December 21.

Wainwright, M. (2000). Street-wise teenagers fight youth crime: We know what gangs get up to, say youngsters masterminding estate projects. *The Guardian,* May 30:1.6.

Waldorf, D. (1993). Don't be your own best customer–Drug use of San Francisco gang drug sellers. *Crime, Law and Social Change.* 19:1-15.

Webber, M. (1991). *Street kids: The tragedy of Canada's runaways.* Toronto: University of Toronto Press.

Weinberg, S.K. (1964). Juvenile delinquency in Ghana: A comparative analysis of delinquents and non-delinquents. *Journal of Criminal Law, Criminology, and Police Science,* 55:471-481.

Weitekamp, E.G.M. (2001). Gangs in Europe: Assessments at the millennium. In M.W. Klein et al. (Eds.), *The eurogang paradox: Street gangs and youth groups in the U.S. and Europe.* Dordrecht, Germany: Kluwer Academic Pubs.

West, D. (1967). *The young offender.* New York: International University Press.

West, D., & Farrington, D. (1977). *The delinquent way of life.* London: Heineman.

Whitfield, R.G. (1982). American gangs and British subcultures: A commentary. *International Journal of Offender Therapy and Comparative Criminology,* 26:90-92.

Williams, C. (2000). Germany bans skinhead group. *The Denver Post,* September 5:2A.

Williams, T. (1989). *The Cocaine Kids: The inside story of a teenage drug ring.* Reading, MA: Addison-Wesley.

Williamson, H. (1996). Tobacco road: Repatriation accord and Vietnamese gang activities. *Far Eastern Economic Review*, 159:21.

Willmontt, P. (1966). *Adolescent boys of East London*. London: Routledge and Kegan Paul.

Willwerth, J. (1991). From killing fields to mean streets. *Time*, 138:(20) 103-106.

Wilson-Smith, A. (1989). Gang warfare, Soviet style. *Maclean's*, May 22, 102:44.

Winter, P. (1998). Pulling the teams out of the dark room: The politicisation of the mongrel mob. In K. Hazlehurst, K. and C. Hazlehurst (Eds.), *Gangs and youth subcultures: International explorations*. New Brunswick, NJ: Transaction.

Womersley, T. (2002). Queen visits the home of yardie drug gangs. *The Scotsman*, February 20:4.

Wooden, W.S. (1995). *Renegade kids, suburban outlaws: From youth culture to delinquency*. Belmont, CA: Wadsworth.

World Press Review. (1995). Brazilian gangs. *World Press Review*, 24: (1) Accession Number 02195649.

World Sources. (2002). Kenya clears street gangs in capital, Xinhua. *Emerging Markets Datafile Xinhua*, March 15.

Wright, H. (1999). Shootings may be linked to yardies. *The Manchester Guardian*, August 14:13.

Xiang, G. (1999). Delinquency and its prevention in China. *International Journal of Offender Therapy and Comparative Criminology*, 43:(1) 61-70.

Yablonsky, L. (1959). The delinquent gang as a near group. *Social Problems*, 7:108-117.

Yablonsky, L. (1970). *The violent gang* (Revised ed.). Baltimore: Penguin.

Yablonsky, L., & Haskell, M. (1988). *Juvenile delinquency*. New York: Harper and Row.

Young, K., & Craig, L. (1997). Beyond white pride: Identity, meaning and contradiction in the Canadian skinhead. *The Canadian Review of Sociology and Anthropology*, 34:175-206.

Zatz, M.S. (1985). Los Cholos: Legal processing of Chicano gang members. *Social Problems*, 33:13-30.

Zatz, M.S. (1987). Chicano youth gangs and crime: The creation of a moral panic. *Contemporary Crisis*, 11:129-158.

Zeldes, I. (1981). *The problem of crime in the USSR*. Springfield, IL: Charles C Thomas.

Zhang, S.X. (2002). Chinese gangs: Familial and cultural dynamics. In C.R. Huff (Ed.), *Gangs in America III*. Newbury Park, CA: Sage.

Zhang, L., & Messner, S.F. (1995). Family deviance and delinquency in China. *Criminology*, 33: 359-387.

Zhang, L., Messner, S.F., Lu, Z., & Deng, X. (1997). Gang crime and its punishment in China. *Journal of Criminal Justice*, 25:289-302.

Zimring, F.E. (1981). Kids, groups, and crime: Some implications of a well-known secret. *Journal of Criminal Law and Criminology*, 72:867-885.

Zu-Yuan, H. (1988). China: Juvenile delinquency and its prevention. *CJ International*, 4:(5) 5-10.

AUTHOR INDEX

SUBJECT INDEX